Metaphor: The Logic of Poetry
A Handbook

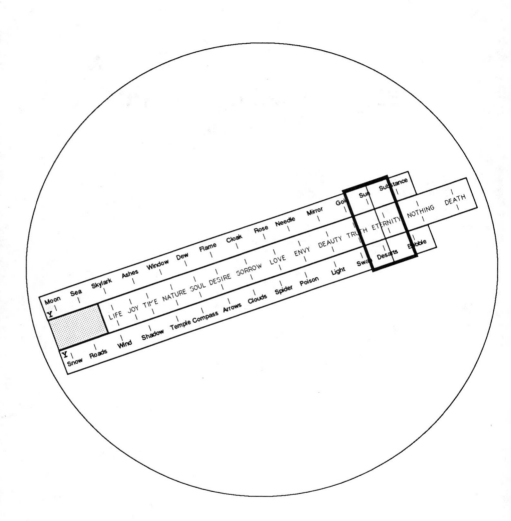

Metaphor: The Logic of Poetry

A Handbook

By John Briggs & Richard Monaco

Pace University Press
New York

This book was set in Galliard Type
The editor was Mark Hussey;
the designer was John Briggs.

Distributed by arrangement with
University Publishing Associates, Inc.

4720 Boston Way
Lanham, MD 20706

British Cataloging in Publication Information Available

Library of Congress Cataloging-in-Publication Data

Logic of poetry.
  Metaphor : the logic of poetry

  Reprint. Originally published: The logic of
poetry. New York; McGraw-Hill, 1974.
  Includes index.
  1. Metaphor. 2. Poetics. I. Briggs, John.
II. Monaco, Richard. III. Title.
PN1059. M4L64   1990   808   90-7654
ISBN 0-944473-03-2
ISBN 0-944473-05-9 (pbk.)

All Pace University Press books are produced on acid-free
paper which exceeds the minimum standards set by the National
Historical Publications and Records Commission.

Acknowledgements

W.H. Auden, "Law Like Love," Copyright © 1940 and renewed 1968 by W.H. Auden. Reprinted from *W.H. Auden: Collected Poems*, edited by Edward Mendelson, by permission of Random House, Inc. & Faber Ltd.

Charles Baudelaire, "Correspondences," translated by Christopher Collins and used with his permission.

John Berryman, "Dream Song # 176," from *The Dream Songs* by John Berryman. Copyright © 1959, 1962, 1963, 1964, 1965, 1966, 1967, 1968, 1969 by John Berryman. Reprinted by permission of Farrar, Straus and Giroux, Inc.

Gwendolyn Brooks, "My Dreams, My Words, Must Wait Till After Hell," from *The World of Gwendolyn Brooks* by Gwendolyn Brooks. Copyright © 1945 by Gwendolyn Brooks Blakely. Reprinted by permission of Harper & Row, Publishers, Inc.

William Cassegrain, "Lucid Prodigy in Snow," from *Complaint of the Invader*. Reprinted by permission of Syzygy Arts, Inc. Copyright © by John Briggs.

Hart Crane, "Moment Fugue" is reprinted from *The Collected Poems and Selected Letters and Prose of Hart Crane*, Edited by Brom Weber, by permission of Liveright Publishing Corporation. Copyright 1933, © 1958, 1966 by Liveright Publishing Corporation.

E.E. Cummings, "Buffalo Bill's" from *Tulips & Chimneys, 1913-1962* by E.E. Cummings. Copyright 1923, 1951 by E. E. Cummings, Edited by George James Firmage, by permission of Liveright Publishing Corporation. Copyright 1923, 1925 and renewed 1951, 1953 by E.E. Cummings. Copyright © 1973, 1976 by George James Firmage.

Allen Ginsberg, "Death on All Fronts" from *Collected Poems 1947-1980* by Allen Ginsberg. Copyright © 1969 by Allen Ginsberg. Reprinted by permission of Harper & Row, Publishers, Inc. and Penguin Books, London.

Emily Dickinson, "There's a Certain Slant of Light," "The Auctioneer of Parting," Copyright 1929, © 1957 by Mary L. Hampson. Reprinted from *The Complete Poems of Emily Dickinson*, edited by Thomas H. Johnson, by permission of Little, Brown and Co.

Alfred Dorn, "The Knowledge of Silence" from *New Orlando Poetry Anthology, Vol. 3*, 1968. Copyright by Alfred Dorn. Reprinted by permission of New Orlando Publications.

Robert Frost, "The Road Not Taken," "A Patch of Old Snow," from *The Poetry of Robert Frost* edited by Edward Connery Lanthem. Copyright © 1916, © 1969 by Holt, Rinehart and Winston, Inc. Copyright 1944, © by Robert Frost. Reprinted by permission of Henry Holt and Company, Inc. and Jonathan Cape, Ltd.

Langston Hughes, "As I Grew Older," Copyright © 1926 by Alfred A. Knopf, Inc. and renewed 1954 by Langston Hughes. Reprinted from *Selected Poems of Langston Hughes*, by permission of Alfred A. Knopf, Inc., and Harold Ober Associates.

Richard Hugo, "Blond Road," Copyright © 1973 by Richard Hugo. Included by permission.

Stanley Kunitz, "The Science of the Night," from Selected Poems, 1928-1958 by Stanley Kunitz. Copyright © 1953 by Stanley Kunitz. First appeared in *New World Writing*. Reprinted by permission of Little Brown and Company and Martin, Secker & Warburg.

JAN -- 2000

ILLUSTRATION CREDITS

John Briggs: Cover, x ; 2, 18, 26, 41, 46, 80, 86, 93, 98, 105, 110, 118, 141, 144, 152, 164, 184, 200, 212, 217, 230, 238, 244, 249, 255, 258, 268, 276, 280, 284, all slide rule illustrations.

Christopher Collins: 57.

Philip Friedman: 124.

Richard Monaco: 205.

SPECIAL ACKNOWLEDGEMENTS

Special thanks to: Diane Golden of Western Connecticut State University for her help on graphics; Adele Leone for her long, frustrating hours gathering permissions; Kristina Masten for patiently scanning and rereading pages and pages of copy; Joanna Myhr for proofreading; and our editor, Mark Hussey, for his good sense and advice on everything.

NOTE ON SPELLING

Archaic spellings have been retained in English language poems after the sixteenth century.

About the Authors

John Briggs is an associate professor of English at Western Connecticut State University and was for fourteen years a member of the faculty of the New School for Social Research in New York City. His book on creativity, *Fire in the Crucible*, was originally published by St. Martin's Press and is now in paperback with Jeremy P. Tarcher. He is also coauthor of *Looking Glass Universe* and *Turbulent Mirror*. A widely published science writer, his doctorate is in aesthetics and psychology. He was for a long time managing editor of the poetry magazine, *New York Quarterly*. His poems have been published in numerous magazines and anthologies.

Richard Monaco is a poet and writer, perhaps best known for his novel *Parsival or a Knight's Tale* which was a main selection in 1977 of the Quality Paperback Book Club and was nominated for the Pulitzer Prize in fiction. More recent novels include *The Final Quest*, *Runes*, *Unto the Beast* and *Journey to the Flame*. In the early 1970's he was editor of McGraw-Hill's anthology *New American Poetry*, and served as poetry editor of *The University Review*. He also studied musical composition at Columbia University under the Pulitzer prize winning composer Charles Wuorinen.

Briggs and Monaco first published *The Logic of Poetry* in 1974 with McGraw-Hill. For three years in the mid 1970's the pair co-hosted "The Logic of Poetry" weekly half-hour radio show on public radio station, WNYC in New York City. *Metaphor: The Logic of Poetry* is a condensed and extensively revised edition of their original anthology.

Contents

Introduction

Poetry has special power. The supernatural "force of the word" (called *Logos* in the West and *Vāc* in the East) is said to be inherent in poetry. Ages ago poetry was used for religious ceremonies because it was considered magical. And poetry *is* magical—it is outside our everyday consciousness of life; it excites an utterly unique awareness and experience. As American poet William Carlos Williams said, "It is difficult to get the news from poems, but men [and women] die every day for the lack of what is found there."

When someone says, "I don't understand poetry," usually this means he or she has become frustrated by the realization that poems don't present "facts," don't serve up information the way a magazine article does, for instance. The person has tried to read poetry as if it were like conversation or expository writing. The problem is that poetry isn't trying to explain events, ideas, feelings, or perceptions in a form or logic we're used to. Poetry isn't explaining experience—it is a state of experiencing. Somehow great poetry has the force to go beyond our feelings or ideas, and even if we disagree with the content or find the sentiments alien, we can still discover a sense of "rightness," of "truth" in a poem. The poem has touched something *beyond* our dislikes and disagreements.

This is poetry's magic. It takes us beyond ourselves, beyond our everyday limitations, or perhaps, in another sense, *into* ourselves.

But poetry baffles the "reasonable" mind. We wonder, "How can I tell when it simply means what it says?" "Why do these poets say one thing and mean something else? Why don't they just say it directly?" The problem is such questions are reasonable but misleading when applied to poetry.

Reading poetry requires a trained attention, a special state of mind that our daily experiences with thought and language don't demand.

Poetic language cannot be understood in the same way that ordinary language is understood. To try to understand it in those terms is frustrating at best, and at worst actually destroys any chance of really experiencing the poem. The words in poems are ordinary words, but something happens to them in the poem, transforms them, and that is what we want to understand.

We could try to do it by looking separately at all the techniques that generations of scholars and critics have painstakingly identified as "poetic" (rhyme, personification, image, symbol, figure, meter, verse forms, etc.) and then observe how some poems have *this*, but don't have *that*, have more of *this* than *that*, and so on. The problem is that if we break poetry up too much in order to see it, we may intensify our difficulty because the poem's magic lies in its wholeness, its complete effect on us. Is there some way to *unify* our perception of the poem, rather than fragmenting it, to learn to think in poetry the way we can learn to think in music or in a foreign language? In this we're asking a fundamental question: Why read poetry at all? And perhaps we'll discover that when we experience poetry as metaphor, the question answers itself.

This text focuses on the terms "metaphor" and "metaphoric language" because understanding how these terms can be extended to cover all the major aspects of poetry will facilitate experience of that special state of insight poems aim to evoke. Aristotle wrote in his *Poetics*, "The greatest thing by far is to be a master of metaphor," and in the *Rhetoric*, "From metaphor we can best get hold of something fresh." And Robert Frost wrote: "There are many other things I have found myself saying about poetry, but the chiefest of these is that it is metaphor, saying one thing in terms of another."

We consider metaphor in detail here specifically because:

1. The operations of the simple metaphor (e.g., "A mighty fortress is our God") provide, when extended as *structural* metaphor, an unusual insight into how poetic language evokes its levels of meaning, and its unique, almost religious power. Perhaps because of this, modern critics have increasingly taken an interest in metaphor, as the *Princeton Encyclopedia of Poetry and Poetics* indicates: "In recent years the view has gathered weight that metaphor is the radical process by which the internal relationships peculiar to poetry are achieved, some critics maintaining that metaphor marks off the poetic mode of vision and utterance from the logical or discursive modes." Many feel that metaphor, in this broader sense, is the essence of poetry. They have observed that no particular technique is common to all poetry, while metaphoric perception appears to be universal. It is consciously or unconsciously involved in all the techniques poets utilize.

2. Many critics often use the terms "image," "symbol," "metaphor," and "figure" interchangeably and endlessly debate fine distinctions. This sort of discussion is of little use to anyone interested in making contact with a poem. Focusing on metaphor simplifies things and leaves us free to concentrate fully on each poem itself. The alternatives involve locating limited examples of each distinction, breaking poetry up into categories (such as period, style, philosophy) and constantly distinguishing between critical terms.

3. Seeing poetry as "metaphoric language" instead of "figurative language," as it is often called, keeps us from confusing "rhetorical" figures with "poetic" figures and has the advantage of allowing us to see, as metaphor, how the dynamics of a poem produce their effect on us.

4. Seeing poetics through metaphor can enable us to encounter *any* kind of poetry as part of one process, poetry from any historical period, school, or national or cultural tradition.

Although traditional critical terms such as irony, symbol, paradox, and tone are introduced and used from time to time in the following pages, our primary purpose is not learning definitions but dealing directly with poems, seeing poems without preconceptions, theories, or anxieties about what they "mean." It is important to grasp that the approach involved in understanding that the logic of poetry is metaphor is not a "method." There are no rules to be learned, no checklists to be followed. It is a gradual process of becoming familiar with how metaphoric language works, of developing your "metaphoric eye." While the principle is simple, every poem is a new case of it, and the only way to really understand is through participation. Let's make an analogy to learning to shoot baskets. A coach can demonstrate the jump shot—can explain, even diagram it so that you understand the reason for all the moves, how to cock your hand, when to release the ball, the principle of spin—but you have to actually participate if you want to make the basket. To do it, you have to work at it, and one day you go up in the air and it happens. Suddenly it seems natural and makes perfect sense. Learn to read metaphorically, sharpen your metaphoric eye, and though you may one day forget just what the definition of metaphor is, you'll always be able to get into poetry, any kind of poetry.

As for the prosody techniques used by poets—rhyme, meter, verse types, and the like, you will see (as we go through the book) that in all the poetic variety, there are no fixed forms or rules. At any point in history poets are influenced by the tradition of those who wrote before them. More often than not the poet will stick with that tradition, write in its forms, and tend to deviate according to his or her personality, interests, and contemporary influences. Since each new generation of poets alters this tradition, we cannot consider any of these techniques the permanent, essential elements of poetry. Consequently, they are dealt with briefly in the discussions and the Glossary.

In all this, we will try to take what amounts to the poet's point of view about poetry, to seize it as an unfragmented perception and expression. Interpretations of poems, should one wish to make them, are left largely to the reader.

The questions that follow and precede many of the poems are not meant to have definite answers. They are simply meant to stimulate exploration of the "unanswerable" aspects of a poem. The questions are intended as a vital part of the discussions of the pieces themselves. *In order to participate in a poem, considering the questions is actually more important than trying to answer them.*

We might think of it this way: A good poem is like a lens through which you can look at the universe, but the vision is yours. The object here is to learn how to focus our minds through a poem and look with our own "sight."

Chapter 1

The Metaphoric Eye: Poetic Vision

Metaphor: The Logic of Poetry

Although we don't usually speak in poetry, when a thing is particularly beautiful, moving, or tragic, even unlikely people become poets for a while. Ask doctors, lawyers, businessmen, almost anyone, and they may admit that at some time or other they have "tried to write poetry." Why? Perhaps because poetry is one of the few things we can do to give voice to our sense of the mystery of life.

In everyday conversations we hope to be clear and simple whenever possible, but we often fail. We know that communicating clearly with one another through a fog of emotion, uncertainty, or opinion is very difficult. Even our knowledge is a kind of fog that obscures the subtle dimensions of existence that we can't really define and categorize. In a way, poetry tries to cut through the fog, expressing not knowledge, opinion or belief but a clear awareness of the mystery, a penetrating "sense of truth."

The essential difference between everyday language (that used in speech, in newspaper writing, on television, and in most fiction and movie scripts, for example) and poetic language is that we can't just sit back with a poem and be entertained or excited by it. We can't imagine we have understood it just because we happen to know what all the words mean; we have to work a little, work with the poet, in order to experience for ourselves the poem's mysterious and elusive sense of truth.

Put yourself in the poet's position for a moment. You may have a subtle awareness of some kind and want to express it, to pass it along to others, but you find that there is no word or expression for what you want to say. It isn't something you already know; it's new, unique, a discovery. You find that expressing your awareness in logical, expository terms doesn't work; you can't really say it that way. You need a new language that goes beyond logic. If you're a poet and you write a successful poem, your poem becomes, in effect, a new word for your new awareness. And if you're really successful the newness will reemerge each time the poem is read. A familiar understanding would not demand a poem. A new understanding does.

In order to communicate new awareness, poetic language relies primarily on metaphor. All language becomes metaphoric at times to make points clear or add color and life to ideas. We continually use metaphors consciously or unconsciously: "the ship of state," "I'm hungry as a wolf" "the mouth of a jar," "one's path through life"—all these are metaphors. But most of the metaphors we hear in everyday speech have been overused and are now cliché or "dead" metaphors (that expression is a metaphor too, of course); they have lost their steam.

In everyday language metaphors generally work either: (1) to clarify ideas and feelings, or (2) to convince us of the value, danger, beauty, ugliness of one thing by comparing it to another which is accepted as valuable, dangerous, beautiful,or ugly—for example, "My enemies are wolves," "He is a pig," "My sister is good as gold."

Poetic metaphor is different from everyday metaphor. Put simply, *a poetic metaphor is the union of unlike things (pictures to ideas, ideas to feelings, feelings to objects, objects to pictures, and so on) such that the mind discovers unexpected relationships and comes upon insight.* While ordinary language sometimes uses metaphor for effect, poetic language is nearly always metaphoric on some level or other. Once you become familiar with this, poetry no longer seems difficult, ambiguous, and recondite.

"Oh my luve is like a red, red rose." Can we look at this well-worn statement by the poet Robert Burns as if for the first time? You have probably heard it much too often; it is always turning up in poetry textbooks or being sung and quoted. But instead of letting it get lost in the background, let's concentrate on it, examine the way it functions. First, notice that SIMILES (comparisons using the words like or as) and metaphors are essentially the same. For example, suppose someone said, "My luve is a red, red rose." Unless you imagine that the speaker is another flower himself or is in love with one, the "like" in such a statement is understood.

What makes metaphor or simile-metaphor work is what might be called the *unlike* factor between the two things being compared. Without the unlike factor there is no metaphoric action at all, just a simple (if sometimes odd) statement of fact. It would be the kind of statement you would have if a boy said of his girlfriend, "My love is like a girl," words lacking impact and real meaning unless his sweetheart was in fact rather old. Second, notice some of the ways "luve" connects with "rose." For instance, the girl the poet is writing about might be soft, sweet, fresh, and pure, smell nice, bloom, blush, and have a certain intensity (the intensity of "red, red") as well as sharp thorns (so be careful how you handle her); and more.

Obviously, if you just say "my love" or "red rose," none of these meanings appears. But juxtaposing them so that the mind brings them together, makes a whole cluster of meanings suddenly flower. It should be noted that not all these meanings necessarily apply; the focus is always provided by the poem as a whole.

So the metaphor's dynamics operate as follows: "my luve" (X) + "a red, red rose" (Y) = a set of new meanings that are not specifically spelled out, a relationship to be discovered by the reader. Even in the simplest case, metaphoric language makes demands on our alertness and requires us to participate with it in a special way in order to understand it.

In "Oh my luve is like a red, red rose" the X and Y terms are compared: X is like Y. But metaphoric terms can be juxtaposed (laid side by side) in other ways that also force the mind to bring them together: For example, the juxtaposed terms can be identified, contrasted, or associated with one another. The following are some examples of other simple X/Y metaphoric juxtapositions. It's not important to remember these as types; just get the feel for how X/Y juxtapositions can show up in poetry:

1. From the eighteenth-century British poet Alexander Pope: "In Folly's cup still laughs the bubble, joy." Here there are actually two metaphors: (*a*) Folly (X)

is identified with a cup (Y), or you could consider Folly a character who uses the cup, in which case Folly (X) is identified as a person (Y), and (*b*) a bubble (X) is identified as joy (Y).

2. From the twentieth-century American poet Wallace Stevens: "The pears are not viols,/ Nudes or bottles!" The pears (X) are contrasted to each of three Y's: viols, nudes, and bottles. This contrast calls attention to the similarity. We realize pears do in fact curiously seem like these three items. Then we ask, But why is the poet saying that pears are *not* viols, nudes or bottles? From this juxtaposition new meanings emerge.

3. From Shakespeare: "Ah, but those tears are pearls which thy love sheds/ And they're rich and ransom all ill deeds." In this metaphor the poet identifies tears (X) with pearls (Y) and then creates an association, seeing the pearls as "ransom."

4. From T. S. Eliot: "The eyes that fix you in a formulated phrase,/ And when I am formulated, sprawling on a pin,/ When I am pinned and wriggling on the wall." This is a more elaborate metaphor where eyes (X) are associated with formulating a phrase (Y), and then a new X/Y relationship is established as eyes + formulated phrase (X) are identified as a pin (Y). At the same time, there is another covert metaphor in which the speaker (X) is identified as some kind of insect (Y).

In all the above instances X and Y are juxtaposed in some fashion so that a spark of meaning jumps between them.

Though they can be helpful, the categories above lack clearly defined boundaries. The point is to be aware of the union of terms in order to experience the poetic effect, the surprising view or insight. *Metaphor, reduced to its essentials, is always a kind of comparison of terms which contain a strong unlike factor*—the eyes as a formulated phrase, the bubble as joy, tears as pearls. But since a poet may choose to juxtapose the terms one way or another, it is useful to be alert to various forms of metaphoric statement.In all the above we are given both terms of the metaphor, the X and the Y, though in the last case the poet does not actually say that the speaker is an "insect."

But the form of the metaphor is not always so obvious as X/Y. Often a single word (an X alone) can create a complete metaphor:

Then Jesus said unto them, Take heed and beware of the leaven of the Pharisees and of the Sadducees. And they reasoned among themselves, saying, It is because we have taken no bread. Which when Jesus perceived, he said unto them, O ye of little faith, why reason ye among yourselves, because ye have brought no bread? . . . How is it that ye do not understand that I spake it not to you concerning bread, that ye should beware of the leaven of the Pharisees? . . . Then they understood that he bade them not beware of the leaven of bread, but of the doctrine of the Pharisees and Sadducees.

Christ points to many rich meanings that do not exist when you substitute the word "doctrine" for the word leaven in the statement. For instance, leaven makes bread rise and puff up; bread is a source of life for mankind; and Christ said (elsewhere) that his teachings were "bread" to sustain people spiritually and give true life, and so it follows that bad "bread" will induce spiritual malnutrition. We see that the whole concept of nourishing and sustaining is compressed here (as metaphor) into a single word. This intensity is what makes poetry live.

A whole poem, like the single word "leaven," can also be a kind of metaphor itself. Sometimes we seem to have a simple statement such as in Robert Frost's poem "The Road Not Taken": "Two roads diverged in a yellow wood,/ And sorry I could not travel both/ And be one traveler, long I stood/ And looked down one as far as I could/ To where it bent in the undergrowth." The poet tells us how the roads looked and how he had to choose between them. On the surface his statement seems to be simple description, but the moment you realize that the roads (X) are not just roads but are pointing to something more (ways of life, experience, events, past hopes and wishes, the pattern of the future, etc.), you know that the situation is an X being juxtaposed to some unstated Y or Y's. The reader implicitly completes the metaphor: The poet choosing between two roads is (like) _____. Obviously there is no one "correct" concept for what the situation represents. It wouldn't be very effective that way—a guessing game rather than a poem. You have to feel your way into this because while there may not be any absolute answers, straining to read anything we wanted into the poem or forcing our opinions on it would be pointless. It would not communicate anything about that subtle awareness or sense of truth that is the real point of the poet's lines.

Notice the unlike factor in Frost's metaphor: roads are just roads, as roses are roses, but when we add them (in our literary equation) to ideas or feelings about life, events, or people, suddenly there is a tension between the terms and a sense of deeper meaning. In the everyday use of metaphors for clarification or persuasion, the emphasis is nearly always on the similarity between terms; in poetic metaphor, *it is on the tension of both the similarities and dissimilarities between them.* Consider the "mouth" of a jar. Somebody noticed the resemblance, and the term stuck. Scholars and philosophers claim that language often extends itself into new areas and includes new objects and experiences by comparing them to old ones. So metaphors of clarification are meant to provide a better picture of something in terms of what we already know. Metaphors used for persuasion also stress the similarity between their terms. If an insurance company compares itself to the Rock of Gibraltar or a cigarette brand is associated with cool water and springtime, the intentions are clear: The qualities of one term (strength/solidarity; freshness/coolness) are meant to be *transferred* to the other. An image is substituted for a categorical word: the Rock of Gibraltar for "solid." Seeing the insurance company as solid is the point of the metaphor. In poetic metaphors similarities are played off against differences. But is there a word which "rose" is substituted for in Robert Burns' famous metaphor? Is there a single, categorical point which the poet wants you to get with the metaphor. Obviously not. The two following sentences are similar: "My company is (like) the Rock of Gibraltar" and "My luve is (like) a red, red rose." But context—in other words, where you find the statement, whether in a poem, an advertisement, or political speech—makes the crucial difference. The poem that surrounds the metaphor focuses on intensity, on discovering meaning, rather than on simply asking you to accept the asserted similarity. Discovering, in this sense, means that you have to keep reacting to the vast difference between the terms. While metaphors of clarification and persuasion are one-leveled, poetic metaphors have many levels and aim at indefinable things rather than obvious fact, belief, or opinion. Everyday metaphors quickly become stale because we know what message they intend. But because of a multiplicity of connections—many of them experienced simultaneously in a poetic context—poetic metaphors don't lose their freshness. In this respect they are never quite experienced the same way twice. To see this for yourself, take some well-worn speech from Shakespeare— say, Hamlet's "to be or not to be" soliloquy—and read it in the context of the whole play. If you really do this, you will find the metaphors come alive with meaning. In a vigorous poem even a thoroughly dead metaphor like the "mouth of a jar" or the "ship of state" might revive itself as other levels and possibilities emerge.

Bear in mind that when we think about these levels or talk about them, we have to do it linearly, make a list, as in the rose metaphor: "The lover referred to is soft, sweet, fresh, smells nice, blooms, blushes, etc." But when we experience the metaphor in its frame of reference (the poem), we feel something happening at once in our minds, something immediate. It is as if our X and Y were joined with a clap, a snap of the fingers: poetic magic. The magic may include all these meanings, but by no means do the meanings exhaust or explain what is going on.

Poetic language frees the reader to "see" in a unique way. We may ask: What is this "seeing"? Is it really seeing at all? What happens when your mind makes these poetic relationships, relates or associates roads and life, tears and pearls, roses and women? Let's deal with images for a moment. IMAGE is a literary term referring to words that suggest or describe sights, sounds, tastes, smells, or the act of touching something—words that relate to the function of the five senses. Obviously, if you say "rose," then perhaps from memory you imagine a rose (though hearing a word is not like actual experience, it recalls it). But can a metaphor be pictured or imagined? When we see what X/Y adds up to, are we really seeing? What happens when we read William Blake's line, "Bring me my Arrows of desire"? It means something; we can relate to it, but can we *see* it? A little reflection shows that in fact we can't. Desires are sharp, piercing, swift; we get all that. But what is actually happening in the mind? Something not at all like seeing, tasting, touching, or remembering these experiences; we can't define the metaphor as an idea, either, but we grasp it all the same. Poetic (metaphoric) language creates these mental effects which seem to be seen, but it is another kind of sight; we might call it *in*sight. We can't store the metaphor in our brains the way we store facts or the words of a poem because the poetic words simply provide the means to approach a sense of truth, to rediscover it in some way each time we read the metaphor or recall it. The very act of finding out something new obviously cannot belong to the past. It happens only now. Looked at this way, the insightfulness of a poem must in an important way be recreated by the insightfulness of the reader.

What is this insight? It is not remembering, not seeing, not imagining, so what is it? Our poetic sense of rightness, truth, reality—even of cosmic proportions— does not come to us logically, that is, through analysis. Essentially, logic is a process of sorting and comparing things we know to make them fit with other things we know. As has often been said, a logical conclusion depends entirely on its premises and cannot meaningfully go beyond them. When people say thus and so is logical, they usually mean it seems to agree with what they already believe or think or know. There is no guarantee that such a process leads to truth; it certainly does not lead to something new. For example, a conservative might assert: "It's logical that we should support big business because that's what makes capitalism work, and capitalism is the backbone of a free society." And a liberal: "Logically, big business must be controlled because it is only out for profit and so is unresponsive to the rights of individuals." Both arguments are based on what the person already believes, and any deductions the speaker makes prove nothing at all. Let's set logic aside, then—the logic that is really a form of presenting opinions—and deal with the "logic" of poetry. That logic has to do with order and harmony and a sense of truth which is not something to agree or disagree about, but simply to perceive. In doing this we will become involved with poetic statements which the rational mind might consider self-contradictory or impossible. We will see that understanding poetic statements often demands that we set aside our intellectual prejudices, memories, and old habits, and move toward the unknown, experiencing the poem (and the mind itself) on a deeper level. Going beyond what the mind already knows, becoming aware and receptive, isn't limited to certain exceptional people. We all can experience this in poetry.

Bear in mind as you go through the text that none of the discussions or questions is meant to be exhaustive. A great poem cannot be worn out by talking about it. We are simply looking for effective ways to make contact with given pieces. When we analyze, we are not providing insight—we are just trying to remove impediments to a direct, insightful experience of poetry.

Read this poem through and then go back and look at individual metaphors. Do you see the series of X/Y juxtapositions? Can you observe how your mind is affected by them?

Archibald MacLeish
ARS POETICA

A poem should be palpable and mute
As a globed fruit

Dumb
As old medallions to the thumb

Silent as the sleeve-worn stone
Of casement ledges where the moss has grown—

A poem should be wordless
As the flight of birds

A poem should be motionless in time
As the moon climbs

Leaving, as the moon releases
Twig by twig the night-entangled trees,

Leaving, as the moon behind the winter leaves,
Memory by memory the mind—

A poem should be motionless in time
As the moon climbs

A poem should be equal to:
Not true

For all the history of grief
An empty doorway and a maple leaf

For love
The leaning grasses and two lights above the sea—

A poem should not mean
But be.

Exploring the Metaphors

1. Consider each of this poem's metaphors in turn, locating the X and Y terms. In several cases there are metaphors within metaphors, something like the Eliot metaphor (eyes/formulated phrase/pin) discussed earlier in the chapter. Can you work these out? What is being compared to what here?
2. What meanings spring out of these X/Y juxtapositions? What do these meanings suggest that "a poem" *is*? Do you see any X/Y paradoxical (self-contradictory) statements in the poem—statements that are contrary to reality or are impossible to observe in the world? Are these effective as poetic statements? Why? What do they tell you about a "poem"?
3. Consider how the poet has compressed various senses into his metaphors (sound, touch, taste, sight). What do the sensations of these senses have to do with "a poem," which is a collection of words?
4. How are the last two lines justified by the preceding lines? Is the effect on you of the last two lines consistent with the effect on you of the previous lines? Do you think the poet has fallen out of the poem in the last two lines and is indulging in argument and opinion?

Technical Notes

The poem is written in COUPLETS. Some of them are given EXACT RHYMES, while others are formed by SLANT RHYMES. The meter and rhyme scheme are irregular.

Oriental poetry, particularly Japanese, has been concerned with the sudden, surprise effects of metaphoric juxtaposition. The following four short Japanese poems aim at flashes of insight. What are the terms of the metaphors here? How do the poems work on us?

Kubonta
HAIKU
Kite like a soul,
dancing,
journeying . . .
Fallen to earth.
Rendition from Japanese

Priest Saigyō
TANKA
Everything is changing
And changes
in this fleeting world . . .
The same still light of the
Changing moon.
                    Rendition from Japanese

Fujiwara Teika (Sadaie)
TANKA
Spring night.
My dream's suspended bridge
Is shattered.
Swirling in the chasm...
Pale light in the east.
                    Rendition from Japanese

Matso Bashō
HAIKU
One's life, a single
dewdrop.
Its lonely savor.
                    Rendition from Japanese

Exploring the Metaphors

1. Consider the Bashō poem. Is "lonely savor" a metaphor?
2. Do you see an apparent contradiction involved in the Saigyō piece? Is this metaphoric? How?

Technical Notes

The four Japanese poems were written in their original language in the HAIKU and TANKA forms, as indicated by the titles.

The twentieth-century poet American Wallace Stevens was attracted to the kind of Oriental poetry which looks to effect a sudden sense of insight through metaphoric contrast. One of Stevens's better-known poems in this mode is "Thirteen Ways of Looking at a Blackbird."

Wallace Stevens

THIRTEEN WAYS OF LOOKING AT A BLACKBIRD

I
Among twenty snowy mountains,
The only moving thing
Was the eye of the blackbird.

II
I was of three minds,
Like a tree
In which there are three blackbirds.

III
The blackbird whirled in the autumn winds.
It was a small part of the pantomime.

IV
A man and a woman
Are one.
A man and a woman and a blackbird
Are one.

V
I do not know which to prefer,
The beauty of inflections
Or the beauty of innuendoes,
The blackbird whistling
Or just after.

VI
Icicles filled the long window
With barbaric glass.
The shadow of the blackbird
Crossed it, to and fro.

The mood
Traced in the shadow
An indecipherable cause.

VII
O thin men of Haddam,
Why do you imagine golden birds?
Do you not see how the blackbird
Walks around the feet
Of the women about you?

VIII
I know noble accents
And lucid, inescapable rhythms;
But I know, too,
That the blackbird is involved
In what I know.

IX
When the blackbird flew out of sight,
It marked the edge
Of one of many circles.

X
At the sight of blackbirds
Flying in a green light,
Even the bawds of euphony
Would cry out sharply.

XI
He rode over Connecticut
In a glass coach.
Once, a fear pierced him,
In that he mistook
The shadow of his equipage
For blackbirds.

XII
The river is moving.
The blackbird must be flying.

XIII
It was evening all afternoon.
It was snowing
And it was going to snow.
The blackbird sat
In the cedar-limbs.

Exploring the Metaphors

We can assume that the poet's use of a blackbird rather than a bluebird or a sparrow was not accidental. In fact, it is probable that he was counting on the word "blackbird" to have some enigmatic, even sinister connotations. "Black" is one of those loaded words poets love to use because they're rich with associations, for example: death, absence of light, evil, mystery, ominousness. The problem is that words like "black" have been overworked. Notice how Stevens avoids this problem by focusing not on black but on a blackbird. The blackbird here becomes a marvelous concentration of contradictory meanings. For instance, on one level the bird evokes some reality beyond the habits of our senses and everyday patterns of thought—a reality haunting our human illusions about what is real. At another level, the blackbird seems to represent the very reality we're in flight from. Such contradictions exist when we talk or think about the blackbird using our conventional logic. But as a fine instance of the logic of poetry, the blackbird makes perfect sense.

The following brief discussions examine a few of the many facets of this poem.

I

In section I, the mammoth, monumentally solid, white, unmoving "twenty snowy mountains" (X) are contrasted with the quick, intensely black, small, extremely mobile eye of the blackbird (Y). Does this intense contrast strike us as an insight, something the mind almost seems to "see"? We might spend hours debating the meaning of this little description. We sense that it means *something*, that some truth has been conveyed, but we would be hard pressed to pin it down, to agree or disagree about it because there is no statement or opinion here. In the long run, the possibilities are so vast and deep that it seems impossible to paraphrase the truth we see in this picture of the blackbird's moving eye against the twenty snowy mountains.

II

The abstract "three minds" are made vividly concrete by the X/Y juxtaposition with the "tree in which there are three blackbirds."

III

The metaphor here is less direct and seems at first like mere description. But notice that the blackbird whirling in the winds (X) is juxtaposed to "a small part of the pantomime" (Y). A pantomime is a story told by movement. We are drawn to wonder what that story is about.

IV

A man and a woman are identified as the abstract concept "one" (as God is one, all people are one). We accept this notion because it is a virtual cliché that men and women in love can unite physically and spiritually. We are startled, however, when Stevens joins this accepted association (X) to a new association (Y) that includes the blackbird as a third term. The blackbird comes in as if to suggest some cosmic mystery, some reality, some portent—and these are only a few of the many rich connotations this black, ambiguous, unsettling bird introduces into the familiar world of men and women.

V

This is a simple metaphoric X/Y contrast: inflections (X) to innuendoes (Y). Or perhaps it's primarily a comparison. We wonder, What are inflections and innuendoes like? Are these also X's with unstated Y's? Can you name a few inflections and innuendoes in the world around you?

VI

The picture of the blackbird crossing back and forth along the window becomes the X term for the Y term embodied in the mysterious lines: "The mood/ Traced in the shadow/ An indecipherable cause." Stevens's use of the word "cause" for this picture raises many questions. Cause for what? The blackbird? Its shadow? Nature? Something beyond nature? The mood itself? Why is the cause "indecipherable"? Does this suggest philosophic ideas about cause and effect?

The metaphoric comparison of the icicles to "barbaric glass" presents the backdrop against which we see the blackbird's shadow. The suggestive power lies in the subtle connection between the picture of the blackbird's shadow in the window and the final statement about the "indecipherable cause."

VII

Here the poet contrasts the golden birds (X) to the blackbird (Y). What kinds of associations do golden birds suggest? Images of the past? The golden age? Images of aspirations? Dreams? Wealth? Beauty? They could be felt as any or all of these things, or others. In the contrast we also see the poet playing off our associations with the blackbird itself. Possibly the sinister element is being stressed here since, like an omen of something impending, the blackbird walks "around the feet of the women." However, other impressions of the section are equally plausible; if, for example, you see the blackbird expressing cosmic, "higher," or absolute reality, then you might say that the "men of Haddam" are living in golden dreams and missing the blunt, black fact of truth right under their noses.

VIII

The "noble accents/ And lucid, inescapable rhythms"(X) are set against the blackbird (Y). But is the blackbird different from them (contrasted), or is it an example of them (compared)? The poet's use of the word "too" in the third line implies that he may feel they are different, but this is not clear. And if different, is the blackbird *escapable*—is it *un*lucid, *ig*noble? How? Again, the poet's metaphoric use of the blackbird makes us sense that it stands for something beyond itself, something as abstract and indefinable as those "lucid, inescapable rhythms" themselves. Or is the bird here a concrete thing, not abstract at all?

IX

The blackbird's flight (X) is associated with a circle (Y), of which the poem claims there are "many." Since we did not see this circle until it was marked by the bird's flight, other circles are suggested, circles invisible to us until marked by something. Circles have rich associations for us: perfection, cycles of life, going around in a circle, being ringed in, the circle as a symbol of unity or infinity. Metaphorically, the blackbird opens a way into understanding the complex circularities of existence.

X

It seems clear from the use of the word "even" that the "bawds of euphony" (literally, the whores of harmonious sound) are hardened or indifferent to most sights. Their dulled sophistication (X) is set against their reaction to "the sight of blackbirds/ Flying in a green light" (Y). It is left for us to discover whether the bawds would cry out sharply from delight, fear, awe, or something else. In any event, the blackbirds suddenly alter the bawds' usual state, perhaps with the impact of something deeper than what they are habituated to, a striking truth about things.

XI

Fear, the blackbird, and the shadow of the glass coach are all intermingled and associated in metaphoric X/Y's. Once more the blackbirds seem to be a portent. But notice how that fear becomes transferred by association ("mistook/ The shadow of his equipage/ For blackbirds") with the glass coach. In this context what does the glass coach mean? Certainly it is evocative, metaphoric. What is the effect of the association of "glass" with "pierce"? Why does the poet use such archaic words as "equipage" and "coach"? How do they add to the meaning? The connotations create a tension between the various terms and seem to point at something beyond the simple description of a traveler looking out the window of his car or train at shadows. Was he frightened, for example, by the ominous shadow of truth? Is his whole existence as fragile as the glass coach?

XII

The river's movement (X) is juxtaposed to the flying blackbird (Y). Is there a causal relation implied between these two? Does the river move and then the blackbird fly, or are they manifestations of the same underlying natural process? Or is it a simple comparison: The river's movement is (like) the blackbird's flying?

All these possibilities might be felt simultaneously. The little two-line metaphor suggests tantalizing depths we can almost plumb.

XIII

The first sentence gives us a complex image of time and movement. The snow is falling continuously; all afternoon it is evening, as if time were somehow stilled in this motion. Against this endless, static time (X) the poet sets a bird in the cedar-limbs (Y). Will it stay still or take flight? The black against white presents a stark visual contrast, and the blackbird, gathered into a dynamic stillness in the tree, contrasts (and compares) with the steadily falling snow. The bird again is "haunting" the peaceful (perhaps illusory) landscape with its total, absolute "realness." Or is it suggesting a deeper reality beyond the real?

In most of the sections discussed so far, Stevens uses the bird as a metaphoric aspect of the unknown. He puts it against contrasting backgrounds—mountains, golden birds, falling snow, the shadow of the glass coach—and all this triggers in us a sense of import, urgency, and meaning. So overall the bird itself is an X for some other Y that we can only dimly sense, something beyond all the comparisons given in the poem and our attempts to discuss them. The blackbird X holds something else in itself; it stands for something beyond the intellect's range and grasp. So through poetry we can sometimes glimpse a vast unknown that waits at the limits of our familiar worlds.

1. *Section I* Is twenty snowy mountains a better number than thirty or fifty? Consider some of the possible meanings for the metaphor in this section. Can you describe what you "see" when you read this metaphor? How does what you see bring home the sense of truth in the image?
2. *Section II* How do you visualize this metaphor? What are some of the possible meanings generated by adding the blackbird as a third term in the cliché? Are some of these meanings contradictory? Can you resolve them?
3. *Section III* What reasons might there be for using the word "whirled"? Do you see an ambiguity here? What possibilities of meaning can you see in the phrase "a small part of the pantomime"?
4. *Section IV* Can you visualize this metaphor? Compare your mental impression of this with your impression of the metaphor in section II.
5. *Section VI* What are some of the possible implications of the last three lines? Do you see any double meanings in the term "traced"—that is, is the blackbird tracing the cause or being traced *by* it? Do you see any tension in the vertical and horizontal lines of the image? Is the blackbird flying or pacing as it casts this shadow? Is there an ambiguity in the way this image can be visualized? If so, is there a significance to the ambiguity?
6. *Section VII* How does the word "thin" relate to the rest of this section? Literally, Haddam is a town in Connecticut. Does Stevens's use of the name

in this context make it metaphoric? Does the fact that it sounds biblical add to the meaning? What kinds of connection do you perceive here between the blackbird and women? And the thin men? Both together?

7. *Section VIII* What are some of the possible meanings for the blackbird in this section of the poem?

8. *Section IX* What is the significance here of the fact that the blackbird is flying "out of sight"?

9. *Section X* What are some of the implications of the phrase "bawds of euphony"? Who might they be? Why is the word "sharply" appropriate in this context? Why "green light"?

10. *Section XI* What is particularly appropriate about the poet's use of the word "pierced"? "Equipage"? Why or how do you think his equipage is like the shadow of blackbirds?

11. *Section XII* Why are these lines separate sentences?

12. Can you see any logic in Stevens's arrangement of the thirteen sections of the poem? For example, what relation do you see between sections VII and VIII or between sections I and XIII?

13. Could you get anything like the impact of the poem from a photograph?

Technical Notes

Stevens uses neither rhyme nor regular meter in this poem. This kind of form, or lack of rigid form, is called FREE VERSE.

The poem below is an example of the simple metaphor extended across a whole poem. Can you see how Frost transcends literal description here?

Robert Frost
A PATCH OF OLD SNOW

There's a patch of old snow in a corner,
    That I should have guessed
Was a blow-away paper the rain
    Had brought to rest.

It is speckled with grime as if
    Small print overspread it,
The news of a day I've forgotten—
    If I ever read it.

Exploring the Metaphors

1. Do you see a central metaphor here, a central X/Y relationship? What is the snow compared to? What about the grime?
2. Do you see how the word "should" in the second line could be taken two ways?
3. Consider some of the implications of the comparison. What kind of "news" could the patch of snow indicate to the narrator?
4. Could the word "read" in the last line be taken metaphorically, as an X, to suggest some unstated Y's. In other words, the narrator says he's "read" this "news"—"read" it in what sense?
5. Is the poet expressing regret over not having read the news or cynicism about it? Are both views possible? If so, are they in contradiction, or do they complement each other in some way?

This poem is based on language rich in direct and indirect metaphor. The poet uses these to explore the subject of melancholy and to make the ABSTRACT (vague or general) word CONCRETE, as if it were an object of the senses, something vivid, not just a distant idea. This is one of the major effects of poetic (metaphoric) language.

John Keats
ODE ON MELANCHOLY

No, no, go not to Lethe, neither twist
   Wolfsbane, tight-rooted, for its poisonous wine;
Nor suffer thy pale forehead to be kiss'd
   By nightshade, ruby grape of Proserpine;
Make not your rosary of yew-berries,
   Nor let the beetle, nor the death-moth be
     Your mournful Psyche,° nor the downy owl
A partner in your sorrow's mysteries;
   For shade to shade will come too drowsily,
     And drown the wakeful anguish of the soul.

But when the melancholy fit shall fall
   Sudden from heaven like a weeping cloud,
That fosters the droop-headed flowers all,
   And hides the green hill in an April shroud;
Then glut thy sorrow on a morning rose,
   Or on the rainbow of the salt sand-wave,
     Or on the wealth of globèd peonies;
Or if thy mistress some rich anger shows,
   Emprison her soft hand, and let her rave,
     And feed deep, deep upon her peerless eyes.

She dwells with Beauty—Beauty that must die;
   And Joy, whose hand is ever at his lips
Bidding adieu; and aching Pleasure nigh,
   Turning to poison while the bee-mouth sips:
Ay, in the very temple of Delight
   Veil'd Melancholy has her sovran shrine,
     Though seen of none save him whose strenuous tongue
     Can burst Joy's grape against his palate fine;
His soul shall taste the sadness of her might,
   And be among her cloudy trophies hung.

°soul

Exploring the Metaphors

In the first STANZA (poetic paragraph) of the poem, the reader's imagination is stimulated by a list of images: Lethe (the mythical river of forgetfulness, oblivion); "wolfsbane" [wolf's-bane], nightshade, and yew-berries (poisons); the beetle, the death-moth, the owl, and shades (the shadowy souls of the dead). All these are classically associated with night, darkness, and death. Each term, however, is unique and adds distinct qualities, illuminating the abstraction "death" from various angles. The combination creates a sense of richness and depth. For example, Lethe suggests a forgetful, almost pleasant oblivion; wolfsbane and nightshade make it sinister; and the beetle, death-moth, and owl add an ominous atmosphere.

Notice how these evocative terms are juxtaposed in metaphoric relationships:

Wolf's-bane is (like) wine grapes (association).
Nightshade is (like) the ruby grape (comparison).
Yew-berries are (like) rosary beads (comparison).
Beetle and death-moth are (like) mournful Psyche (identification) .
Downy owl is (like) a partner (identification).
Shades are (like) water—since they drown the soul (association).

"Lethe" is similar to "leaven" in Christ's parable, where we are given only the X term and have to supply the Y ourselves.

Observe how the the other metaphors interact; for example, the metaphor rosary/yew-berries suggests religious overtones. What sort of overtones are created by the other metaphors?

Notice that we are concerned not with the DENOTATIONS, the dictionary definitions or literal meanings of the words in the metaphors—with the fact that the beetle is an insect, for instance—but with their CONNOTATIONS, their reverberations in our experience. In fact, poetic language is concerned mainly with these connotative levels. Here, the connotations of the images produce a mood and a sense of death that cannot be summed up by saying: "No, no, don't commit suicide." In effect, suicide (X) is (like) (Y) going to Lethe, twisting wolf's-bane, and so on. It is an act full of these connotations. Death as an overall metaphor (X) is being associated with melancholy (Y). This sets the stage for a more intense juxtaposition in which melancholy + death (X) is juxtaposed to life (Y) in the second stanza, for example "glut thy sorrow on a morning rose. . ." (Can you see in that line the X/Y juxtaposition life/death?) Stanza one ends enjoining against letting death drown the "wakeful anguish of the soul." Why does the poet call anguish "wakeful"? Is some beneficial, positive aspect of melancholy implied?

The second stanza opens with an extended metaphor identifying the "melancholy fit" (X) with a rain shower (Y). Notice that inside this metaphor is another (like those we looked at in "Ars Poetica"): Instead of "rain cloud," Keats writes "weeping cloud." So we have a compressed identification: rain is (like) weeping.

In the third line of the second stanza the rain from the "melancholy fit" falls on a landscape—flowers, a green hill—making a transition to a fresh series of metaphors with a whole new slant on the subject.

In the lines beginning "Then glut thy sorrow," sorrow (X) is associated with three Y's: (1) a "morning rose," (2) a "rainbow on a wave," and (3) "globèd peonies." Melancholy is now somehow involved with *joy*. Notice that there is a metaphor within a metaphor here, too: wealth (X) is identified with "globèd peonies" (Y). Since we usually think of wealth in terms of money and material possessions, what effect does applying these associations to natural objects have on your mental "seeing"?

In the final lines of this stanza two descriptive words (images) act as forceful covert metaphors (one-word metaphors like "leaven " or "Lethe"). In the phrase "emprison her soft hand," the word "emprison" is implicitly compared (or, if you like, contrasted) with a lover holding the beloved's hand. This might suggest restrictions on freedom, love as a restriction, the binding effect of melancholy. Next consider the word "feed" in the last line of the stanza. There is desperation and hunger here. Why? The following line and stanza provide a partial answer: "She dwells with Beauty—Beauty that must die."

In stanza three we read: "And Joy, whose hand is ever at his lips/ Bidding adieu..." The technical word for a metaphor comparing or identifying a thing or concept (like joy) with human attributes or actions is PERSONIFICATION. Here joy (X) is personified as a lover (Y), that is, Joy is (like) this lover. (The rain cloud in the second stanza was also personified by its identification with "weeping.") This metaphor explores the melancholy of love and its connection with the pleasure of love. Joy and melancholy, life and death, are now seen as part of one process. Next, "and aching Pleasure nigh,/ Turning to poison where the bee-mouth sips" would be absurd if we tried to vizualize it. It is certainly not true to nature: Nectar does not become deadly as the bee ingests it. Does this weaken the metaphor in any way? Notice that the line vividly echoes the poison and death theme in stanza one, as well as giving new vigor to the cliché sentiment: "Your sweetness will turn bitter in your mouth, your pleasures will be pain."

The following two lines identify "Delight" as a temple and "Melancholy" as a shrine in it, suggesting religious connotations, as the rosary did in stanza one. Is it implied that delight is something we worship? Is it a pagan worship? Pagan in what sense? If we worship delight, then don't we have to worship "veil'd Melancholy" as well?

The dramatic intensity of the poem reaches a peak in the next comparison. Joy is now sensual and sensuous, identified metaphorically with a grape. The tongue bursting it focuses the whole subtle, complex entanglement of joy and melancholy that the poem has been manifesting. The single image unites them: We have to know melancholy to know joy, and vice versa. Why do you think Keats says, "Though seen of none save him. . ."? Why is he asserting that the union of the two can be grasped only by someone with a "palate fine"? Can you see how "palate" might suggest a necessary sensitivity to poetic metaphor, for instance? Logic might demonstrate that bursting joy's grape is a contradiction in terms, but is it? Compressed into this dense little metaphor is the sense of transience that the whole poem has been suggesting ("Beauty that must die") and the pain of life ("wakeful anguish").

So we have seen how metaphoric language (sometimes called FIGURATIVE LANGUAGE) spins an intricate web of connotation and association and gives a form to difficult abstractions. If you follow this—if you experience this as you work through the poem, you will discover how metaphors always go beyond the literal and outdistance "logic."

1. An ODE is a poem of praise. Why is this poem called "Ode on Melancholy"?
2. Consider the metaphor in the phrase "nightshade, ruby grape of Proserpine." Proserpine (Persephone) was the goddess associated with spring and rebirth, but she also served as Queen of Hades or Hell, Pluto's wife in his domain. What are the implications of comparing nightshade to a grape of Proserpine? How does this connection relate to others in the poem ?
3. Consider the comparison "Nor let the beetle, nor the death-moth be / Your mournful Psyche." What are the implications of this comparison (beetle/ death-moth is (like) mournful Psyche) for the rest of the poem?
4. In the last line of the first stanza, "And drown the wakeful anguish of the soul," how is the sense of "wakeful anguish" illustrated by what follows?
5. Consider the phrase "on a morning rose" in the second stanza. A PUN is a play on words with the same or similar sound but with sharply different meanings. What is the pun in this line, and how do you think it adds meaning to the poem?
6. What kinds of meanings does the word "feed" in the last line of the second stanza suggest about melancholy? Are there any other words in this stanza that relate to "feed"?
7. Consider Keats's use of the expression "palate fine." Aside from the question of rhyme, why is the word "fine" so appropriate to this line?
8. How are joy, melancholy, and transience embodied throughout the poem?
9. In the last two lines, why does the poet say "*sadness* of her might"? Why are the trophies "cloudy"?
10. Consider any descriptive phrase or adjective in the poem. What are the connotations? How does it relate to the rest of the poem?
11. This poem and many others in the tradition of older English poetry refers to the poet's (or poetic voice's) "mistress." The social status of women in nineteenth century British society was obviously different from what women's status is now in our culture. You might want to consider whether the old idea of the poet's mistress affects the impact of the metaphors of this poem in any way. See also "To His Coy Mistress" (page 27) and "My Mistress' Eyes" (page 31) in this chapter.

Technical Notes

The poem is an ode, with the stanza rhyme scheme *a b a b c d e c d e*. The METER is predominately IAMBIC PENTAMETER.

Since this poem happens to be about both poetry and melancholy, two subjects we have already encountered, you can compare its effect on you with the effects of "Ode on Melancholy" and "Ars Poetica."

Gerald Francis
POETRY AND MELANCHOLY

A poem is meant to give relief,
To soothe all pangs of dread and grief.
To hear the truth of love or woe,
Then to a good poem you should go.
The poem is like a faithful friend,
It helps a broken heart to mend,
It makes a gloomy day turn bright,
Because its words have secret might.

Exploring the Metaphors

1. What do you think of this poem? If you like it, what makes it effective? If you dislike it, what do you think is wrong with it?
2. Can you find any metaphors here? What are the X and Y terms?
3. What are some of the essential differences between this poem and "Ode on Melancholy" and "Ars Poetica"?
4. What effect do the meter and rhyme of the poem have on you?

The poet is trying to tell us how he feels about poetry, how it brightens his life. Do we get anything new here, any depth, excitement, or discovery? Does the poet get beyond trying to convince us to agree with him?

The first stanza is straight statement, telling us what to think. The second attempts some metaphors: (1) a poem (X) is compared to a faithful friend (Y), (2) a heart (X) is identified as something which can be broken and mended (Y), and (3) the poem (X) is given the properties of sunlight (Y).

Of these, the first asserts a similarity which falls flat because there is no tension between the terms, nothing concrete in "faithful friend" to give the abstraction ("poem") life. Does the expression "faithful friend" do any more than try to persuade us that a poem is nice by comparing it to something everyone likes? This resembles a politician supporting motherhood to get votes. Of course, we can't be sure of the poet's intentions, but we can see the effect of the finished product. The second quasi-metaphor is an out-and-out cliché. What about the third? In each case the unlike factor is weak, and so the union of terms looks on the surface like a metaphor but the effect is not really metaphoric.

What about the form of the poem? Many people believe that if a statement rhymes and has regular meter, it's a poem. "Poetry and Melancholy" has both. After reading it, do you think that definition of poetry is reasonable?

How do you react to the implications and levels in this little metaphor? What does it suggest about Mistress Southwell—her personality?

Robert Herrick
UPON MISTRESS SUSANNA SOUTHWELL, HER FEET

Her pretty feet
Like snails did creep
A little out, and then,
As if they played at bo-peep,
Did soon draw in again.

This is the complete poem from which the first line was extracted as an example in the introduction to this chapter. Here, as in "Ars Poetica," a poet is making his case by employing a series of metaphors. Now that we have the whole poem, see how the rose comparison works in context.

Robert Burns
A RED, RED ROSE

Oh my luve is like a red, red rose,
That's newly sprung in June:
Oh my luve is like the melodie,
That's sweetly play'd in tune.

As fair art thou, my bonie lass,
So deep in luve am I;
And I will luve thee still, my dear,
Till a' the seas gang dry.

Till a' the seas gang dry, my dear,
And the rocks melt wi' the sun;
And I will luve thee still, my dear,
While the sands o' life shall run.

And fare thee weel, my only luve!
And fare thee weel a while!
And I will come again, my luve,
Tho' it were ten thousand mile!

Exploring the Metaphors

1. The poet writes that his "luve" is like a rose. Does "luve" mean his girl friend or his love for her? Or both? Consider how this ambiguity might add depth to the poem.
2. In the second, third, and fourth stanzas of the poem, the poet makes exaggerated comparisons in which the quality of his love is compared to impossible or heroic actions. How do these exaggerations contribute to the poem's effectiveness as a statement of love?
3. What would you get from the photograph accompanying this poem without the poem itself? Do you think it would be possible to convey the sense of this poem in an illustration? Why or why not?
4. Consider the rhyme and meter of the poem. How do they contribute to the poem's effectiveness as a love poem? Does this poem remind you of a song?

On the surface the next piece is a carpe diem "seduction poem," in which the narrator is supposedly talking a lady into surrendering her virginity. The argument of the poem is clever and straightforward. Whether it would actually accomplish its purpose is a matter for conjecture, but a deeper poetic purpose is served. The seduction framework becomes the poet's opportunity to discover things about our relation to love and time.

Andrew Marvell
TO HIS COY MISTRESS

Had we but world enough, and time,
This coyness, Lady, were no crime.
We would sit down, and think which way
To walk, and pass our long love's day.
Thou by the Indian Ganges' side
Should'st rubies find: I by the tide
Of Humber would complain. I would
Love you ten years before the Flood:
And you should, if you please, refuse
Till the Conversion of the Jews.
My vegetable love should grow
Vaster than empires, and more slow.
An hundred years should go to praise

Thine eyes, and on thy forehead gaze;
Two hundred to adore each breast:
But thirty thousand to the rest:
An age at least to every part,
And the last age should show your heart.
For, Lady, you deserve this state;
Nor would I love at lower rate.
    But at my back I always hear
Time's wingèd chariot hurrying near:
And yonder all before us lie
Deserts of vast eternity.
Thy beauty shall no more be found;
Nor, in thy marble vault, shall sound
My echoing song: then worms shall try
That long preserved virginity:
And your quaint honor turn to dust;
And into ashes all my lust.
The grave's a fine and private place,
But none I think do there embrace.
    Now therefore, while the youthful hue
Sits on thy skin like morning dew,
And while thy willing soul transpires
At every pore with instant fires,
Now let us sport us while we may;
And now, like am'rous birds of prey,
Rather at once our time devour,
Than languish in his slow-chapt ° power.
Let us roll all our strength, and all
Our sweetness, up into one ball:
And tear our pleasures with rough strife,
Thorough the iron gates of life.
Thus, though we cannot make our sun
Stand still, yet we will make him run.

° slowly chewed

Exploring the Metaphors

   The poem begins with a complicated comparison of the hours of "love's long day" (X) to the ages of history (Y) and a comparison of the local terrain of the lover's walk (X) to the geography of the world (Y). Brooks in a seventeenth-century suburban field become great rivers, the Humber and the Ganges; the lady's body becomes something that could literally take ages to properly explore.

If there were time, the poet says, he could do all this.

The overall structure follows the form of a classical three-part logical argument: (1) if ("Had we but world enough . . ."), (2) but ("But at my back. . .") and (3) therefore ("Now therefore, while . . .")

Having opened his piece by emphasizing the shortness of life, the poet moves through the second and third stages of the argument using a series of forceful local metaphors that set abstractions against concrete details. Among other things, this demonstrates how metaphors can give immediacy and uniqueness to the abstract. The major direct and indirect metaphors are listed below.

X	Y
1. Time	1. A wingèd chariot
2. Deserts	2. Vast eternity
3. Virginity	3. Something (like a corpse) that can be "tried" by worms (note the sexual implication of worms)
4. Honor	4. Quaintness, a quaint object °
5. Honor	5. Subject to decay (turning to dust)
6. Lust	6. Combustible material (since it can be turned to ashes)
7. The grave	7. Something like a bed chamber (it is a "fine and private place" except that none "do there embrace")
8. Youth (as reflected in the skin)	8. Like morning dew (which, after all, vanishes soon enough)
9. Willing soul	9. Fire burning out through the skin (probably burning off the dew)
10. The lovers	10. "Am'rous birds of prey"
11. Time	11. Something which can be devoured
12. The lovers' strength and sweetness	12. Something that can be rolled up into a ball—(like) birds rolling up into a ball when tearing their "pleasures with rough strife"
13. Life	13. Iron gates
14. Sun	14. Unspecified, probably time (though it might be love or other things as well)

° "Quaint" was also a period sexual pun.

As you can see, many of the metaphors are implicit. The point here is not to become an expert at uncovering and analyzing hidden metaphors but to see that poetic language is essentially metaphoric language: to become sensitive to this level of communication.

Marvell's use of words relies, not always obviously, on the union of dissimilar things, the unlike factor. In some cases—for example, item 7 in the preceding list—the two terms are contrasted. In other cases there is comparison—X is (like) Y: youth equals morning dew (item 8), and lovers equal amorous birds of prey (item 10). Several of the metaphors are associations: time with wingèd chariot (item 1), life with iron gates (item 13), and honor with dust and with quaintness (items 4 and 5).

What sort of effect does the surrealist landscape sketched by the metaphors have on your understanding? Do you sense a unique perception of love and living where the "iron gates of life" open on those "deserts of vast eternity" as the two "am'rous birds of prey" roll through "tearing their pleasures"? Look at this last metaphor: Through this identification (lovers are birds) Marvell develops a complex psychological vision with love as hunger, violence, raw survival. As often happens, there is a twist or ironic play on an old cliché here: Commonly, poetic lovers were compared to turtledoves and the like. How do you react to the savage humor of Marvell's slant? What dimension does it add to the general attitude (in the poem) about lovemaking? Remember, the piece is supposed to be arguing in favor of this love. Is the poet really making fun of it too? If we dynamically balance the basic seriousness with the mocking humor undercutting it, we discover a form of poetic irony, a surprising reversal of the general drift and expected direction of the poet's point of view. Comparing romantic love to worms, graves, and ashes is one way of mocking it. Romantic images are continually compared with images usually considered unpleasant. The effect is partly to shock readers into reexamining their ideas and habits of thought.

1. Honor—generally thought of as something lofty and significant—is associated with the word "quaint." What effect does this have?
2. The lovers as birds of prey are going to "devour" time. Since what they are devouring is each other, do you see that there is an implication that the lovers *are* time themselves?
3. Consider the line "My vegetable love should grow/ Vaster than empires, and more slow." What are the connotations (suggested meanings) of Marvell's association of love's growth with vegetable growth? In what ways does this metaphor relate to the central comparison of the first part of the poem, that is, the comparison of love's time to historical time?
4. Consider in detail some of the possible comments on love and time implied by the language of the poem.
5. Marvell opens the poem by suggesting that time is short. Consider the last two lines. Is there a contradiction here? What kinds of relations can you develop

between the opening statements and this one?

Technical Notes

The poem is written in couplets of IAMBIC TETRAMETER.

Here the poet pokes fun at the exaggerated and overdone metaphors used by his fellow poets to praise their lovers. Shakespeare calls attention to the grotesqueness and absurdity of these comparisons and illustrates the dangers of misusing metaphoric language, dangers anyone who has ever tried to write poetry will be familiar with.

Male poets in Western culture traditionally have treated "mistresses" as objects of poetic contemplation. Do you think Shakespeare falls merely falls prey to this tradition or that he transcends it here in some way?

William Shakespeare
MY MISTRESS' EYES . . .

My mistress' eyes are nothing like the sun;
Coral is far more red than her lips' red:
If snow be white, why then her breasts are dun;
If hairs be wires, black wires grow on her head.
I have seen roses damask'd, red and white,
But no such roses see I in her cheeks;
And in some perfumes is there more delight
Than in the breath that from my mistress reeks.
I love to hear her speak; yet well I know
That music hath a far more pleasing sound;
I grant I never saw a goddess go,
My mistress, when she walks, treads on the ground:
And yet, by heaven, I think my love as rare
As any she belied with false compare.

Exploring the Metaphors

In the first line Shakespeare mocks a comparison which was an old favorite at that time and had been much used by earlier poets: the comparison of the lover's eyes with the sun. The purpose of this was to exalt the woman by identifying her with lofty, impressive objects.

Here the way Shakespeare puts the metaphors makes them ridiculous; we have a lady's snow white breast, her rosy cheeks, her lips as red as coral. But Shakespeare's phrasing stresses the real, denotative, literal aspect of the terms in each comparison—the snow, the rose, the coral—and draws our attention to the difference, the impossible difference, between these and a real woman's features. So he compels us to imagine a grotesque lady, whom he compares to his mistress, to the latter's definite advantage. By setting the artificial mistress created out of clumsy and cliché metaphor beside his own realistically presented, unadorned, but "rare" mistress, Shakespeare focuses on basic humanness with fresh eyes. We might explicate this structure as follows: overdone "fancy" depiction (X) +

realistic description of the real mistress (Y) = fresh insight into love, language, and poetry. So cliché and absurd metaphor are made a term in Shakespeare's own very original and acute metaphor.

1. What different kinds of bad or cliché metaphor is he ridiculing here?
2. What is the real purpose of his mockery of bad metaphor?
3. Consider the picture the poem gives you of Shakespeare's mistress. What details do we know about her? First, is there a double irony in words like "reeks" and "wires"—that is, does the poet evoke both the woman's beauty and her earthy, even gross, reality? Second, consider the poet's use of the word "rare" in the last line. How does this word relate to the argument in favor of his mistress?
4. Does the word "love" in the phrase "my love as rare" have a double meaning? What are the implications of this?
5. Consider the last line. Why does the poet use the word "belied"?
6. Could Shakespeare have as effectively described his mistress's naturalness without referring to the artifice of other poets?
7. Compare this poem with the Burns piece.

Technical Notes

This poem is a SHAKESPEAREAN SONNET written in iambic pentameter.

Here's another poem about a "mistress." Does this poet escape sexism through metaphor? Herrick's poetic observation would probably make sense to most men. What about women readers? If you think so, why? If not, why not?

In everyday speech we might talk about a woman's "flowing gown" or describe a dress as "flowing." But this poem's comparison of the motion of water to the fit and fall of a dress has lost its impact. It is a dead metaphor (like the eye of a needle or leg of a table); it has become so common that we no longer react to it metaphorically at all. How does Herrick bring the dead metaphor to life?

Robert Herrick
UPON JULIA'S CLOTHES

When as in silks my Julia goes,
Then, then (me thinks) how sweetly flowes
That liquefaction of her clothes.
Next, when I cast mine eyes and see
That brave Vibration each way free;
O how that glittering taketh me!

Exploring the Metaphors

1. Consider Herrick's use of "brave Vibration." How might this describe Julia's clothes? Julia herself?
2. Make the same consideration for "glittering" in the last line.
3. Consider how Herrick's overall description of Julia's clothes is a description of Julia and of Julia's effect on him.
4. Could "each way free" also suggest that she is finally naked? Suppose you read the last line with the emphasis: "Oh how *that* glittering taketh me."
5. Why does the poet repeat the word "then" in the second line? Does this fit with the metaphor of "liquefaction"?

The late-eighteenth-century poet William Blake was both poet and painter, famed for his "visionary" images. How do the metaphors work here?

William Blake

AUGURIES OF INNOCENCE

To see a World in a Grain of Sand,
And a Heaven in a Wild Flower,
Hold Infinity in the palm of your hand,
And Eternity in an hour.
A Robin Redbreast in a Cage
Puts all Heaven in a Rage.
A dove-house fill'd with Doves and Pigeons
Shudders Hell thro' all its regions.
A dog starv'd at his Master's Gate
Predicts the ruin of the State.
A Horse misus'd upon the Road
Calls to Heaven for Human blood.
Each outcry of the hunted Hare
A fibre from the Brain does tear.
A Skylark wounded in the wing,
A Cherubim does cease to sing.
The Game Cock clip'd and arm'd for fight

Does the Rising Sun affright.
Every Wolf's and Lion's howl
Raises from Hell a Human Soul.
The wild Deer, wand'ring here and there,
Keeps the Human Soul from Care.
The Lamb misus'd breeds Public Strife
And yet forgives the Butcher's knife.
The Bat that flits at close of Eve
Has left the Brain that won't Believe.
The Owl that calls upon the Night
Speaks the Unbeliever's fright.
He who shall hurt the little Wren
Shall never be belov'd by Men.
He who the Ox to wrath has mov'd
Shall never be by Woman lov'd.
The wanton Boy that kills the Fly
Shall feel the Spider's enmity.
He who torments the Chafer's Sprite
Weaves a Bower in endless Night.
The Catterpiller on the Leaf
Repeats to thee thy Mother's grief.
Kill not the Moth nor Butterfly,
For the Last Judgment draweth nigh.
He who shall train the Horse to war
Shall never pass the Polar Bar.
The Beggar's Dog and Widow's Cat,
Feed them and thou wilt grow fat.
The gnat that sings his Summer's Song
Poison gets from Slander's tongue.
The poison of the Snake and Newt
Is the sweat of Envy's Foot.
The poison of the Honey Bee
Is the Artist's Jealousy.
The Prince's Robes and Beggar's Rags
Are Toadstools on the Miser's Bags.
A Truth that's told with bad intent
Beats all the Lies you can invent.
It is right it should be so;
Man was made for Joy and Woe;
And when this we rightly know,
Thro' the World we safely go,

Joy and Woe are woven fine,
A Clothing for the soul divine.
Under every grief and pine
Runs a joy with silken twine.
The Babe is more than Swadling Bands;
Throughout all these Human Lands
Tools were made, and Born were hands,
Every Farmer Understands.
Every Tear from Every Eye
Becomes a Babe in Eternity;
This is caught by Females bright
And return'd to its own delight.
The Bleat, the Bark, Bellow and Roar,
Are Waves that Beat on Heaven's Shore.
The Babe that weeps the Rod beneath
Writes Revenge in realms of Death.
The Beggar's Rags, fluttering in Air,
Does to Rags the Heavens tear.
The Soldier, arm'd with Sword and Gun,
Palsied strikes the Summer's Sun.
The poor Man's Farthing is worth more
Than all the Gold on Afric's Shore.
One Mite wrung from the Lab'rer's hands
Shall buy and sell the Miser's Lands;
Or, if protected from on high,
Does that whole Nation sell and buy.
He who mocks the Infant's Faith
Shall be mock'd in Age and Death.
He who shall teach the Child to Doubt
The rotting grave shall ne'er get out.
He who respects the Infant's faith
Triumphs over Hell and Death.
The Child's Toys and the Old Man's Reasons
Are the Fruits of the Two seasons.
The Questioner, who sits so sly,
Shall never know how to Reply.
He who replies to words of Doubt
Doth put the Light of Knowledge out.
The Strongest Poison ever known
Came from Caesar's Laurel Crown.
Nought can Deform the Human Race

Like to the Armour's iron brace.
When Gold and Gems adorn the Plow
To Peaceful Arts shall Envy Bow.
A Riddle, or the Cricket's Cry,
Is to Doubt a fit Reply.
The Emmet's Inch and Eagle's Mile
Make Lame Philosophy to smile.
He who Doubts from what he sees
Will ne'er Believe, do what you Please.
If the Sun and Moon should Doubt,
They'd immediately Go Out.
To be in a Passion you Good may do,
But no Good if a Passion is in you.
The Whore and Gambler, by the State
Licensed, build that Nation's Fate.
The Harlot's cry from Street to Street
Shall weave Old England's winding Sheet.
The Winner's Shout, the Loser's Curse,
Dance before dead England's Hearse.
Every Night and every Morn
Some to Misery are Born.
Every Morn and every Night
Some are Born to Sweet Delight.
Some are Born to Sweet Delight,
Some are Born to Endless Night.
We are led to Believe a Lie
When we see not Thro' the Eye,
Which was Born in a Night to perish in a Night,
When the Soul Slept in Beams of Light.
God Appears, and God is Light,
To those poor souls who dwell in Night,
But does a Human Form Display
To those who Dwell in Realms of Day.

Exploring the Metaphors

Like other poets, Blake makes his metaphoric juxtapositions in several different
ways:

Comparison: "The Bleat, the Bark, Bellow and Roar/Are Waves that Beat on
Heaven's Shore."

Identification: "Runs a joy with silken twine."
Contrast: "Some are Born to Sweet Delight,/ Some are Born to Endless Night."
Association: "Each outcry of the hunted Hare/ A fibre from the Brain does tear."
Personification: "Poison gets from Slander's tongue."

Notice how many of the associations take the form of cause and effect. If X, then Y; if "A Robin Redbreast in a Cage," then "all Heaven in a Rage"; if a man "the Ox to wrath has moved," then he "shall never be by Woman lov'd." Notice also that it is by linking commonplace things (a beggar's rags, the maltreatment of a horse) with grand cosmic consequences that Blake projects his vision.

The poet says that "To see a World in a Grain of Sand,/ And a Heaven in a Wild Flower," is his intention, and so he sets out to show us the great in the small, the universal in the particular, the celestial in the mundane. The contrasts are merged into metaphoric unity. Is he implying that the action of metaphor (where the uniting of seemingly unlike, fragmentary things reveals a whole truth) is a universal, spiritual law?

In concluding, Blake extends his union of opposites—big and little—to man and God. For "those poor souls who dwell in Night" (and "night," like "black," in "Thirteen Ways of Looking at a Blackbird" is a loaded word that operates metaphorically connoting ignorance, evil, blindness), God appears as "light." But the ones who live in God's realms (day) observe that God wears a human face. Anyone who can see a world in a grain of sand will grasp this immediately.

1. How does the line "And Eternity in an hour" resemble Marvell's language in the first section of "To His Coy Mistress"?
2. Consider the lines "The Game Cock clip'd and arm'd for fight/Does the Rising Sun affright." What are the similarities and differences between the two terms of this metaphor (the game cock and the sun)? Make this kind of consideration for other metaphors in the poem.
3. What possible reasons might Blake have had for calling this poem "Auguries of Innocence"?
4. Consider any of the local metaphors in the poem. What new perceptions of things result from the metaphors?

Technical Notes

The poem has a feeling of regular meter, partly because of Blake's use of couplets—most of them separate, self-contained thoughts—and partly because of his use of ACCENTUAL MEASURE, four STRESSES to a line. Note the change of meter in the sixth line from the end. What does this change accomplish?

The contemporary Russian poet Voznesensky plays on the metaphoric idea that this world (X) is really an antiworld (Y). See for yourself how he works this out. Notice what effect his individual, or local, metaphors have on this concept.

Andrei Voznesensky
ANTIWORLDS

The clerk Bukashkin is our neighbor:
His face is grey as blotting-paper.

But like balloons of blue or red,
Bright Antiworlds
         float over his head!
On them reposes, prestidigitous,
Ruling the cosmos, a demon-magician,
Anti-Bukashkin the academician,
Lapped in the arms of Lollobrigidas.

But Anti-Bukashkin's dreams are the color
Of blotting-paper, and couldn't be duller.

Long live Antiworlds! They rebut
With dreams the rat-race and the rut.
For some to be clever, some must be boring.
No deserts? No oases, then.
There are no women—
         just anti-men.
In the forests, anti-machines are roaring.
There's the dirt of the earth, as well as the salt.
If the earth broke down, the sun would halt.

Ah, my critics, how I love them.
Upon the neck of the keenest of them,
Fragrant and bald as fresh-baked bread,
There shines a perfect anti-head . . .

. . . I sleep with windows open wide;
Somewhere a falling star invites,
And skyscrapers,
                    like stalactites,

Hang from the planet's underside.
There, upside down
                    below me far,
Stuck like a fork into the earth,
Or perching like a carefree moth,
My little Antiworld,
                    there you are!

In the middle of the night, why is it
That Antiworlds are moved to visit?

Why do they sit together, gawking
At the television, and never talking?

Between them, not one word has passed.
Their first strange meeting is their last.

Neither can manage the least *bon ton*.
Oh, how they'll blush for it later on!

Their ears are burning like a pair
Of crimson butterflies, hovering there . . .

. . . A distinguished lecturer lately told me,
"Antiworlds are a total loss."

Still, my apartment-cell won't hold me;
I thrash in my sleep, I turn and toss.

And, radio-like, my cat lies curled
With his green eye tuned in to the world.

Translation from Russian by Richard Wilbur

1. The Metaphoric Eye: Poetic Vision   **39**

The poem below is a statement of traditional Christian doctrine, but it is made through metaphors which give it a humorous twist and revitalize the idea—as well as giving you something to think about next time you crave a smoke.

Anonymous

A RELIGIOUS USE
OF TAKING TOBACCO

The Indian weed withered quite,
Green at morn, cut down at night,
   Shows thy decay;
   All flesh is hay:
Thus think, then drink tobacco.

And when the smoke ascends on high,
Think thou behold'st the vanity
   Of worldly stuff,
   Gone with a puff:
Thus think, then drink tobacco.

But when the pipe grows foul within,
Think of thy soul defiled with sin.
   And that the fire
   Doth it require:
Thus think, then drink tobacco.

The ashes that are left behind,
May serve to put thee still in mind
   That into dust
   Return thou must:
Thus think, then drink tobacco.

Exploring the Metaphors

1. What are the terms of the major metaphoric comparison in this poem?
2. How is this comparison extended into other metaphors ?
3. Would you argue about doctrine put in this way or experience the "truth" of it no matter what your beliefs? Why?

Unlike most of the poems we have looked at up to now, the one below may seem at first to be no more than a series of obliquely related statements. The connections between them are not very clear until we see that violence, anger, war, death are continually being referred to.

Philip Levine
HOW MUCH CAN IT HURT?

The woman at the checkstand
Who wishes you cancer

The fat man who hates his mother
The doctor who forgets

The soup bubbling on the back of the stove
The stone staring into the sun

The girl who kisses her own arms
The girl who fries her hair

The egg turning brown under the spoon
The lemon laughing all night long

My brother in his uniform over Dresden
The single thrill of fire going for the bed

The kindergarten blowing its windows out
Chalk burning the little fingers

The newspaper waiting all weekend
Dozing in rain with the deaths smeared on its lips

The oiling and the loading and the springing
The bullets sucking quietly in their cradles

How much can it hurt in the wood
In the long nerve of lead, in the fattened head

How much can it hurt
In each ration of meat hooked and hanging

In the unfinished letter, the dried opened socket
The veil of skin flapping, the star falling

My face punctured with glass
The teeth eating themselves in dreams

Our blood refusing to breathe, refusing to sleep
Asking the wounded moon

Asking the pillow, asking, asking
How much can it hurt?

Exploring the Metaphors

What we really have in this poem is an extension of the principle of covert or implied metaphoric language: The statements are comparisons, and we have to explore what lies unstated, what connects X to Y. As we have seen, in poetry the unstated meanings really matter most.

There are many examples here of metaphoric usage dealt with in previous poems, for example, "The newspaper waiting all weekend/ Dozing in rain with deaths smeared on its lips. " The newspaper is a personification, as joy is in "Ode on Melancholy ."

1. What examples of metaphoric language can you find in the poem?
2. "The girl who fries her hair" seems somehow to connect with the images of burning children in Dresden. (Dresden, an open city, was bombed by the Allies during World War II; 100,000 civilians were killed, many of them women and children who had been sent there for safety.) Can you find other such relationships between the opening ten lines and the rest of the poem?
3. Consider whether it is possible to write a simple explication of this particular piece. If not, why not?

Here we see a medieval French poem that has something in common with the twentieth-century piece we have just looked at. The poet lists things—in this case the names of famous women in history—without making any overt comment. Though this list is not as studded with individual metaphors as the one in the Levine poem, there is obviously something metaphoric here. Can you see it? Remember that we are looking for a relationship that creates a tension, an X/Y.

François Villon
BALLAD OF THE LADIES OF OLD

Tell, where, what country is Flora,
The girl who was called the fair Roman?
Or where is Archipiades, [1] or Thais, [2]
Who was her incomparable cousin?
Or Echo, who whispered of love
Over rivers and desolate marsh?
Her beauty was far more than human, they say.
And last year's snows, where are they?

Where is sweet Eloise, the wise, [3]
For whose love Peter Abelard endured
The loss of the flame of his manhood,
And the pain of a monk coldly cloistered?
And where the tyrannical queen [4]
Who decreed that poor Buridan, her lover,
Be tossed in a sack in the bay?
And last year's snows, where are they?

Oh, where is the lily pale princess
Who sang in a lily pale voice?
Bertha bigfoot, [5] Alice, Beatrice,
Lady Haremburgis, [6] and others of choice?
And good Joan of Arc, where is she,
Whose brave body kept Englishmen warm?

Where are they, Oh Virgin, I pray?
And last year's snows, where are they?

ENVOY
Prince, don't ask me this week or this year
To divulge where these ladies have gone.
The refrain of this song only stays.
Last year's snows, where are they?

Translation from French by John Briggs

[1] a celebrated Athenian woman
[2] no doubt beautiful
[3] Eloise was a student of Abelard, the twelfth-century philosopher.
He was castrated by agents of her father. He subsequently retired to
a monastery, and she to a convent.
[4] wife of Louis X
[5] Charlemagne's mother.
[6] the twelfth- or thirteenth-century daughter of a count

Exploring the Metaphors

Notice that each group in the list is followed by a line saying simply, "They're gone, and where are yesterday's snows?" We might compare this with the Levine line: "How much can it hurt?" You *know* the answer, perhaps, but you cannot say what it is. The simple answer is unstated, and you have to bring to it your own fresh understanding of death, pain, and loss. The extension here associates and unites X (the ladies in question are all gone) and Y (where are the snows?). In a sense the poet has actually said that the women have melted away like the snow, but by keeping the connection less obvious, he produces a sense of distance, mystery, and intensity.

1. Do you think the length of the Villon poem adds anything to its effect? If so, how do you think it does?
2. Are the questions asked in the Villon and the Levine poems really meant to be answered? Can they be?

In this early English poem the poet laments the loss of his young daughter and likens her to a lost pearl. What other things might the pearl stand for? The entire poem, of which these two stanzas are a modern translation, contains 100 stanzas, each twelve lines long. In the poem the poet dreams he finds his pearl in the heavenly kingdom.

Anonymous
from THE PEARL

I

Perfect pearl, a pleasure for princes
To cleanly enclose in gold so clear,
Not in the orient, am I convinced,
Can any preciousness equal her,
So round, so right in every way,
So small, so smooth her curvings were
Of every jewel I've seen, I say,
I call her clearly beyond compare.
   Alas! in an arbor I lost her;
   Hidden in the high tangled grass;
   For love's lost soul my griefs were:
   Pearl, spotless, perfect, peerless.

II

Since in that spot it from me fell,
I have often stood still, dreaming
Of the good that's gone, my wealth
Weighs on my worn heart false, seeming;
Within I swell and burn and strain.
Yet such a sweet song stays
From that hushed hour, pain
Seems soothed in dreams of other days;
   Images float past in fierce distress:
   To see her set in sullen dirt!
   O earth you stain that sweetness—
   My pearl without a spot or hurt.

Translated from Middle English by Richard Monaco

1. The Metaphoric Eye: Poetic Vision **45**

46   *Metaphor:* The Logic of Poetry

Chapter 2

Metaphoric Language in Poetry

We have seen how the metaphoric experience goes beyond subject matter such as mistresses, tobacco, or melancholy, and can excite an awareness, an intuitive state, in the reader's mind. Now, to go further, let's consider some varieties of metaphoric language in order to understand how that special poetic language and metaphoric logic contributes to the overall mood and attitude of a poem—what is called the poem's TONE.

Most of the fairly simple metaphors we have seen fall into three basic categories. In these, the metaphoric X/Y juxtapositions either compare, contrast, associate, or identify:

1. An *abstraction* with something *concrete* (or vice versa), e.g., joy/grape; time/wingéd chariot. Most simple metaphors are of this type. Sometimes, however, the second (or Y) term is unstated, for example, the metaphor of the blackbird in the Stevens poem, where we have a concrete X (blackbird) which implies many abstract Ys such as mystery, truth, danger.

2. Something *concrete* with something *concrete*, e.g., Keats's "yew-berries" (X) and the "ruby grape of Proserpine" (Y). Concrete to concrete metaphors are not very common.

3. An *abstraction* with an *abstraction*. This is rarer still; we will see one in Donne's "A Valediction: Forbidding Mourning," where ordinary lovers have souls which are said to be "like sense." Usually at least one of the terms in an abstract to abstract metaphor is arranged to *seem* concrete.

In the case of combination 1, the abstract term is generally the main subject—the focus of the metaphor (Joy, Time, etc.)—but in combinations 2 or 3 it may be more difficult to tell. For instance, suppose we turn our example around and say: "This red, red rose is like my luve." What is the main subject here? It could still be "my luve," but it might alternatively be the rose. Only the context, the situation in which the statement is made, can tell us for certain which term is the main one. Notice how the main subject directs the metaphor. Sometimes we can discover the subject only through the context, or tone.

What if we said, "The red rose of my luve"? The same X/Y relationship would exist, but now there's a new angle. Now love is *clearly* abstract. (Of course, we're assuming a context that doesn't refer to a flower on her evening dress.) Then if we alter our choice of words slightly, using more conversational or colloquial diction, we might say: "My girlfriend's a real rose." Each of these changes affects the metaphor and how we take it. *Tone* is considered to be the apparent attitude a piece takes toward its subject matter, and so the way a given metaphor is "put" reflects or expresses the tone.

Another expression or reflection of tone is IRONY. People have talked about socratic irony, verbal irony, cosmic irony, tragic irony, and so on, but what is really taking place in an ironic statement? Perhaps it is not too complicated: "If you don't smoke enough cigarettes, you'll never get lung cancer." The writer says one thing (X) but really means something else (Y), though, the words of the statement might be perfectly true. Irony has to do with being aware of the speaker's intentions in making her statement. Dynamically, irony works more or less like metaphor: There is a tension between the literal level and the connotations—for instance, "Nations have been known to make war from time to time." You might call that an ironic UNDERSTATEMENT. It plays off the fact that human beings have been continually fighting for thousands of years. But because this is not just said outright, the unlike factor between our knowledge of the seriousness of our continual war making (X) and a statement of it as if it were a trivial matter (Y) intensifies the statement, puts it in a new light, makes us stop and see it freshly for a moment.

There are many forms of irony. For instance, in understatement the expressed meaning is mild and the intended meaning is intense, as above, while in ironic overstatement (HYPERBOLE) the reverse is true. In some irony a character or statement considered foolish may actually prove wise, or an apparently wise one may prove foolish. In dramatic irony a character may think he is doing one thing while he is really doing something else (Oedipus, when he looks for his father's murderer, is really finding out that the murderer is himself), or something may have one meaning in its immediate context and then turn out to mean something else later on (ironic FORESHADOWING). In heavy irony, called SARCASM, apparent praise is actually dispraise (for example, a conservative commenting on a liberal President: "Oh, he's a great man for the White House!"). So in all irony there is a difference, a tension between what a thing means on the surface (X) and our recognition of another "real" meaning (Y).

There is a vital difference, however, between literary irony and everyday irony, just as there is a difference between literary metaphors and everyday metaphors. Saying that someone is a great man for the White House and meaning that you think he is really *not* a great man, is ironic only until the listener understands your real message. Everyday irony, like everyday metaphors, resolve themselves in the end to a fairly clear, singleminded message. Not so with literary irony. In *Oedipus Rex* we will never really get to the bottom of the irony that Oedipus, determined to find his father's murderer, finds the truth about himself. Students and critics of Sophocles have been arguing about that irony for over 2,000 years. Literary irony, like literary metaphor, maintains the tension of its unlike factor. The point of literary irony isn't a message, but a perception of truth.

Other elements that help establish a poem's tone are pun and PARADOX. A pun, which we have already touched on, works similarly to irony and metaphor: "Would he had been one of my rank!" a Shakespeare character says, and another replies, "To have smell'd like a fool." So rank as status (X) is juxtaposed to rank as a bad smell (Y). The similarity between X and Y (they are the same word) emphasizes the *unlike* factor, the contrast, between them.

In a paradox, X is set up to be equal to its opposite; thus the Y in a paradox is the same as X's contradiction, as in Marvell's line (from "Eyes and Tears"), "Yet happy they whom *grief* does bless." So in the paradox, too, the unlike factor gives power to the asserted similarity.

The Shakespeare and Marvell examples of pun and paradox are also examples of irony. Pun and paradox frequently have an ironic effect.

Poetic *images* refer to something perceived by the human senses. These are sometimes called "word pictures," although there are images of sound, touch, taste, and smell as well.

An image, in itself, is a description—for example, the wind blowing, a river flowing, the smell or feel of grass or earth, the sound of a gun. At the very least it is a noun: wind, river, grass, gun—in other words, a sound, sight, taste, smell, or touch. The act of poetry is to make the images of experience or imagination (an imaginary animal or place, for instance) metaphoric, that is, to make them mean things they *cannot* describe. This is done either by (1) combining the image into a metaphor (associating time to the image "wingèd chariot" for example) or by (2) placing it in a context where it *functions* as a metaphor (i.e., the image of the eye of the blackbird as the only moving thing among twenty snowy mountains, where the blackbird's eye becomes an X with many unstated Y's).

The type of image helps determine tone. In order to see this more clearly, let's look at some of the types of images possible.

1. *Natural images* These employ objects in the world, such as flowers, the sea, and the stars, that have intrinsic connotative depth and mystery for the observer regardless of how familiar they are to her.

2. *Technological images* These involve objects that are fashioned for a particular purpose, such as typewriters, guns, and washing machines, and which have little resonance or depth in themselves since familiarity and science define and explain them thoroughly for the most part. These images can easily become metaphoric, however.

3. *Literary-technological images* These involve technological objects that possess a kind of imposed depth and connotation because they have been used in literature so often—for example, a lyre, an urn, a sword, or a bow. We can even, in certain cases, speak of CONVENTIONAL IMAGES or CLICHÉ images, such as Cupid's arrow.

4. *Literary-natural images* These involve the use of specific natural images that have added color because of their association with myth, religion, or historical events—for instance, the Styx, holly or yew-berries, and Olympus.

Often they are ALLUSIONS, references to a person, place, or event with which the reader is assumed to be familiar, such as the Styx and Olympus.

5. *Natural, nonliterary images, infrequently occurring in literature* These involve things which are generally thought of as being prosaic, ugly, unpleasant, and/or lacking in depth and mystery *in themselves.* Obviously, if they are used skillfully in a poem they work as well as anything else. These images include things like fecal matter, zinc oxide, and fungus.

The tendency of a poet to use one or another of these types of imagery is considered an element of the author's "style."

Now, if we were to use these types of images to make simple metaphors, we might have something like:

1. *Natural* Grandmother is (like) a rose.
2. *Technological* Grandmother is (like) a sewing machine.
3. *Literary-technological* Grandmother is (like) a lyre.
4. *Literary-natural* Grandmother is (like) Venus.
5. *Natural, nonliterary* Grandmother is (like) cabbage.

Again, imagery when used as (*a*) contrast, comparison, association, or identification or (*b*) in a context where the tone suggests that we ought to be comparing, associating, contrasting, or identifying it with something unstated becomes metaphoric language. So even putting an individual metaphor in the X/Y form (as in the above examples) may not be enough to highlight the similarities and differences and cause the terms to interact. In example 1 the metaphoric relationship is obvious, but in example 2 it isn't since a sewing machine does not have basic poetic associations for us, the way a rose does. The relationship between it and Grandmother is obscure. We need a clearer context, a background, an attitude to establish in what way she is like a sewing machine. Does she stitch her life together? Taken alone, the sentence lacks direction. Try writing a few lines that might bring this image to metaphoric life. For example, what happens if you add the word "rusty"?

Notice that because there is no context, example 1 is rather vague and general, whereas example 2 is virtually nonmetaphoric, though it has possibilities. So in a sense, tone (the total context) directs, focuses. For instance, if we were to write a poem obviously suggesting that warfare is dreadful and if we capped it with natural images expressed as metaphor—"The soldier's blood like dew upon the grass"—the tone (war is horrible) would condition how we associated the terms of the metaphor. If our imaginary poem treated war as a glorious struggle, honorable necessity, an activity of grim beauty, then the same metaphor would have quite different connotations, suggesting some mystical splendor associated with dying.

In example 3 we can make some connections to the lyre of Orpheus and so the metaphor, as with examples 1 and 4, is there, if vague and unfocused. Example 5 certainly needs focus, as example 2 does.

So, unlike everyday language, which demands logical, obvious relationships, poetry can contain virtually any number of things linked as X/Y. For example, fill in the blank: "Grandmother (or Grandfather) is like___." Provide a context, set up an unlike factor, and see how it works. You do not have to write great poetry to test this principle.

A "white dove" is a natural image. If we had the white dove "circling the bloody battlefield," we would create a tone of violent contrast: innocent bird (X) contrasted to carnage (Y). Through this contextual association we might have a kind of metaphor developed by contrast. But, someone may point out, a dove *stands for* (is a symbol of) peace, and thus another kind of meaning is involved. We associate doves with peace, and so in another sense the fact that we have chosen a dove to float over the combat (a canary would not do, clearly) provides an additional contrast, peace versus war.

We might say that a SYMBOL is an image that has meanings *asserted* of it. We just say that the dove means peace; it is a special connotation for the word. Except in a few cases, all symbols are *conventional*. Various examples are the cross, the hammer and sickle, the Magen David (Jewish Star), the hourglass, and the scythe. We know pretty well what these symbols stand for, and so when we assert that dove equals peace, we are making the image "dove" a kind of code word for an idea. Remember that an image without a context is not metaphoric, but it might be a symbol. For example, "I'm thinking of a dove" *might* mean "I'm considering peace." But there is clearly no metaphor. A poetic context might be: "The soldier with a mind of razor steel is thinking of a dove," where the image is obviously to be contrasted: steel thoughts (X) with soft dove qualities (Y). This context then also *includes* the symbol for peace.°

Symbol and metaphor, like image and metaphor, are terms often used interchangeably by critics and scholars. What we have called *metaphors with unstated Y terms*, like the overall metaphor of Stevens's blackbird, are sometimes referred to as *symbols*.

In order to avoid confusion, we can define "symbol" in a way commonly agreed on: *In a symbol the Y term is always obvious*—that is, it's obvious once you know what meanings or connotations have been assigned to the image, such as that a dove stands for peace. Paradoxically, you have to know it is a symbol to get the

---

° On the other hand, suppose we had a nightingale flying over our supposed battlefield. There is no metaphoric action unless we know that the nightingale is a symbol of eternal sorrow, grief, immortality. Then we have eternal sorrow (represented by the bird) associated with the local carnage. Many technological and literary-natural images have symbolic meanings attached to them.

meaning, and you must know what it means to see that it is a symbol.

When a poet drops a conventional symbol into a poetic context, it turns metaphoric, just as an image does. For instance, the "natural image" of the beetle is sometimes considered a symbol of death, but in Keats's "Ode on Melancholy" this image-symbol is metaphoric because of its general relationship to "melancholy," and its specific one to "mournful Psyche," and because Keats relies not only on its assigned symbolic meaning (death) but also on its connotations (such as the insectlike quality).

Suppose we write: "She is in the Lethean forest." Lethe is an *allusion* to classical mythology; it was the river of forgetfulness from which the dead drank upon their entrance into Hades. Lethe is a symbol because it has come to *stand for* forgetfulness. A sip of its waters, and you forgot all you had known and been in life. But there is an implicit comparison here. She is in a forest which is (like) (1) the shadowy trees around Lethe, (2) a wood of death, (3) a place of forgetfulness, and so on. So Lethe is metaphoric. If you are familiar with the allusion, you pick up meanings like the first two listed above, but unless you know that Lethe is a symbol, meanings along the line of the third one are lost. If you don't know that it's an allusion or a symbol, there is no metaphoric effect at all. The tension, the unlike factor, comes in only when you perceive the strain between what Lethe refers to and what an ordinary forest is.

In addition to conventional symbols, with which readers are supposed to be familiar, some poets sometimes use symbols of their own devising—PRIVATE SYMBOLS. The principle is the same: The poet (often over the course of her career) assigns some specific meaning or meanings to an image, or she may take a conventional symbol and extend it. The important thing is to experience how it becomes metaphoric.

Look at the following extracts from the poem "Byzantium" by W. B. Yeats (for entire poem see page 233):

The unpurged images of day recede;
The Emperor's drunken soldiery are abed;
Night resonance recedes, night-walker's song
After great cathedral gong;
A starlit or a moonlit dome disdains
All that man is,
All mere complexities,
The fury and the mire of human veins.

. . . .

Miracle, bird or golden handiwork,
More miracle than bird or handiwork,

Planted on the star-lit golden bough °. . . .

There are a number of images here that might be symbols: the "moonlit dome," the golden bird, and "Byzantium" itself. Sometimes we "feel" that something is a symbol because we sense that if we just knew more about the image, there would be metaphoric action. You might feel that is the case here, with good reason. Let's just consider "Byzantium." Probably we all know something about what that city was and when it was. The poem itself might even suggest things to us about a way of life and a certain time. But only if we study Yeats's works do we discover that it had a special, private symbolic meaning for him (representing, among other things, the poetic imagination). You do not have to know this, however, to experience the poem on a great many levels.

Another element of tone is the sound and pattern of the poem's language: whether the poet uses meter or rhyme or words with similar consonant or vowel sounds. In practice this aspect cannot really be separated from other elements (like metaphor, irony, images, symbols). For example, in Shakespeare's line (from *Macbeth*), "Life's but . . . a poor player that struts and frets his hour upon the stage," can we really say whether Shakespeare chose "struts" and "frets" because of their sound or because of their meaning? Obviously, the sound and the meaning are one unit. The connotation of any word includes its sound (e.g., "small" and "tiny"). Similarly, on one level, arranging words in a regular pattern (meter) or repeating similar sounds (rhyme) in a line pattern (verse form) is one way poets shape and direct connotations, a written version of our inflecting or stressing certain words when we talk. In most cases, a poet may use rhyme and meter (or not use it) largely because it is traditional to do so. Sometimes the rhyme-meter form may have a more immediate effect on tone; a singsong meter and clever rhyme might connote irony, humor, or satire, for example, and so become a kind of metaphor where the mechanical sound (X) plays off the mechanical attitudes or gestures of the ridiculed object (Y). In addition, meter, rhyme, measure, stress, or other aspects of sound may serve to give a sense of order to a poem—and by establishing a sound pattern and then varying or contrasting it, emphasis and tension can be produced. Certainly, the ordering of sound as words in poetry (by whatever techniques) sets the poem dynamically off from ordinary speech and other writing. The poetic sound pattern, then, adds intensity to the way metaphoric language is put.

So everything we have been discussing helps determine tone. A poem's tone is clearly a composite of many factors—irony, metaphor types, intensity, use of symbols, puns, and the choice of words and their particular order or sound. There is no mechanical way to define tone. You have to experience it as the movement of metaphoric language.

° The Golden Bough is a conventional literary symbol connoting special privilege, sovereignty, the key to seeing the world beyond.

This poem contains so few of the familiar poetic devices that it seems only to describe attending a lecture. Unlike the simple-seeming Frost poem, "A Patch of Old Snow," this one doesn't even include traditional meter or rhyme to make you think of poetry when you read it. Only the way it is printed on the page suggests a relationship to poetic tradition. What is the poet's tone here?

Walt Whitman

WHEN I HEARD THE LEARN'D ASTRONOMER

When I heard the learn'd astronomer,
When the proofs, the figures, were ranged in columns before me,
When I was shown the charts and diagrams, to add, divide, and measure
    them,
When I sitting heard the astronomer where he lectured with much applause
    in the lecture-room,
How soon unaccountable I became tired and sick,
Till rising and gliding out I wander'd off by myself,
In the mystical moist night-air, and from time to time,
Look'd up in perfect silence at the stars.

Exploring the Metaphors

Can you discover a metaphor that works the way those we discussed in Chapter 1 did? There doesn't seem to be one, does there? How, then, does a reader get into this piece?

The whole point, climax, and impact of this poem lies in intense metaphoric irony. In this case, it is totally serious irony. The astronomer's theories, the limited logic of the human brain (X), are contrasted with the vast, absolute reality of the universe (Y)—overwhelmingly visible to anyone who takes the trouble simply to look at it without prejudice, without some theory to expound. This contrast, made through simple, descriptive images with virtually no comment, appears totally to demolish the pedantic, speculative, limited world of the lecturer and, at the same time, to expand our sense of awe. The poet does not overtly say anything negative about the astronomer. The reader has to pick up on that for himself. Whitman apparently does not even want to dignify what men can say about reality to the extent of making any kind of argument in the manner of, say, Marvell or Blake. In effect, he says: "I couldn't listen to it, I went outside and looked at the sky." This is put very subtly: "Looked up in perfect silence at the stars." Notice the contrast of the droning lecture with the "perfect silence." So the comparison that makes the metaphor here is between man's presumptions and the vast, unfathomable universe. The tone results from seemingly artless speech plus deep irony. If you didn't feel the tension between the two areas that are compared, the poem wouldn't have much impact. It would be little more than a description of an evening out.

1. How does the use of the word "learn'd" add to the ironic tone?
2. Is there any irony in the poet's use of the word "unaccountable"?
3. Throughout the poem, Whitman gives us images of what he saw. How do these images react with one another? For example, how does the image "mystical moist night-air" contrast with the astronomer's lecture?
4. What would the effect of this poem have been if the poet had actually drawn attention to the irony? Would it have remained ironic?
5. Does the irony of this poem resolve itself into a message, or is there something about the ironic juxtaposition that keeps the tension between the X and Y terms, and the meaning alive?

Technical Notes

This poem is in free verse, which Whitman popularized.

You should not have any trouble spotting the colossally ironic tone in this poem.

Percy Bysshe Shelley
OZYMANDIAS

I met a traveller from an antique land
Who said: Two vast and trunkless legs of stone
Stand in the desert . . . Near them, on the sand,
Half sunk, a shattered visage lies, whose frown,
And wrinkled lip, and sneer of cold command,
Tell that its sculptor well those passions read
Which yet survive, stamped on these lifeless things,
The hand that mocked them, and the heart that fed:
And on the pedestal these words appear:
'My name is Ozymandias, king of kings:
Look on my works, ye Mighty, and despair!'
Nothing beside remains. Round the decay
Of that colossal wreck, boundless and bare
The lone and level sands stretch far away.

2. Metaphoric Language in Poetry   57

Exploring the Metaphors

1. What is ironic about the legend on the pedestal of Ozymandias's statue?
2. What are the implications of the image in the final two lines?

In this poem, a contemporary poet uses metaphoric irony derived from metaphoric imagery which takes us beyond description into some complex emotional territory.

James Merrill
LABORATORY POEM

Charles used to watch Naomi, taking heart
And a steel saw, open up turtles, live.
While she swore they felt nothing, he would gag
At blood, at the blind twitching, even after
The murky dawn of entrails cleared, revealing
Contours he knew, egg-yellows like lamps paling.

Well then. She carried off the beating heart
To the kymograph and rigged it there, a rag
In fitful wind, now made to strain, now stopped
By her solutions tonic or malign
Alternately in which it would be steeped.
What the heart bore, she noted on a chart,

For work did not stop only with the heart.
He thought of certain human hearts, their climb
Through violence into exquisite disciplines
Of which, as it now appeared, they all expired.
Soon she would fetch another and start over,
Easy in the presence of her lover.

Exploring the Metaphors

   In this poem we view a gruesome scene in a biology lab, observing and participating in Charles's reaction to the dissection. Through careful use of detail, the poet subtly and ironically juxtaposes love (X) to the procedures Naomi performs on the turtles (Y).

As the poem opens, we find her taking "heart and a steel saw" to begin the dissection. The word "heart" is central: It is an idiom here, as in "You have to have the heart to do it" or "Don't give up, take heart," but we immediately see the pun—Naomi is "taking heart" another way too.

Naomi tells Charles that the turtles feel no pain; nevertheless, he is upset by the sight: "he would gag/ At blood, at the blind twitching." "Blood" and "blind twitching" are literal descriptive images of what Charles sees, but notice that already we begin to understand that something more is involved. Perhaps we feel the impact of the words' associations and connotations: blood as a well-recognized symbol for life and pain; "blindness" as a metaphor suggesting blindness to others and ourselves; the blind fate in which we all "twitch," etc. Naomi's opening up the turtles lays bare a whole area of questions and feelings we have about existence. Do we begin to sense that what Charles sees has something to do with his love for Naomi too?

The image that follows (line five) takes us further into life/death/love implications. "The murky dawn of entrails" is actually a covert metaphor; that is, the turtles' entrails (X) are (like) a "murky dawn" (Y). Both terms of the comparison associate richly with questions of life and death. We commonly connect entrails with emotions or feelings: "I feel it in my guts"; or with basics: "the guts of something." We connect dawning with coming into being or awareness, as in "the dawn of life" or "it dawned on me." Perhaps the meaning of the dissection itself is dawning on Charles.

When the "dawn of entrails" clears, what Charles observes is "contours he knew." The word "contours" becomes an X for a number of possible Y's. What contours? The shape of his relation to Naomi? Of love? Of life? Of death? Of violence? The image of the "egg-yellow" color of the entrails like "lamps paling" is a double comparison: eggs (X) to entrails (Y) and then entrails (X) to paling lamps (Y). What possibilities of meaning do you see here?

The entrails/ lamps metaphor also continues a tension introduced earlier by the "steel saw": a tension between the cold technological world of dissection and the organic world of life and death.

Stanza two extends this juxtaposition of the technological to the organic as Naomi carries the "beating heart" to a "kymograph." We do not have to know what a kymograph is to sense its passionless, calculating purpose. The whole process of the dissection is being carried out with an inhuman efficiency symbolized by this machine, which measures and tests the disembodied heart for its responses but ignores its essence—life.

The heart subjected to this fatal observation is no more than a "rag in a fitful wind." In Naomi's scientific and logical hands it is "now made to strain, now stopped/ By her solutions tonic or malign" and watched for reactions. Note the pun on "solutions." Literally they are chemical solutions to speed up or depress the heart's action, but figuratively what are they? Her solutions to life? Her solutions to love? Something she manifests that affects her lover: different moods? The phrase "what the heart bore" refers literally to the turtle's heart, but metaphorically what does it imply?

Stanza three breaks away more sharply from the descriptive tone to reveal the poem's metaphoric intent: The dissection of the turtle's heart (X) is associated directly with "human hearts" (Y). And the "violence" and "exquisite discipline" of Naomi's skill at dissection are identified with death ("they all expired"). But what kind of death? Physical? Psychological? Moral? Spiritual? Does "they" refer to her past lovers? She "broke" all their hearts? What or who is it really that is expiring? Obviously, this is all complexly metaphoric. Though it is never really stated, we feel that what Naomi is doing to the turtles she also does with life and love, and Charles.

The poem's major irony comes clear in the last line. Despite Naomi's cold violence as she slices the turtles, she is "easy in the presence of her lover." But the dissecting skill which she has mastered and which puts her at ease with Charles makes him decidedly *un*easy with her. Love is mentioned for the first time in this line: a word which connotes unity and tenderness is here ironically set.

So the tone of the poem is largely the result of (1) a conversational description of the dissection and Charles's reaction to it, (2) a contrast of the mechanical elements of the dissection (X) with the organic elements of the thing dissected (Y), and (3) the central implied comparison of the dissection (X) to love (Y). Of course we do not know anything at all about the "love" between these lovers except through the description of Charles's reaction to the dissection. But we fill in the gaps as the poem begins to extend past the literal statements and images.

1. Could the word "saw" in the phrase "steel saw" be a pun, or is that stretching it? Where should we draw the line between "reading into" a poem implications that aren't there and being sensitive to implications that are there?
2. The egg is associated with birth. Consider the implications of Merrill's identifying the egg with the entrails of the turtle and with "lamps paling."
3. Could the word "dissection" itself be taken metaphorically (as an X)? Aside from the literal cutting into bodies, are other kinds of dissection possibly suggested here?
4. Look at the verb tenses in which this poem is written. What do they tell you?
5. Consider the lines "tonic or malign/ Alternately in which it would be steeped." What are some of the metaphoric possibilities here? In other words, what thoughts, feelings, and ideas could this refer to?
6. What insights do you gain from this poem?

Technical Notes

The poem includes exact rhymes (heart-chart, gag-rag) and some slant rhymes (revealing-paling). Iambic meter is the background.

The tone here is obviously not ironic—or at least not obviously ironic—but clear and straightforward. The poem appears to be a sincere, direct inspirational statement based on "inspired" metaphoric imagery. In fact, the poem became a standard hymn in English liturgy.

William Blake
from MILTON

And did those feet in ancient time
Walk upon England's mountains greens?
And was the holy Lamb of God
On England's pleasant pastures seen?

And did the Countenance Divine
Shine forth upon our clouded hills?
And was Jerusalem builded here
Among these dark Satanic Mills?

Bring me my Bow of burning gold!
Bring me my Arrows of desire!
Bring me my Spear! O clouds unfold!
Bring me my Chariot of fire!

I will not cease from Mental Fight,
Nor shall my Sword sleep in my hand,
Till we have built Jerusalem
In England's green and pleasant Land.

Exploring the Metaphors

Look at the line "Bring me my Bow of burning gold!" How is it metaphoric? It is obviously an image we can picture; for example, we can imagine a Walt Disney cartoon of a burning golden bow. It is not a picture of something real, of course, it can be put together *only* by the imagination. Notice that this line contains an implicit comparison of the form "the bow is (like) burning gold." The bow could be made of burning wood, and though it would be hard to hold, it would not be a metaphor. Can you see why not? Because a mental picture is drawn, *the image itself*—apart from the metaphoric relationship of bow to gold—becomes an X, and we have Y levels such as a glorious war, a war of gold, fire and light, a spiritual war.

In the "arrows of desire" metaphor, mentioned before, you cannot actually imagine arrows which are (like) desires. You can only sense this combination; there is no picture. So we discover that the effect of linking a *concrete* term with a *concrete* term, as with the bow and gold, can produce a picture (and it might, in other cases, cause us to imagine sounds or smells, etc.), while linking an *abstract* with a *concrete* term (desires/arrows) has a different impact, perhaps more interesting, because it forces the mind instantly to give up its familiar patterns of association—like imagining pictures, for instance. Poetry, for the most part, aims at this dynamic state of awareness beyond imagination.

What about "these dark Satanic Mills"? What do we "see" here? Does "Satanic Mills" mean mills that are *like* Satan? Satan is a symbol. Are these mills that Satan operates? Blake says they are in England, but did they come from hell? Are they incarnate evil ideas? Are workers there in a kind of hell? "Satanic" might call up images of fire and brimstone: Imagine in the lush English countryside the sight of squat, soot-darkened factories belching black smoke and orange flame. It might recall paintings of hell. So there is a kind of *concrete* term in "Satanic." On the other hand, we have never actually seen what this *literary image* refers to (unlike gold, burning or otherwise), and much of the metaphor's suggestive intensity results from linking an *abstract* symbolic term (Satanic) with a *concrete* one (mills).

In the last line, "built Jerusalem" is another kind of symbol-metaphor. Jerusalem has traditional symbolic meanings, and these are applied to the context. Certainly the poet does not mean to move the actual city to England. What does he mean?

1. Do you think the last two lines of the poem are as intense as the bow-and-arrow pair? How does this affect the tone?
2. What is meant by "Mental Fight"?
3. Does the metaphoric image "bow of burning gold" seem symbolic to you, as if it had conventional meanings assigned to it, as if the poet had said, "Bring me my cross"? Part of the symbolic feeling of this metaphoric image is the result of the poem's tone. Can you see how?

Technical Notes

The second and fourth lines of each stanza rhyme—a BALLAD STANZA. Note in the last stanza the additional slant rhyme of "land" and "Jerusalem." The background rhythm is iambic.

The next piece uses metaphoric image in the context of a direct and philosophic tone—as if the poet wants to explain some ideas about "the knowledge of silence," to express what it is. But while a philosopher might take hundreds of pages and invent a complicated logical system to explain the relation of silence to self, the poet does it in a few lines. And while the philosopher's system might be refuted in argument, the poet has no system to refute. Since he does not start with a premise, he has no conclusions. He offers instead images and metaphors which point at what he sensed—at the momentary flash of truth which is understood not as a thought but as a perception.

Alfred Dorn

THE KNOWLEDGE OF SILENCE

Silence is not an empty room
Where entering mind grows void in vacancy,
But a museum where the self collects
Its past in marble.
               Here is yet the bloom
Of vanished laughter held in tinted stone,
For here is all that sculpting mind has known.
Here is the white lucidity of tasks
Perfected; here stand jagged blocks of pain
Broken from time.
               And here the mind at last
Endures the pitiless light beneath its masks.

Exploring the Metaphors

1. Look at the opening line. Although the poet denies that silence (X) is like an empty room (Y), are these terms united in some way? How?
2. Consider the images in the poem (such as "vanished laughter held in tinted stone" or "the white lucidity of tasks"). Are these also metaphors?
3. How do all the metaphors and metaphoric images relate to one another in this poem? What things is the marble related to, for example?
4. What are the masks, and what do they have to do with sculpture and silence? Do you see how, in effect, the last two lines are juxtaposed to the rest of the poem as an X to a Y? What is the "pitiless light"?
5. What is the "knowledge" of silence?
6. Though this poem does not have the if-then logician's tone of "To His Coy Mistress," there is a definite feeling of reasonableness about it. Can you account for this tone?

Technical Notes

Although not a regular pattern, the rhyme scheme of the poem is *a b c d a a a e f f e*. Note the use of INTERNAL RHYME. Rhyme is employed to give the poem a sense of closure and adds to the "reasonable" tone, as if the thoughts were neat and complete. Note the slant rhyme at the end. All lines except the third are iambic pentameter.

This Wallace Stevens poem takes as its ostensible subject metaphoric imagery itself. In "Thirteen Ways of Looking at a Blackbird" we found that, overall, the blackbird was an X with many possible Y's. Here, Stevens reveals the world is full of images that stand as the metaphoric X. What is the tone of this poem?

Wallace Stevens
THE MOTIVE FOR METAPHOR

You like it under the trees in autumn,
Because everything is half dead.
The wind moves like a cripple among the leaves
And repeats words without meaning.

In the same way, you were happy in spring,
With the half colors of quarter-things,
The slightly brighter sky, the melting clouds,
The single bird, the obscure moon—

The obscure moon lighting an obscure world
Of things that would never be quite expressed,
Where you yourself were never quite yourself
And did not want nor have to be,

Desiring the exhilarations of changes:
The motive for metaphor, shrinking from
The weight of primary noon,
The A B C of being,

The ruddy temper, the hammer
Of red and blue, the hard sound—
Steel against intimation—the sharp flash,
The vital, arrogant, fatal, dominant X.

Exploring the Metaphors

Who is the "you" the poet addresses in the first line? The reader? The poet himself? Another poet? Perhaps all these. But whoever it is, the narrator (or VOICE) of the poem obviously treats the "you" in an ironic tone, approaching sarcasm. The irony comes out of contrasting the you's rather pale, timid preference for "half colors" and "quarter-things" (X) with a hard, vital, dominant reality (Y) represented as the "weight of primary noon,/ The ABC of being." In the face of this reality the "you" and his "motive for metaphor" are "shrinking."

Notice Stevens' use of images: "The slightly brighter sky, the melting clouds,/ The single bird, the obscure moon." Sky, clouds, birds, and the moon are natural images that already have a great many associations for us. On one level, Stevens is showing us that they are potential metaphoric terms, and the list suggests that the world is alive with such phenomena: The raw material of the poet's trade. Stanza three describes the tone of this world of potential metaphor; it could as well be a description of our reader's reaction to a good poem, our entry, through a good poem, into a world "of things that would never be quite expressed,/ Where you yourself were never quite yourself/ And did not want nor have to be."

Against this poetic world of "intimation" the poet contrasts the world of "steel" in the final stanza, a world where things are clear, hammered out, "vital, arrogant, fatal, dominant." One way of seeing this is to take Stevens's poem as a contrast of the blunt, undeniable facts of reality (X) with vague, shadowy "intimation" (Y), a kind of shrinking back from reality. But could we also see this whole idea as subtly ironic? Stevens calls this blunt reality the "dominant X," so it is presented not as itself but through metaphor. Isn't the letter "X" itself a metaphor? Can you see this? Obviously, we can get at the reality "X" only through metaphoric images such as those Stevens has given us (in this case, *technological images*): the red and blue hammer, the steel, the "*weight* of primary noon." So from this angle the motive for metaphor may be the desire not to shrink from reality but to *discover* it, though this comes about only through "intimation," indirectly, because the poet's image-metaphors can never actually be the Absolute; they can only suggest it. Seen this way, the time of moons and birds and the one of steel and primary noon are really the same, though one is a gentle season, and the other is harsh. These metaphoric images become tools for discovering the unknown, the "dominant X." So the poem's irony folds back on itself. Stevens is able to have it both ways. He criticizes poetry for not being the absolute reality and yet through the very metaphors of his criticism he evokes that reality.

1. Can you see other ways in which the ironic contrast between the gentle and harsh worlds accounts for this poem's tone? What effect do the ironies have on our interpretations?
2. What do you think the motive for metaphor is? Can we give this a final answer?

3. Can we really tell whether Stevens's "X" refers to the blunt outward facts of existence or to the unknown that lies behind existential facts? Or both? Are these two ways of looking at the poem contradictory?
4. Who do you feel the "you" of the poem is? Why?
5. Consider individual lines and phrases, such as "The wind moves like a cripple among the leaves" or "Desiring the exhilarations of changes." What relation do they bear to the central metaphor, which juxtaposes the poet's world to reality? What are the levels of meanings?
6. Look at the line "And repeats words without meaning." What are some of the possible implications of this line in terms of the whole poem?
7. Why is the "you" of the poem said to be "happy" in the autumn and spring?
8. Stevens used the color blue in many of his poems as a *private symbol* for the aesthetic or artistic function. How does the color relate to this particular poem if that meaning is added? What do you associate with blue? Do you have other associations that might be relevant here? What about red?
9. Might the seasons themselves be private symbols for Stevens? Do you sense this possibility here? Find out what Stevens wanted these symbols to stand for.
10. Compare this poem with Paul Verlaine's "Claire De Lune" on page 129. Do you see how Verlaine is using the very types of images Stevens appears to criticize. Stevens himself was particularly influenced by French symbolist poetry such as Verlaine wrote. With that in mind, how would you explain Stevens's approach in this poem?

Technical Notes

Note the use of ASSONANCE (spring-slightly-bright-bird-melting). The rhythm is a recurrent accentual TRIMETER.

Contemporary poet Gwendolyn Brooks takes a traditional form—the Shakespearean sonnet—and some traditional symbols—bread and honey—and forges them into an evocative statement of frustration. But frustration may not be quite the right term. The tone of the poem on the next page is curious and rich. How would you describe it?

Gwendolyn Brooks

MY DREAMS, MY WORKS, MUST WAIT TILL AFTER HELL

I hold my honey and I store my bread
In little jars and cabinets of my will.
I label clearly, and each latch and lid
I bid, Be firm till I return from hell.
I am very hungry. I am incomplete.
And none can tell when I may dine again.
No man can give me any word but Wait,
The puny light. I keep eyes pointed in;
Hoping that, when the devil days of my hurt
Drag out to their last dregs and I resume
On such legs as are left me, in such heart
As I can manage, remember to go home,
My taste will not have turned insensitive
To honey and bread old purity could love.

Exploring the Metaphors

Bread is the classic biblical symbol of nourishment, the staff of life. Honey is symbolically nourisment as well, but has different connotations. While bread is basic, a sort of minimum requirement for sustaining life, honey connotes richness and surplus, life's sweetness. Honey as manna was the gift of God; in a religious context honey symbolizes God's grace.

Brooks sets these symbols to work metaphorically. The speaker of the poem says that her honey and bread (her forms of nourishment) are stored in metaphoric cabinets of her "will." Perhaps there is a pun on the word "will" here: in one sense the speaker's determination, in another her future, as in "That's something I *will* do eventually."

The speaker appears to be undergoing some trial, or awful journey, some "hell" of indefinite duration. She is keeping the bread and honey preserved until this "hell" is over. Hell is, of course, a symbol, but it is used here so ambiguously that it becomes metaphoric, an X with an unstated Y or Y's.

The problem with hoarding away the bread and honey—the nourishment— becomes evident at the beginning of the second QUATRAIN of the sonnet (in line five). Initially it may have appeared to the reader that the bread and honey were nourishing valuables that the speaker meant to give out to others, bread that a woman bakes, honey that she collects to feed her family, for example. In line five, however, we see that what she means to give out to nourish others, also nourishes her. The irony is that by hoarding these things she will go hungry, spiritually or in some other way. She is "incomplete" unless she can "dine again."

But she won't get her nourishment (what she both gives and receives) until this "hell" is over, the next seven lines tell us.

Here the metaphoric question grows—what the hell is this hell? We have some information. It is something the speaker is going through that involves a "hurt." It may also involve an experience so distracting that it might deflect the speaker from even remembering to go home where she has left the nourishment. But the worst of it may be that this hell has the power to make the speaker insensitive.

The last line suggests that one needs to be pure to taste the bread and honey, and that the speaker fears being corrupted by the hell. Bread, honey, love and purity all entwine metaphorically in this last line. Can you tease out the implications of their relationship?

1. Why do you think the narrator of the poem calls the jars she holds the honey in "little"? Is she being ironic? Humble?
2. What do you think the tone of this poem is? Bitter? Depressed? Resigned? Determined? What sense of truth about the human condition do you think is embodied in the ambiguity of this tone?
3. What kinds of experiences could constitute the "hell," "the devil days of my hurt" the speaker refers to?
4. We are not told the sex of the speaker of the poem but it has become the convention with so-called "confessional" poets in our day to identify the poet as the real speaker of the poem. Brooks is a black woman. How would this information affect your perception of the line "No man can give me any word but Wait"? How would it affect your sense of what the "hell" is the speaker is going through? Would this information about Brooks add to the depth of the poem for you or contract it into a political statement about black women artists being held back by contemporary American society?
5. How is your understanding of what the "hell" of the poem is affected by the title?

Technical Notes

This modern Shakespearean sonnet—three quatrains of alternating rhymed lines and a concluding rhymed couplet—makes deft use of SLANT RHYME. Look at the final couplet, for example. The *ive* sound in the word "insensitive" rhymes on a slant with the *ove* sound in "love." The accentual stress does not fall on the last syllable in "insensitive" but does fall on the word "love," making the last word in the poem particularly forceful. The poem's background rhythm is loose iambic pentameter.

Here an early-twentieth-century poet uses conventional symbols to enrich his brief, violent vision of modern life.

Hart Crane
MOMENT FUGUE

The syphilitic selling violets calmly
    and daisies
By the subway news-stand knows
       how hyacinths

This April morning offers
    hurriedly
In bunches sorted freshly—
       and bestows
On every purchaser
         (of heaven perhaps)

His eyes—
      like crutches hurtled against glass
Fall mute and sudden (dealing change
    for lilies)
Beyond the roses that no flesh can pass.

Exploring the Metaphors

A man suffering from a sexual disease is selling flowers. The tone of violent vision results largely from the clashing ironic juxtaposition of disease (X) with (Y) fresh flowers, natural objects considered pure, sweet, delicate.

The flowers are obviously metaphoric, an X we are meant to connect with some Y or Y's. In the last line of the second stanza the poet gives us one possible connection: flowers stand for heaven ("perhaps") .

In the third stanza, the flowers are used symbolically, as discussed earlier in the chapter: Lilies are the conventional symbol for death and resurrection, and roses are the symbol for God, love, redemption. Could April also be a symbol? Thus the basic metaphoric association of the flowers with heaven is extended here by specific symbolic associations .

1. Consider some of the implications of the fact that it is a "syphilitic" selling these flowers. What kinds of things has the flower seller come to represent by the end of the poem?
2. Why might the flower seller be offering his flowers "hurriedly"?

3. What are some of the implications of the line "His eyes—/ like crutches hurled against glass/ Fall mute and sudden"?
4. Can you see several puns in this poem? If so, what levels do they add?
5. Look at the title of the poem. What is a fugue? Why is the poem a "moment fugue"? (You will probably want to look at the poem's shape and line arrangement when you consider this.) How do the meter and grammatical structures intensify this piece?
6. What are some of the possible levels of meaning in the last line?

Technical Notes

The poem is iambic pentameter irregularly broken into HEMISTICHES. Only the final line is whole. There are occasional rhymes (eyes-lilies, glass-pass).

Roses, as we saw in the last poem, have symbolic associations. In this poem the familiar rose is obviously metaphoric, but Blake also had some specific private symbolic meanings in mind. First see how much you can get from the poem directly; then you might want to find out what specific things Blake wanted his sick rose to stand for. Does the idea of a sick rose itself contribute to the poem's tonal effect?

William Blake
THE SICK ROSE

O Rose, thou art sick.
The invisible worm
That flies in the night,
In the howling storm,
Has found out thy bed
Of crimson joy,
And his dark secret love
Does thy life destroy.

Baudelaire was the first great French "symbolist" poet. He believed that the phenomena of the world were symbols through which we could contact spiritual realities and transform our sense perceptions. So he used many private and conventional symbols in his poems. But whatever symbolic meanings he assigned to his images, we can see in this poem how they combine into metaphors, and we can understand the piece well enough without knowing what Baudelaire wanted his symbols to mean. How would you describe the tone of this next piece?

Charles Baudelaire
CORRESPONDENCES

The whole world is a temple from whose living columns
Issue forth at times a host of commingled words;
Man passes through, surrounded by such forests of symbols,
Symbols that watch him out of kindred interest.
As, at a distance, overlapping echoes merge
To mingle in a unity of depth and shadow,
Vast as the night, vast as the effulgence of the day,
So scents and sounds and colors tally with one another.

Perfumes there are, fresh and cool as the flesh of children,
Sweet to the taste as oboes, green as meadows—
And there are other perfumes, rich, corrupt, triumphant,
Able to expand in space like infinite things:

Musk and amber, benjamin and frankincense.
These are what sing the ecstasies of soul and sense.

Translation from French by Christopher Collins

Exploring the Metaphors

1. Obviously, the key metaphor of the poem is that the terrain of the world (X) is a living (organic) temple of symbols (Y). What are the other metaphors based on this one?
2. Consider in detail some of these secondary metaphors, for example, the one beginning "As, at a distance. . . ." What kinds of levels does the word "tally" add to this metaphor? How are these secondary metaphors linked to the main one? What part do all the metaphors play in creating the tone of the poem?
3. Consider the thesis of the poem. Is the world full of symbols? If so, in what way? Do you think Baudelaire could be using the word symbol to mean something like what we are calling here metaphor? What would be the evidence for that? What part does the thesis that the world is full of symbols (or metaphors) play in the tone of the poem?
4. You might want to do some research to find out what private symbols Baudelaire used in this poem and then reread it to see what meaning your knowledge of these symbols adds to the poem.

5. What are some of the many possibilities in the line "Able to expand in space like infinite things"?
6. Compare this piece to "Motive for Metaphor." Stevens showed us the intimate relation between *image* and metaphor; how does this Baudelaire poem demonstrate the connection between *symbol* and metaphor?

Technical Notes

The poem in the original French is a sonnet. In this translation the rhymes have been omitted, but the original iambic HEXAMETER (ALEXANDRINES) has been retained.

The tone of this poem is based on a series of puns.

Stephen Spender
SUBJECT: OBJECT: SENTENCE

A subject thought: because he had a verb
With several objects, that he ruled a sentence.
Had not Grammar willed him these substantives
Which he came into, as his just inheritance?

His objects were *wine, women, fame* and *wealth*,
And a subordinate clause—*all life can give.*
He grew so fond of having these that, finally,
He found himself becoming quite subjective.

Subject, the dictionary warned means *someone ruled by*
Person or thing. Was he not having's slave?
To achieve detachment, he must be *objective*
Which meant to free himself from the verb *have.*

Seeking detachment, he studied the context
Around his sentence, to place it in perspective:
Paraphrased, made a critical analysis,
And then re-read it, feeling more *objective.*

Then, with a shock, he realized that *sentence*
Like *subject-object* is treacherously double.
A sentence is condemned to stay as stated—
As in *life-sentence, death-sentence,* for example.

Exploring the Metaphors

1. What puns do you see here, and how does the poet play on the double meanings of these words?
2. Besides using direct puns, in what ways does the poet play off of grammar itself in order to evoke levels of meaning?

In this piece, the poet is employing sound as a metaphoric device, juxtaposing tightly held meter and rhyme patterns (X) with a complaint against them (Y). A humorous tone results.

Ben Jonson
A FIT OF RIME AGAINST RIME

Rime, the rack of finest wits,
That expresseth but by fits,
      True Conceipt,[1]
Spoyling Senses of their Treasure,
Cosening Judgement with a measure,
      But false weight.
Wresting words, from their true calling;
Propping Verse, for feare of falling
      To the ground.
Joynting Syllabes, drowning Letters,
Fastning Vowells, as with fetters
      They were bound!
Soone as lazie thou wert knowne,
All good Poetrie hence was flowne,
      And Art banish'd.
For a thousand yeares together,
All *Parnassus*[2] Greene did wither,
      And wit vanish'd.
Pegasus[3] did flie away,
At the Wells no Muse did stay,
      But bewailed
So to see the Fountaine drie,
And *Apollo's*[4] Musique die,
      All light failed!
Starveling rimes did fill the Stage,
Not a Poet in an Age,

Worth a crowning.
Not a worke deserving Baies,[5]
Nor a lyne deserving praise,
   Pallas[6] frowning.
Greeke was free from Rimes infection,
Happy Greeke, by this protection,
   Was not spoyled.
Whilst the Latin, Queene of Tongues,
Is not yet free from Rimes wrongs,
   But rests foiled.
Scarce the Hill againe doth flourish,
Scarce the world a Wit doth nourish,
   To restore
Phoebus[7] to his Crowne againe;
And the Muses to their braine:
   As before.
Vulgar Languages that want
Words, and sweetnesse, and be scant
   Of true measure,
Tyran[8] Rime hath so abused,
That they long since have refused
   Other ceasure.[9]
He that first invented thee,
May his joynts tormented bee,
   Cramp'd for ever;
Still may Syllabes jarre with time,
Still may reason warre with rime,
   Resting never.
May his Sense, when it would meet
The cold tumor in his feet,
   Grow unsounder.
And his Title be long foole,
That in rearing such a Schoole,
   Was the founder.

[1] conceit: poetic conception, wit, a possible pun
[2] mountain in Greece, symbolic of poetic inspiration
[3] winged horse, symbolic of poetry
[4] Greek god of poetry
[5] Bays: prize for excellence
[6] Athena, Greek goddess of the arts
[7] Apollo
[8] tyrant
[9] caesura: a pause within a line of verse

Exploring the Metaphors

1. In what ways is Jonson's technique in this poem similar to Spender's in "Subject: Object: Sentence"?
2. What things does Jonson associate with rhyme("rime") in this poem?
3. In what ways does Jonson's own use of rhyme add to the meaning of the poem?
4. What is Jonson's complaint against rhyme? Is that complaint ironic? That is, is there a sense in which he is really praising rhyme too? Consider the title.
5. Notice the poet's use of allusions (references) to Greek mythology (Pegasus, Apollo, Pallas, for example). What implicit connections does this make between poetry and myth?

A central paradox sparks the Earl of Rochester's witty tone and creates surprising reversals and twists of association. We said that a paradox is like a metaphoric relationship except that instead of X/Y, we have X = not-X. In other words, paradoxical statements seem self-contradictory. You will be able to spot the major paradox in this poem fairly easily.

John Wilmot, Earl of Rochester
UPON NOTHING

Nothing! thou Elder Brother ev'n to Shade,
Thou hadst a being ere the World was made,
And (well fixt) art alone, of Ending not afraid.

Ere Time and Place were, Time and Place were not,
When Primitive Nothing something streight begot,
Then all proceeded from the great united—What.

Something, the gen'ral Attribute of all,
Sever'd from thee, its sole Original.
Into thy boundless self must undistinguish'd fall.

Yet Something did thy mighty Pow'r command,
And from thy fruitful Emptiness's Hand,
Snatch'd Men, Beasts, Birds, Fire, Air, and Land.

Matter, the wickedest Off-spring of thy Race,
By Form assisted, flew from thy Embrace,
And Rebel Light obscur'd thy reverend dusky Face.

With Form and Matter, Time and Place did join;
Body, thy Foe, with thee did Leagues combine,
To spoil thy peaceful Realm, and ruin all thy Line.

But Turn-Coat Time assists the Foe in vain,
And, brib'd by thee, assists thy short-liv'd Reign,
And to thy hungry Womb drives back thy Slaves again.

Tho' Mysteries are barr'd from Laick ° Eyes,
And the Divine alone, with Warrant, pries
Into thy Bosom, where the Truth in private lies:

Yet this of thee the Wise may freely say,
Thou from the Virtuous nothing tak'st away,
And to be part with thee the Wicked wisely pray.

Great Negative, how vainly wou'd the Wise
Enquire, define, distinguish, teach, devise?
Didst thou not stand to point their dull Philosophies.

Is, or *is not*, the Two great Ends of Fate,
And, true or false, the Subject of Debate,
That perfect, or destroy, the vast Designs of Fate;

When they have rack'd the *Politician*'s Breast,
Within thy Bosom most securely rest,
And, when reduc'd to thee, are least unsafe and best.

But, *Nothing*, why does *Something* still permit,
That Sacred Monarchs should at Council sit,
With Persons highly thought at best for nothing fit.

Whilst weighty *Something* modestly abstains,
From Prince's Coffers, and from Statesmen's Brains
And Nothing there like stately *Nothing* reigns.

Nothing, who dwells with Fools in grave Disguise,
For whom they reverend Shapes, and Forms devise,
Lawn Sleeves, and Furrs, and Gowns, when they like
     thee look wise.

French Truth, *Dutch* Prowess, *British* Policy,
Hibernian Learning, *Scotch* Civility,
Spaniard's Dispatch, *Dane's* Wit, are mainly seen in thee.

The Great Man's Gratitude to his best Friend,
Rings Promises, Whores Vows, towards thee they bend,
Flow swiftly into thee, and in thee ever end.

° layman's

Exploring the Metaphors

The trick is, of course, that the poet has personified the abstraction "nothing" as if it were some god, and so has turned nothing into something. This something/ nothing becomes the creator whose creations are all reversed: "And from thy fruitful Emptiness's Hand,/ Snatch'd men, Beasts, Birds, Fire, Air, and Land." The tone of praise for this god becomes SATIRE, in which the poet undercuts the vanities (the somethings) of scholars and philosophers and virtually everything we accept as substance—because we ironically see it all as nothing. So though the poem is humorous, it points to a rather serious insight.

1. Consider the paradoxical elements of "And Rebel Light obscur'd thy reverend dusky Face." The implicit terms of this metaphor-paradox rely on the simple reversal: light (X) equals darkness (Y), since we normally think of darkness as obscuring things. Find other examples of metaphor relying on this kind of reversal. What might "Rebel" in "Rebel Light" be an allusion to?
2. Beyond satire, what are some of the other implications of the poet's identification of nothing with the various somethings of the poem? What levels of meaning does he generate through this paradox?

This Marvell poem is laced with paradox. What other dimensions of tone do you perceive?

Andrew Marvell
EYES AND TEARS

How wisely Nature did decree,
With the same eyes to weep and see!
That, having viewed the object vain,
They might be ready to complain.

And, since the self-deluding sight,
In a false angle takes each height;

These tears which better measure all,
Like wat'ry lines and plummets fall.

Two tears, which sorrow long did weigh
Within the scales of either eye,
And then paid out in equal poise,
Are the true price of all my joys.

What in the world most fair appears,
Yea even laughter, turns to tears:
And all the jewels which we prize,
Melt in these pendants of the eyes.

I have through every garden been,
Amongst the red, the white, the green;
And yet, from all the flowers I saw,
No honey, but these tears could draw.

So the all-seeing sun each day
Distills the world with chemic ray;
But finds the essence only showers,
Which straight in pity back he pours.

Yet happy they whom grief doth bless,
That weep the more, and see the less:
And, to preserve their sight more true,
Bathe still their eyes in their own dew.

So Magdalen, in tears more wise
Dissolved those captivating eyes,
Whose liquid chains could flowing meet
To fetter her Redeemer's feet.

Not full sails hasting loaden home,
Nor the chaste lady's pregnant womb,
Nor Cynthia teeming shows so fair,
As two eyes swoln with weeping are.

The sparkling glance that shoots desire,
Drenched in these waves, does lose its fire.
Yea oft the Thund'rer pity takes
And here the hissing lightning slakes.

The incense was to Heaven dear,
Not as a perfume, but a tear.

And stars show lovely in the night,
But as they seem the tears of light.

Ope then mine Eyes your double Sluice,
And practise so your noblest Use.
For others too can see, or sleep;
But only humane Eyes can weep.

Now like two Clouds dissolving, drop,
And at each Tear in distance stop:
Now like two Fountains trickle down:
Now like two floods o'return and drown.

Thus let your Streams o'erflow your Springs,
Till Eyes and Tears be the same things:
And each the other's difference bears;
Those weeping Eyes, those seeing Tears.

Exploring the Metaphors

Paradox and irony can be very close, as witness the opening stanza here. The poet says that ironically, almost paradoxically, nature gives us eyes to see the world *in order to weep* because the world we see is utterly vain. Moving through the poem, we discover that this ironic-paradoxical tone persists to the very end.

Alternately and together, "eyes" and "tears" are terms of individual metaphors throughout the piece. In the last stanzas, they are united as in the opening lines: Eyes become tears, which is to say that eyes = tears, a paradoxical relationship. Marvell's paradox conveys profound seriousness without losing distance: "Those weeping eyes, those seeing tears." How is the intensity of those last three words bound up with the very paradox of the statement? One level of "those seeing tears" might be paraphrased as "Grief or grieving allows us to 'see' things as they really are." In various ways the whole poem echoes this.

1. Identify the paradoxes.
2. Try putting the irony here into words.
3. What can you say about the tone? Is it really serious? Funny?
4. Consider the different things the poet relates metaphorically to eyes and/or tears. What are some of the levels of meaning a reader might get from each of these metaphoric relationships?
5. Is the word "garden" in the fifth stanza a metaphor? Could it also be a symbol?
6. In the last stanza, what kinds of things does the poet mean by "And each the other's difference bears"? How is that related to the eyes/tears paradox?

Metaphor: The Logic of Poetry

The tone of this poem is established by the voice of a man thoughtfully talking about his sense of approaching death. The overall attitude of the speaker is easy to perceive and is conveyed through several direct metaphors which give the ideas great force.

William Shakespeare
THAT TIME OF YEAR . . .

That time of year thou mayst in me behold
When yellow leaves, or none, or few, do hang
Upon those boughs which shake against the cold,
Bare ruined choirs, where late the sweet birds sang.
In me thou see'st the twilight of such day
As after sunset fadeth in the west,
Which by and by black night doth take away,
Death's second self that seals up all in rest.
In me thou see'st the glowing of such fire,
That on the ashes of his youth doth lie,
As the death-bed, whereon it must expire
Consumed with that which it was nourished by.
    This thou perceiv'st, which makes thy love more strong
    To love that well, which thou must leave ere long.

Exploring the Metaphors

1. Notice that the narrator of the poem implicitly compares life (X) to a year (Y). This spring/youth, winter/age, is almost cliché poetic association. How does Shakespeare put life into it?
2. Consider the metaphor of the fire and ashes. Is it a paradox?
3. What is the relation of the final couplet to the rest of the poem?

Contrast the previous poems in this chapter with this one. What is the tone here? How is it achieved? Does the moon function metaphorically here?

George Gordon, Lord Byron
SO WE'LL GO NO MORE A-ROVING

1
So we'll go no more a-roving
So late into the night,
Though the heart be still as loving,
And the moon be still as bright.

2
For the sword outwears its sheath,
And the soul wears out the breast,
And the heart must pause to breathe,
And Love itself have rest.

3
Though the night was made for loving,
And the day returns too soon,
Yet we'll go no more a-roving
By the light of the moon.

In this next poem the seventeenth-century poet John Donne achieves a remarkable tone by consciously and artfully keeping the distance between the X and Y terms so great that the unlike factor borders on being absurd. This poem is considered particularly difficult. Chapter 7 deals with poems of this order, but let's see how far we can go into it with the experience we already have.

John Donne
A VALEDICTION:
FORBIDDING MOURNING

As virtuous men passe mildly away,
     And whisper to their soules, to goe,
Whilst some of their sad friends doe say,
     The breath goes now, and some say, no:

So let us melt, and make no noise,
      No teare-floods, nor sigh-tempests move,
T'were prophanation of our joyes
      To tell the layetie our love.

Moving of th'earth brings harmes and feares,
      Men reckon what it did and meant,
But trepidation of the spheares,
      Though greater farre, is innocent.

Dull sublunary lovers love
      (Whose soule is sense) cannot admit
Absence, because it doth remove
      Those things which elemented it.

But we by a love, so much refin'd,
      That our selves know not what it is,
Inter-assured of the mind,
      Care lesse, eyes, lips, and hands to misse.

Our two soules therefore, which are one,
      Though I must goe, endure not yet
A breach, but an expansion,
      Like gold to airy thinnesse beate.

If they be two, they are two so
      As stiffe twin compasses are two,
Thy soule the fixt foot, makes no show
      To move, but doth, if th'other doe.

And though it in the center sit,
      Yet when the other far doth rome,
It leanes, and hearkens after it,
      And growes erect, as that comes home.

Such wilt thou be to mee, who must
      Like th'other foot, obliquely runne;
Thy firmnes drawes my circle just,
      And makes me end, where I begunne.

Exploring the Metaphors

The important tonal elements are immediately apparent in this poem: (1) exaggeration (a characteristic of Donne's poetry) and (2) an exposition that seems logical. Remember we also saw this poetic logic, as well as exaggerated or strange metaphors, in "To His Coy Mistress." Poets who used these techniques in the seventeenth-century came to be called METAPHYSICAL POETS. Both Marvell and Donne are prime exponents of this STYLE.

In order to keep his exaggerations from becoming absurd, Donne speaks (in the poem) as though he were making a reasoned argument. In the first two stanzas he says, in effect, "*Since* good men die peacefully in a subtle way, *therefore* he and his lady should part without weeping or showing their feelings." If you separate this argument from the poem, it's clearly not very convincing, but is it really meant to convince?

Donne maintains the premise-conclusion form (since-therefore, if-then) for almost the entire poem. In addition, he maintains exaggeration on at least two levels: (1) the distance between the things compared (dying men to lovers, compasses to lovers, etc.) and (2) exaggeration of emotion and idea ("virtuous men" whispering to their souls or Donne telling his lover to produce no "tearefloods, no sigh-tempests"). This kind of intensification cannot be reduced to something like: "Don't be upset when I leave, honey, because I'll love you wherever I am." Donne goes deeply into the idea and experience of love and parting while still keeping his sense of humor and irony. This attitude also helps prevent the extremes from becoming silly: He establishes the tone by revealing his feelings without losing a certain distance and perspective. Compare this with the Burns rose poem, where the voice of the poet becomes increasingly melodramatic and sentimental.

Though in the first two stanzas the speaker has not actually said he is parting from his lover, the idea of separation is certainly implicit: The image of the soul leaving the body (X) in stanza one is compared to the second-stanza image of lover parting from lover (Y). Through this relationship a sense of quiet beauty, holiness, sadness, and virtue, is suggested. The most important meanings in this relationship are actually unstated. They exist, as in other examples, as a sum of X + Y. When we paraphrase them, they instantly lose their power, and the poetic tension dissipates. Since poetic tension is a state of insight, coming to a conclusion (by making a paraphrase) puts an end to that state.

In the second stanza, we also have an example of a single word acting as metaphor: "layetie," which means laymen, worldly people. Would this term have much force if instead Donne had said "other people"? Not only does "layetie" connect with the mood of sacredness already established, it also suggests that only other lovers in the purest state of love, only those who truly love (without worldly, egotistical desires), are fit to hear of these feelings or capable of understanding them. Notice that you can perceive and experience this immediately in the poem, but to discuss it takes a disproportionate amount of space and time.

Right from the first two stanzas the idea of spirit versus flesh is being played on. Donne keeps hinting that even if bodies are apart, souls remain in touch. In the third stanza we are told that the earth (which is physical *like* the body—a covert metaphor) moves (experiences earthquakes, tidal waves, for example); we are also told that when the spheres ° tremble, though their motion is as vast as space and proportionately profound, it is undetectably subtle and troubles no one. So from this angle we have returned to the idea that souls are mild and gentle and cause no problems when they act. Desires (particularly physical desires) cause trouble. This same metaphoric relationship has been extended from stanza one.

In the fourth stanza the expression "sublunary lovers" continues the metaphoric contrast between earth/body (X) and soul/heaven (Y). "Sublunary" (under the moon) refers not only to the earth—earthly concerns—but also to the place ruled by the moon (from astrology), where there is birth, death, and corruption. The sublunary was the lowest of the spheres. Here Donne continues the "logical," reasonable tone: "Dull sublunary lovers love/ (whose soule is sense) cannot admit/ Absence, because it doth remove/ Those things which elemented it." In other words, things bound to the senses in the physical world perish, and so if all you want is your lover's body, then when she (or he) is gone—when you have parted from each other—you have nothing. The fifth stanza completes the contrast of spirit versus flesh begun in stanza four by showing that the narrator and his lover are beyond these worldly miseries, having arrived at a higher state or point of view.

In stanza six we see the first explicit metaphor of the poem. Souls parting from each other are compared to beaten gold. What was hidden before, suggested by covert metaphoric operations, is now (as a kind of dramatic conclusion) being exposed in open form. All the previous suggestions are united in a single, complex extended metaphor* possessing added meaning because of the extensive buildup. Because of all the levels of meaning already in the air, the tension between "compasses" (X) on the one hand (a technological image, very unpoetic by most standards—like a TV set or washing machine) and lovers (Y) on the other pulls these meanings together with great force. The feeling of "truth" that comes out of this rather bizarre association can't be stated. It has to be sensed, intuited, or "felt." The most abstract of concepts (soul, love, etc.) are tied to the most dead and concrete of objects. This is *extreme* metaphor and results in an extreme, almost shocking tone. And since the two terms are incredibly far apart, almost as a function of this distance the piece gains terrific, surprising depth and impact.

° Spheres were considered to be invisible forces that sustain and shape the visible universe, each one defined by the orbit of a particular planet; thus there was a "lower" sphere, like the sphere of the moon, and a higher sphere—the sphere of Jupiter, for example.

* These are sometimes called CONCEITS today, though the term meant metaphors with extreme stress on the unlike factor.

1. Can you see any further parallels between the situation in the poem and the pair of compasses?
2. In what ways does Donne refer to the world (the earth)? How are the "teare-floods" and "sigh-tempests" related to the world? How is the compass conceit related to the world? What kinds of meanings does the world take on here?
3. Consider the second line in the fourth stanza. In what ways do the "dull sublunary lovers" have souls that are sense?
4. If other people are the "layetie" (lay people, nonchurchmen), what are the lovers implicitly compared to ?
5. In stanza five, why don't the lovers know what their love is?
6. Consider the implications of each of the details in the metaphor of the compasses. "Thy firmnes draws my circle just," for example. What are some of the possibilities in the word "circle"? (Remember section IX of Stevens' blackbird poem.) What does it refer to? What might it mean? You can make these kinds of considerations for many of the words in the poem.
7. Consider the different effect when metaphors are made—as in "Ode on Melancholy"—with "poetic" literary or natural images (goddesses, grapes) and with the "unpoetic" technological objects here. How does the type of image seem to affect the tone of each kind of poem?
8. Consider the two lines "Inter-assured of the mind,/ Care lesse, eyes, lips, and hands to misse." How does the stress pattern in the first line contrast with the stress pattern in the second? How does this reflect the sense of the lines? Can you find other examples of this kind of metric contrast in the poem?
9. Does Donne's "distance" from the subject of love necessarily show a lack of deep feeling? Would you imagine a poet feels more intensely just because he says he does? How can we gauge his feeling?

Technical Notes

The rhyme scheme is simple *a b a b*. The meter is iambic tetrameter.

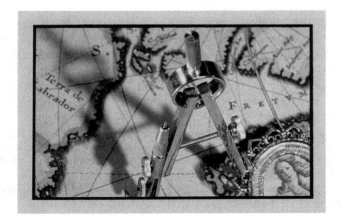

Compare this next poem with the Donne piece. Notice the same type of exaggerated metaphoric comparisons. What is the effect of the tone in the Wills piece?

William Wills
IN PRAISE OF MARRIAGE

Just as this ruler measures off the floor
In inches and feet, where I the carpet lay,
So you, my bride, are the measure of me.

My love is like the rug I struggle with:
It must be cut and fitted to your needs;
It must be shaped to the room of our life;

It must cover the bare boards,
The imperfections and the old shellac,
Brushed on by others, and the worn-out

Places where other boots have scraped.
O take the scissors and the hammer, love,
Square me off and nail me into place!

Exploring the Metaphors

1. Is the poet being witty or sincere? Can you find any clues to his attitude, the mood, or the atmosphere? How are we supposed to take this poem?
2. Is the writing overdone? If so, can you give clear reasons why? If not, what do you think are its merits?
3. Do you see a difference between this and the Donne piece in terms of the depth and intensity of insight? If so, how do you account for it?

What would you say about the tone here? What does it depend on? At first this piece may seem more complex than it actually is. The relation between the hourglass (X) and what it is associated with (Y) is fairly simple, and you should be able to work it out easily.

Ben Jonson
THE HOURE-GLASSE

Doe but consider this small dust,
      Here running in the Glasse,
         By Atomes mov'd;
    Could you beleeve, that this,
        The body was
           Of one that lov'd?
And in his Mistris flame, playing like a flye,
      Turn'd to cinders by her eye?
Yes; and in death, as life unblest,
      To have't exprest,
Even ashes of lovers find no rest.

Exploring the Metaphors

1. Contrast the humorous irony here with the deadly serious, exalted feeling of "When I Heard the Learn'd Astronomer." How much of this difference is due, in effect, to Jonson's use of the technological image of the hourglass?
2. Consider the individual images and metaphors of the poem. How do they affect the tone (for example, the fly metaphor)? What insights do they generate?
3. Consider the last statement. Try stressing "lovers" and then try stressing "ashes." How does this alter the tone?
4. Do you see a connection between the continuous movement in the hourglass and the process of love? Could the metaphor be suggesting that the lovers are continually afflicting their minds with doubt and hope, sighing, weeping, etc.? How? What does the fact that this all takes place in an hourglass add?
5. Consider the shape of the poem, the way the lines are indented. Does this also add to the poem's metaphor?

Christopher Marlowe
THE PASSIONATE SHEPHERD TO HIS LOVE

Come live with me and be my love,
And we will all the pleasures prove,
That hills and valleys, dales and fields,
And all the craggy mountains yields.

There we will sit upon the rocks,
And see the shepherds feed their flocks,
By shallow rivers to whose falls
Melodious birds sing madrigals.

And I will make thee beds of roses
With a thousand fragrant posies,
A cap of flowers, and a kirtle
Embroidered all with leaves of myrtle;

A gown made of the finest wool
Which from our pretty lambs we pull;
Fair lined slippers for the cold,
With buckles of the purest gold;

A belt of straw and ivy buds,
With coral clasps and amber studs:
And if these pleasures may thee move,
Come live with me and be my love.

The shepherds' swains shall dance and sing
For thy delight each May morning:
If these delights thy mind may move,
Then live with me and be my love.

2. Metaphoric Language in Poetry **89**

Sir Walter Raleigh
THE NYMPH'S REPLY
TO THE SHEPHERD

If all the world and love were young,
And truth in every shepherd's tongue,
These pretty pleasures might me move,
To live with thee, and be thy love.

Time drives the flocks from field to fold,
When rivers rage, and rocks grow cold,
And Philomel ° becometh dumb,
The rest complains of cares to come.

The flowers do fade, and wanton fields,
To wayward winter reckoning yields,
A honey tongue, a heart of gall,
Is fancy's spring, but sorrow's fall.

Thy gowns, thy shoes, thy beds of roses,
Thy cap, thy kirtle, and thy posies,
Soon break, soon wither, soon forgotten:
In folly ripe, in reason rotten.

Thy belt of straw and ivy buds,
Thy coral clasps and amber studs,
All these in me no means can move,
To come to thee, and be thy love.

But could youth last, and love still breed,
Had joys no date, nor age no need,
Then these delights my mind might move,
To live with thee and be thy love.

° a figure in Greek mythology (see page 161)

John Donne
THE BAITE

Come live with mee, and bee my love,
And wee will some new pleasures prove
Of golden sands, and crystal brookes,
With silken lines, and silver hookes.

There will the river whispering runne
Warm'd by thy eyes, more than the Sunne.
And there th'inamor'd fish will stay,
Begging themselves they may betray.

When thou wilt swimme in that live bath,
Each fish, which every channell hath,
Will amorously to thee swimme,
Gladder to catch thee, than thou him.

If thou, to be so seene, beest loath,
By Sunne, or Moone, thou darknest both,
And if my selfe have leave to see,
I need not their light, having thee.

Let others freeze with angling reeds,
And cut their legges, with shells and weeds,
Or treacherously poore fish beset,
With strangling snare, or windowie net:

Let coarse bold hands, from slimy nest
The bedded fish in banks out-wrest,
Or curious traitors, sleavesilke flies
Bewitch poore fishes wandring eyes.

For thee, thou needst no such deceit,
For thou thy selfe art thine owne bait;
That fish, that is not catch'd thereby,
Alas, is wiser farre than I.

Exploring the Metaphors

As you see, the Marlowe piece is serious and straightforward. The poet speaks with a shepherd's voice, associating his love with an ideal or mythical world. Implicit in this is a comparison of his contemporary environment with a place or state of perfection. Poets have done this for ages and still do. In the Marlowe and Raleigh poems we have the shepherd's world (X) expressing the poet's world (Y). This metaphoric technique has been used so often that it is called a LITERARY CONVENTION, something like a dead metaphor. Unless handled with consummate skill and energy, a literary convention is always in danger of becoming a stylistic cliché. If everybody is comparing his love relationships to the affairs of shepherds and nymphs, there is little that is vital or fresh about the idea.

Marlowe's poem is an example of a fairly clever use of convention, but few would call it outstanding. Raleigh read it and reacted, it would seem, to the tone of simple sincerity and (he must have thought) excessive optimism. So Raleigh stays within the convention, but gives it a whole new twist. The basic difference in tone has nothing to do with metaphors, images, diction, or technique (the styles are similar); instead it is established by a note of cynicism against a background of realistic appraisal of the facts of life. Notice how the effect of the convention is completely changed by this. If you read the Marlowe poem first and it seems dead, when you follow up with the Raleigh poem the metaphoric situation comes to life. It suddenly has bite and depth.

Donne goes further: He extends the cynical tone and mocks the convention itself, and he creates a totally independent poem. Raleigh's piece is literally an answer to the Marlowe poem and thus depends on it for full value. Donne sets up an atmosphere of absurd humor together with a very sophisticated sense of the reality of love.

1. What effect does the comparison of lovers to fish have in the Donne poem?
2. Compare the tone of the first two poems with Donne's tone, the result of striking, even grotesque natural, nonliterary images against natural and literary-natural images. What is the effect of this on the convention which John Donne is mocking?

Technical Notes

The poems are all written in what amounts to iambic tetrameter. The rhyme schemes are obviously parallel.

This long poem, one of the wittiest in the language, is satiric in tone. Pope, who flourished in a cultured eighteenth-century English social atmosphere, aims barb after barb at London high society and hits home by making clever juxtapositions that set the capricious, petty concerns and foolishness of the local upper classes against eternal EPIC *drama: the trivial (X) to the heroic (Y). A gentleman's idle prank on a young lady is treated as if it were an event in the battle of Troy. In his dedication Pope said: "For the ancient Poets are in one respect like many modern Ladies: Let an Action be never so trivial in itself, they always make it appear of the utmost Importance." Pope was not being negative about the ancient poets; he admired them greatly, and so the dedication is ironic: he is pointing out that his representation of London society (in which its trivia are treated as important) is equivalent to its own self-image, the difference being that he sees it as absurd comedy.*

Pope's descriptions of insignificant doings at court, in the manner of Homer and Virgil, form the structure supporting this satire: In the Iliad *great battles are fought; in London society the battles consist of playing card games (games of "Ombre") and throwing snuff. The battle of Troy was ignited by the abduction of Helen; in London society war is waged because the Baron snipped off a lock of Belinda's hair. In Virgil's* Aeneid, *Queen Dido performs rites before immolating herself for love of the hero, Aeneas. In "The Rape of the Lock," Belinda performs the "rites of pride" at her dressing table. In the epics, universal Olympian gods and goddesses take sides and offer aid to the heroes in the great human battles. In Pope's poem, spiteful gnomes and prankish sprites and sylphs, spirits of vanity, guard Belinda's earrings and pamper her sacred lock. Beaus and Belles, men and women, are equally satirized by Pope here.*

Don't be intimidated if you miss many of the things the poet refers to. One of the beauties of this poem is its richness. You don't even have to be very familiar with the epics Pope is playing on to appreciate much of the humor here. No matter how much you miss, there is always more to enjoy and more to gain in later readings. But even on the first reading you should be able to appreciate that beneath the witty surface, Pope penetrates into the nature of human values, going past London society and epic legends to present an incisive vision of human folly and pretentiousness.

Alexander Pope

THE RAPE OF THE LOCK

CANTO I
What dire Offence from am'rous Causes springs,
What mighty Contests rise from trivial Things,
I sing—This Verse to *Caryll*, [1] Muse! is due;
This, ev'n *Belinda* may vouchsafe to view:

[1] A friend of Pope

Slight is the Subject, but not so the Praise,
If She inspire, and He approve my Lays.
    Say what strange Motive, Goddess! cou'd compel
A well-bred *Lord* t'assault a gentle *Belle*?
Oh say what stranger Cause, yet unexplor'd,
Cou'd make a gentle *Belle* reject a *Lord*?
In Tasks so bold, can Little Men engage,
And in soft Bosoms dwells such mighty Rage?
    Sol thro' white Curtains shot a tim'rous Ray,
And op'd those Eyes that must eclipse the Day;
Now Lapdogs give themselves the rowzing Shake,
And sleepless Lovers, just at Twelve, awake:
Thrice rung the Bell, the Slipper knock'd the Ground, [2]
And the press'd Watch return'd a silver Sound. [3]
Belinda still her downy Pillow prest,
Her Guardian *Sylph* prolong'd the balmy Rest.
'Twas he had summon'd to her silent Bed
The Morning-Dream that hover'd o'er her Head.
A Youth more glitt'ring than a *Birth-night Beau* [4]
(That ev'n in Slumber caus'd her Cheek to glow)
Seem'd to her Ear his winning Lips to lay,
And thus in Whispers said, or seem'd to say.
    Fairest of Mortals, thou distinguish'd Care
Of thousand bright Inhabitants of Air!
If e'er one Vision touch'd thy infant Thought,
Of all the Nurse and all the Priest have taught,
Of airy Elves by Moonlight Shadows seen,
The silver Token, and the circled Green,
Or Virgins visited by Angel-Pow'rs,
With Golden Crowns and Wreaths of heavn'ly Flow'rs,
Hear and believe! thy own Importance know,
Nor bound thy narrow Views to Things below.
Some secret Truths from Learned Pride conceal'd,
To Maids alone and Children are reveal'd:
What tho' no Credit doubting Wits may give?
The Fair and Innocent shall still believe.
Know then, unnumber'd Spirits round thee fly,
The light *Militia* of the lower Sky;
These, tho' unseen, are ever on the Wing,

[2] Belinda's handbell unanswered, she knocked with her slipper.
[3] The watch sounded the quarters of the hour when pressure
was applied to the pin near the pendant.
[4] birthday dress

2. Metaphoric Language in Poetry   95

Hang o'er the *Box*, and hover round the *Ring*.[5]
Think what an Equipage thou hast in Air,
And view with scorn *Two Pages* and a *Chair*.[6]
As now your own, our Beings were of old,
And once inclos'd in Woman's beauteous Mold,
Thence, by a soft Transition, we repair
From earthly Vehicles to these of Air.
Think not, when Woman's transient Breath is fled,
That all her Vanities at once are dead:
Succeeding Vanities she still regards,
And tho' she plays no more, o'erlooks the Cards.
Her Joy in gilded Chariots, when alive,
And Love of *Ombre*,[7] after Death survive.
For when the Fair in all their Pride expire,
To their first Elements their Souls retire:
The Sprights of fiery Termagants[8] in Flame
Mount up, and take a *Salamander's* Name.
Soft yielding Minds to Water glide away,
And sip with *Nymphs*, their Elemental Tea.
The graver Prude sinks downward to a *Gnome*,
In search of Mischief still on Earth to roam.
The light Coquettes in *Sylphs* aloft repair,
And sport and flutter in the Fields of Air.
    Know farther yet; Whoever fair and chaste
Rejects Mankind, is by some *Sylph* embrac'd:
For Spirits, freed from mortal Laws, with ease
Assume what Sexes and what Shapes they please.
What guards the Purity of melting Maids,
In Courtly Balls, and Midnight Masquerades,
Safe from the treach'rous Friend, the daring Spark,[9]
The Glance by Day, the Whisper in the Dark;
When kind Occasion prompts their warm Desires,
When Musick softens, and when Dancing fires?
'Tis but their *Sylph*, the wise Celestials know,
Tho' *Honour* is the Word with Men below.
Some Nymphs there are, too conscious of their Face,[10]
For Life predestin'd to the *Gnomes'* Embrace.

[5] a fashionable parade for coaches in Hyde Park
[6] a sedan chair
[7] a card game like bridge
[8] an overbearing, nagging woman
[9] a lively, showy, fellow. A term of contempt
[10] their beauty

96   *Metaphor:* The Logic of Poetry

These swell their Prospects and exalt their Pride,
When Offers are disdain'd, and Love deny'd.
Then gay Ideas crowd the vacant Brain;
While Peers and Dukes, and all their sweeping Train,
And Garters, Stars and Coronets appear,
And in soft Sounds, *Your Grace* salutes their Ear.
'Tis these that early taint the Female Soul,
Instruct the Eyes of young *Coquettes* to roll,
Teach Infant-Cheeks a bidden Blush [11] to know,
And little Hearts to flutter at a *Beau.*
  Oft when the World imagine Women stray,
The *Sylphs* thro' mystick Mazes guide their Way,
Thro' all the giddy Circle they pursue,
And old Impertinence [12] expel by new.
What tender Maid but must a Victim fall
To one Man's Treat, [13] but for another's Ball?
When *Florio* speaks, what Virgin could withstand,
If gentle *Dæmon* did not squeeze her Hand?
With varying Vanities, from ev'ry Part,
They shift the moving Toyshop of their Heart;
Where Wigs with Wigs, with Sword-knots Sword-knots [14] strive
Beaus banish Beaus, and Coaches Coaches drive.
This erring Mortals Levity may call,
Oh blind to Truth! the *Sylphs* contrive it all.
  Of these am I, who thy Protection claim,
A watchful Sprite, and *Ariel* is my Name.
Late, as I rang'd the Crystal Wilds of Air,
In the clear Mirror of thy ruling *Star*
I saw, alas! some dread Event impend,
Ere to the Main this Morning Sun descend.
But Heav'n reveals not what, or how, or where:
Warn'd by thy *Sylph*, oh Pious Maid beware!
This to disclose is all thy Guardian can.
Beware of all, but most beware of Man!
  He said; when *Shock*, who thought she slept too long,
Leapt up, and wak'd his Mistress with his Tongue.
'Twas then *Belinda*! if Report say true,
Thy Eyes first open'd on a *Billet-doux;*
Wounds, Charms, and *Ardors,* were no sooner read,

[11] with rouge
[12] trifle
[13] an entertainment of food and drink
[14] a ribbon tied to the hilt of a sword

But all the Vision vanish'd from thy Head.
   And now, unveil'd, the *Toilet* stands display'd,
Each Silver Vase in mystic Order laid.
First, rob'd in White, the Nymph intent adores
With Head uncover'd, the *Cosmetic* Pow'rs.
A heav'nly Image in the Glass appears,
To that she bends, to that her Eyes she rears;
Th'inferior Priestess, at her Altar's side,
Trembling, begins the sacred Rites of Pride.
Unnumber'd Treasures ope at once, and here
The various Off'rings of the World appear;
From each she nicely culls with curious Toil,
And decks the Goddess with the glitt'ring Spoil.
This Casket *India*'s glowing Gems unlocks,
And all *Arabia* breathes from yonder Box.
The Tortoise here and Elephant unite,
Transform'd to *Combs*, the speckled and the white.
Here Files of Pins extend their shining Rows,
Puffs, Powders, Patches, Bibles, Billet-doux.
Now awful Beauty puts on all its Arms;
The Fair each moment rises in her Charms,
Repairs her Smiles, awakens ev'ry Grace,
And calls forth all the Wonders of her Face;
Sees by Degrees a purer Blush arise,

And keener Lightnings quicken in her Eyes. [15]
The busy *Sylphs* surround their darling Care;
These set the Head, and those divide the Hair,
Some fold the Sleeve, whilst others plait the Gown;
And *Betty's* prais'd for Labours not her own.

CANTO II
Not with more Glories, in th' Etherial Plain,
The Sun first rises o'er the purpled Main,
Than issuing forth, the Rival of his Beams
Lanch'd on the Bosom of the Silver *Thames.*
Fair Nymphs, and well-drest Youths around her shone,
But ev'ry Eye was fix'd on her alone.
On her white Breast a sparkling *Cross* she wore,
Which *Jews* might kiss, and Infidels adore.
Her lively Looks a sprightly Mind disclose,
Quick as her Eyes, and as unfix'd as those:
Favours to none, to all she Smiles extends,
Oft she rejects, but never once offends.
Bright as the Sun, her Eyes the Gazers strike,
And, like the Sun, they shine on all alike.
Yet graceful Ease, and Sweetness void of Pride,
Might hide her Faults, if *Belles* had Faults to hide:
If to her share some Female Errors fall,
Look on her Face, and you'll forget 'em all.
    This Nymph, to the Destruction of Mankind,
Nourish'd two Locks, which graceful hung behind
In equal Curls, and well conspir'd to deck
With shining Ringlets the Smooth Iv'ry Neck.
Love in these Labyrinths his Slaves detains,
And mighty Hearts are held in slender Chains.
With hairy Sprindges we the Birds betray,
Slight Lines of Hair surprize the Finny Prey,
Fair Tresses Man's Imperial Race insnare,
And Beauty draws us with a single Hair.
Th' Adventrous *Baron* the bright Locks admir'd,
He saw, he wish'd, and to the Prize aspir'd:
Resolv'd to win, he meditates the way,
By Force to ravish, or by Fraud betray;
For when Success a Lover's Toil attends,

[15] She is using either eyeshadow or the juice of belladona
(nightshade), which enlarges the pupils of the eyes and
was popular in the eighteenth century.

Few ask, if Fraud or Force attain'd his Ends.
  For this, ere *Phoebus* rose, he had implor'd
Propitious Heav'n, and ev'ry Pow'r ador'd,
But chiefly *Love*—to *Love* an Altar built,
Of twelve vast *French* Romances, neatly gilt.
There lay three Garters, half a Pair of Gloves;
And all the Trophies of his former Loves.
With tender *Billet-doux* he lights the Pyre,
And breathes three am'rous Sighs to raise the Fire.
Then prostrate falls, and begs with ardent Eyes
Soon to obtain, and long possess the Prize:
The Pow'rs gave Ear, and granted half his Pray'r,
The rest, the Winds dispers'd in empty Air.
  But now secure the painted Vessel glides,
The Sun-beams trembling on the floating Tydes,
While melting Musick steals upon the Sky,
And soften'd Sounds along the Waters die.
Smooth flow the Waves, the Zephyrs gently play,
Belinda smil'd, and all the World was gay.
All but the *Sylph*—With careful Thoughts opprest,
Th'impending Woe sate heavy on his Breast.
He summons strait his Denizens of Air;
The lucid Squadrons round the Sails repair:
Soft o'er the Shrouds Aerial Whispers breathe,
That seem'd but *Zephyrs* to the Train beneath.
Some to the Sun their Insect-Wings unfold,
Waft on the Breeze, or sink in Clouds of Gold.
Transparent Forms, too fine for mortal Sight,
Their fluid Bodies half dissolv'd in Light.
Loose to the Wind their airy Garments flew,
Thin glitt'ring Textures of the filmy Dew;
Dipt in the richest Tincture of the Skies,
Where Light disports in ever-mingling Dies,
While ev'ry Beam new transient Colours flings,
Colours that change when'er they wave their Wings.
Amid the Circle, on the gilded Mast,
Superior by the Head, was *Ariel* plac'd;
His Purple Pinions opening to the Sun,
He rais'd his Azure Wand, and thus begun.
  Ye *Sylphs* and *Sylphids*, to your Chief give Ear,
Fays, Fairies, Genii, Elves, and *Dæmons* hear!
Ye know the Spheres and various Tasks assign'd,
By Laws Eternal, to th' Aerial Kind.

Some in the Fields of purest *Æther* play,
And bask and whiten in the Blaze of Day.
Some guide the Course of wandring Orbs on high,
Or roll the Planets thro' the boundless Sky.
Some less refin'd, beneath the Moon's pale Light
Pursue the Stars that shoot athwart the Night,
Or suck the Mists in grosser Air below,
Or dip their Pinions in the painted Bow,
Or brew fierce Tempests on the wintry Main,
Or o'er the Glebe distill the kindly Rain.
Others on Earth o'er human Race preside,
Watch all their Ways, and all their Actions guide:
Of these the Chief the Care of Nations own,
And guard with Arms Divine the *British Throne*.
　　Our humbler Province is to tend the Fair,
Not a less pleasing, tho' less glorious Care.
To save the Powder from too rude a Gale,
Nor let th' imprison'd Essences exhale,
To draw fresh Colours from the vernal Flow'rs,
To steal from Rainbows ere they drop in Show'rs
A brighter Wash; to curl their waving Hairs,
Assist their Blushes, and inspire their Airs;
Nay oft, in Dreams, Invention we bestow,
To change a *Flounce*, or add a *Furbelo*.[16]
　　This Day, black Omens threat the brightest Fair
That e'er deserv'd a watchful Spirit's Care;
Some dire Disaster, or by Force, or Slight,
But what, or where, the Fates have wrapt in Night.
Whether the Nymph shall break *Diana's* Law,
Or some frail *China* Jar receive a Flaw,
Or stain her Honour, or her new Brocade,
Forget her Pray'rs, or miss a Masquerade,
Or lose her Heart, or Necklace, at a Ball;
Or whether Heav'n has doom'd that *Shock* must fall.
Haste then ye Spirits! to your Charge repair;
The flutt'ring Fan be *Zephyretta's* Care;
The Drops to thee,[17] *Brillante*, we consign;
And, *Momentilla*, let the Watch be thine;
Do thou, *Crispissa*, tend her fav'rite Lock;
Ariel himself shall be the Guard of *Shock*.

[16] a piece of material plaited and puckered together, either below or
above, on women's petticoats or gowns
[17] diamond(s) hanging in the ear

To Fifty chosen *Sylphs*, of special Note,
We trust th' important Charge, the *Petticoat*:
Oft have we known that sev'nfold Fence to fail,
Tho' stiff with Hoops, and arm'd with Ribs of Whale.
Form a strong Line about the Silver Bound,
And guard the wide Circumference around.
  Whatever Spirit, careless of his Charge,
His Post neglects, or leaves the Fair at large,
Shall feel sharp Vengeance soon o'ertake his Sins,
Be stopt in *Vials*, or trans'fixt with *Pins*;
Or plung'd in Lakes of bitter *Washes* lie,
Or wedg'd whole Ages in a *Bodkin's* Eye: [18]
Gums and *Pomatums* shall his Flight restrain,
While clog'd he beats his silken Wings in vain;
Or Alom-*Stypticks* with contracting Power
Shrink his thin Essence like a rivell'd Flower. [19]
Or as *Ixion* fix'd, the Wretch shall feel
The giddy Motion of the whirling Mill,
In Fumes of burning Chocolate shall glow,
And tremble at the Sea that froaths below!
  He spoke; the Spirits from the Sails descend;
Some, Orb in Orb, around the Nymph extend,
Some thrid the mazy Ringlets of her Hair,
Some hang upon the Pendants of her Ear;
With beating Hearts the dire Event they wait,
Anxious, and trembling for the Birth of Fate.

CANTO III
Close by those Meads for ever crown'd with Flow'rs,
Where *Thames* with Pride surveys his rising Tow'rs,
There stands a Structure of Majestick Frame,
Which from the neighb'ring *Hampton* takes its Name.
Here *Britain's* Statesmen oft the Fall foredoom
Of Foreign Tyrants, and of Nymphs at home;
Here Thou, Great *Anna*! [20] whom three Realms obey,
Dost sometimes Counsel take-and sometimes *Tea*.
  Hither the Heroes and the Nymphs resort,
To taste awhile the Pleasures of a Court;

[18] Pope plays on the various meanings of "bodkin": (1) a blunt-pointed needle; (2) a hair ornament; and (3) a dagger.
[19] contracted into wrinkles and corrugations
[20] Queen Anne of England

In various Talk th' instructive hours they past,
Who gave the *Ball*, or paid the *Visit* last:
One speaks the Glory of the *British Queen*,
And one describes a charming *Indian Screen*;
A third interprets Motions, Looks, and Eyes;
At ev'ry Word a Reputation dies.
Snuff, or the *Fan*, supply each Pause of Chat,
With singing, laughing, ogling, and all that.

   Mean while declining from the Noon of Day,
The Sun obliquely shoots his burning Ray;
The hungry Judges soon the Sentence sign,
And Wretches hang that Jury-men may Dine;
The Merchant from th' *Exchange* returns in Peace,
And the long Labours of the *Toilette* cease—,
Belinda now, whom Thirst of Fame invites,
Burns to encounter two adventrous Knights,
At *Ombre* singly to decide their Doom;
And swells her Breast with Conquests yet to come.
Strait the three Bands prepare in Arms to join,
Each Band the number of the Sacred Nine.
Soon as she spreads her Hand, th' Aerial Guard
Descend, and sit on each important Card:
First *Ariel* perch'd upon a *Matadore*,
Then each, according to the Rank they bore;
For *Sylphs*, yet mindful of their ancient Race,
Are, as when Women, wondrous fond of Place.

   Behold, four *Kings* in Majesty rever'd,
With hoary Whiskers and a forky Beard;
And four fair *Queens* whose hands sustain a Flow'r,
Th' expressive Emblem of their softer Pow'r,
Four *Knaves* in Garbs succinct, a trusty Band,
Caps on their heads, and Halberds in their hand;
And Particolour'd Troops, a shining Train,
Draw forth to Combat on the Velvet Plain.

   The skilful Nymph reviews her Force with Care;
Let Spades be Trumps! she said, and Trumps they were. [21]

   Now move to War her Sable *Matadores*,
In Show like Leaders of the swarthy Moors.
Spadillio first, unconquerable Lord!
Led off two captive Trumps, and swept the Board.
As many more *Manillio* forc'd to yield,

[21] Remember Gen. 1:3: "And God said, 'Let there be
light:' and there was light."

And march'd a Victor from the verdant Field.
Him *Basto* follow'd, but his Fate more hard
Gain'd but one Trump and one *Plebeian* Card.
With his broad Sabre next, a Chief in Years,
The hoary Majesty of *Spades* appears;
Puts forth one manly Leg, to sight reveal'd;
The rest his many-colour'd Robe conceal'd.
The Rebel-*Knave*, who dares his Prince engage,
Proves the just Victim of his Royal Rage.
Ev'n mighty *Pam* that Kings and Queens o'erthrew,
And mow'd down Armies in the Fights of *Lu*,
Sad Chance of War! now, destitute of Aid,
Falls undistinguish'd by the Victor *Spade*!
　　Thus far both Armies to *Belinda* yield;
Now to the *Baron* Fate inclines the Field.
His warlike *Amazon* her Host invades,
Th' Imperial Consort of the Crown of *Spades*.
The *Club*'s black Tyrant first her Victim dy'd,
Spite of his haughty Mien, and barb'rous Pride:
What boots the Regal Circle on his Head,
His Giant Limbs in State unwieldy spread?
That long behind he trails his pompous Robe,
And of all Monarchs only grasps the Globe?
　　The *Baron* now his *Diamonds* pours apace;
Th' embroider'd *King* who shows but half his Face,
And his refulgent *Queen*, with Pow'rs combin'd,
Of broken Troops an easie Conquest find.
Clubs, Diamonds, Hearts, in wild Disorder seen,
With Throngs promiscuous strow the level Green.
Thus when dispers'd a routed Army runs,
Of *Asia*'s Troops, and *Africk*'s Sable Sons,
With like Confusion different Nations fly,
Of various Habit and of various Dye,
The pierc'd Battalions dis-united fall,
In Heaps on Heaps; one Fate o'erwhelms them all.
　　The *Knave of Diamonds* tries his wily Arts,
And wins (oh shameful Chance!) the *Queen of Hearts*.
At this, the Blood the Virgin's Cheek forsook,
A livid Paleness spreads o'er all her Look;
She sees, and trembles at th' approaching Ill,
Just in the Jaws of Ruin, and *Codille*.
And now, (as oft in some distemper'd State)

On one nice *Trick*[22] depends the gen'ral Fate.
An Ace of Hearts steps forth: The *King* unseen
Lurk'd in her Hand, and mourn'd his captive *Queen*.
He springs to Vengeance with an eager pace,
And falls like Thunder on the prostrate *Ace*.

The Nymph exulting fills with Shouts the Sky,
The Walls, the Woods, and long Canals reply.
    Oh thoughtless Mortals! ever blind to Fate,
Too soon dejected, and too soon elate!
Sudden these Honours shall be snatch'd away,
And curs'd for ever this Victorious Day.
For lo! the Board with Cups and Spoons is crown'd,
The Berries crackle, and the Mill turns round.
On shining Altars of Japan [23] they raise
The silver Lamp; the fiery Spirits blaze.
From silver Spouts the grateful Liquors glide,
While *China*'s Earth receives the smoking Tyde.
At once they gratify their Scent and Taste,
And frequent Cups prolong the rich Repast.

[22] a pun
[23] Lacquered tables

Strait hover round the Fair her Airy Band;
Some, as she sip'd, the fuming Liquor fann'd,
Some o'er her Lap their careful Plumes display'd,
Trembling, and conscious of the rich Brocade.
Coffee,[24] (which makes the Politician wise,
And see thro' all things with his half-shut Eyes)
Sent up in Vapours to the *Baron*'s Brain
New Stratagems, the radiant Lock to gain.
Ah cease rash Youth! desist ere 'tis too late,
Fear the just Gods, and think of *Scylla*'s Fate!
Chang'd to a Bird, and sent to flit in Air,
She dearly pays for *Nisus*' injur'd Hair![25]
    But when to Mischief Mortals bend their Will,
How soon they find fit Instruments of Ill!
Just then, *Clarissa* drew with tempting Grace
A two-edg'd Weapon from her shining Case;[26]
So Ladies in Romance assist their Knight,
Present the Spear, and arm him for the Fight.
He takes the Gift with rev'rence, and extends
The little Engine on his Fingers' Ends,
This just behind *Belinda*'s Neck he spread,
As o'er the fragrant Steams she bends her Head:
Swift to the Lock a thousand Sprights repair,
A thousand Wings, by turns, blow back the Hair,
And thrice they twitch'd the Diamond in her Ear,
Thrice she look'd back, and thrice the Foe drew near.
Just in that instant, anxious *Ariel* sought
The close Recesses of the Virgin's Thought;
As on the Nosegay in her Breast reclin'd,
He watch'd th' Ideas rising in her Mind,
Sudden he view'd, in spite of all her Art,
An Earthly Lover lurking at her Heart.
Amaz'd, confus'd, he found his Pow'r expir'd,
Resign'd to Fate, and with a Sigh retir'd.

[24] Coffeehouses were frequented by amateur politicians.
[25] King Nisus' daughter Scylla, fell in love with Minos. The
safety of Nisus' kingdom was known to depend on a purple
hair which grew on his head. Scylla plucked out the hair and
took it to Minos, but met with nothing but horror for her
action. After Minos's victory he sailed away; Scylla attempted
to cling to his ship till, beaten off by Nisus, who had become
an osprey; she also became a bird.
[26] tweezer case

The Peer now spreads the glitt'ring *Forfex* wide,
T'inclose the Lock; now joins it, to divide.
Ev'n then, before the fatal Engine clos'd,
A wretched *Sylph* too fondly interpos'd;
Fate urg'd the Sheers, and cut the *Sylph* in twain,
(But Airy Substance soon unites again)
The meeting Points the sacred Hair dissever
From the fair Head, for ever and for ever!
    Then flash'd the living Lightning from her Eyes,
And Screams of Horror rend th' affrighted Skies.
Not louder Shrieks to pitying Heav'n are cast,
When Husbands or when Lap-dogs breathe their last,
Or when rich *China* Vessels, fal'n from high,
In glittring Dust and painted Fragments lie!
    Let Wreaths of Triumph now my Temples twine,
(The Victor cry'd) the glorious Prize is mine!
While Fish in Streams, or Birds delight in Air,
Or in a Coach and Six the *British Fair*,
As long as Atalantis [27] shall be read,
Or the small Pillow grace a Lady's Bed,
While *Visits* shall be paid on solemn Days,
When numerous Wax-lights in bright Order blaze,
While Nymphs take Treats, or Assignations give,
So long my Honour, Name, and Praise shall live !
    What Time wou'd spare, from Steel receives its date,
And Monuments, like Men, submit to Fate!
Steel cou'd the Labour of the Gods destroy,
And strike to Dust th' Imperial Tow'rs of *Troy*;
Steel cou'd the Works of mortal Pride confound,
And hew Triumphal Arches to the Ground.
What Wonder then, fair Nymph! thy Hairs shou'd feel
The conqu'ring Force of unresisted Steel?

CANTO IV

But anxious Cares the pensive Nymph opprest,
And secret Passions labour'd in her Breast.
Not youthful Kings in Battel seiz'd alive,
Not scornful Virgins who their Charms survive,
Not ardent Lovers robb'd of all their Bliss,
Not ancient Ladies when refus'd a Kiss,

[27] Mrs. Manley's *Secret Memories and Manners of Several Persons of Quality, of Both Sexes. From the New Atalantis, an island in the Mediterranean, 1700.*

Not Tyrants fierce that unrepenting die,
Not *Cynthia* when her *Manteau's* [28] pinn'd awry,
E'er felt such Rage, Resentment and Despair,
As Thou, sad Virgin! for thy ravish'd Hair.
    For, that sad moment, when the *Sylphs* withdrew,
And *Ariel* weeping from *Belinda* flew,
Umbriel, a dusky melancholy Spright,
As ever sully'd the fair face of Light,
Down to the Central Earth, his proper Scene,
Repair'd to search the gloomy Cave of *Spleen*. [29]
    Swift on his sooty Pinions flitts the *Gnome*,
And in a Vapour reach'd the dismal Dome.
No cheerful Breeze this sullen Region knows,
The dreaded *East* is all the Wind that blows. [30]
Here, in a Grotto, sheltred close from Air,
And screen'd in Shades from Day's detested Glare,
She sighs for ever on her pensive Bed,
Pain at her Side, and *Megrim* [31] at her Head.
    Two Handmaids wait the Throne: Alike in Place,
But diff'ring far in Figure and in Face.
Here stood *Ill-nature* like an *ancient Maid*,
Her wrinkled Form in *Black* and *White* array'd;
With store of Pray'rs, for Mornings, Nights, and Noons,
Her hand is fill'd; her Bosom with Lampoons.
    There *Affectation* with a sickly Mien
Shows in her Cheek the Roses of Eighteen,
Practis'd to Lisp, and hang the Head aside,
Faints into Airs, and languishes with Pride;
On the rich Quilt sinks with becoming Woe,
Wrapt in a Gown, for Sickness, and for Show.
The Fair-ones feel such Maladies as these,
When each new Night-Dress gives a new Disease.
    A constant *Vapour* o'er the Palace flies;
Strange Phantoms rising as the Mists arise;
Dreadful, as Hermit's Dreams in haunted Shades,
Or bright as Visions of expiring Maids.
Now glaring Fiends, and Snakes on rolling Spires, [32]
Pale Spectres, gaping Tombs, and Purple Fires:

[28] a loose upper garment worn by women
[29] name for an ancient malady of malice
[30] The east wind was thought to provoke ill will.
[31] a severe headache
[32] coils

Now Lakes of Liquid Gold, *Elysian* Scenes,
And Crystal Domes, and Angels in Machines. [33]
 Unnumber'd Throngs on ev'ry side are seen
Of Bodies chang'd to various Forms by *Spleen*.
Here living *Teapots* stand, one Arm held out,
One bent; the Handle this, and that the Spout:
A Pipkin [34] there like *Homer's Tripod* walks;
Here sighs a Jar, and there a Goose-pye talks,
Men prove with Child, as pow'rful Fancy works,
And Maids turn'd Bottels, call aloud for Corks.
 Safe past the *Gnome* thro' this fantastick Band,
A Branch of healing *Spleenwort* in his hand.
Then thus addrest the Pow'r—Hail wayward Queen!
Who rule the Sex to Fifty from Fifteen,
Parent of Vapours and of Female Wit,
Who give th' *Hysteric* or *Poetic* Fit,
On various Tempers act by various ways,
Make some take Physick, others scribble Plays;
Who cause the Proud their Visits to delay,
And send the Godly in a Pett, to pray.
A Nymph there is, that all thy Pow'r disdains,
And thousands more in equal Mirth maintains.
But oh! if e'er thy *Gnome* could spoil a Grace,
Or raise a Pimple on a beauteous Face,
Like Citron-Waters Matrons' Cheeks inflame,
Or change Complexions at a losing Game;
If e'er with airy Horns I planted Heads,
Or rumpled Petticoats, or tumbled Beds,
Or caus'd Suspicion when no Soul was rude,
Or discompos'd the Head-dress of a Prude,
Or e'er to costive Lap-Dog gave Disease,
Which not the Tears of brightest Eyes could ease.
Hear me, and touch *Belinda* with Chagrin;
That single Act gives half the World the Spleen.
 The Goddess with a discontented Air
Seems to reject him, tho' she grants his Pray'r.
A wondrous Bag with both her Hands she binds,
Like that where once *Ulysses* held the Winds;
There she collects the Force of Female Lungs,

[33] a satiric catalog of the scenic effects of contemporary opera
and pantomime
[34] a small earthen boiler

Sighs, Sobs, and Passions, and the War of Tongues.
A Vial next she fills with fainting Fears,
Soft Sorrows, melting Griefs, and flowing Tears.
The *Gnome* rejoicing bears her Gifts away,
Spreads his black Wings, and slowly mounts to Day.
   Sunk in *Thalestris'* [35] Arms the Nymph he found,
Her Eyes dejected and her Hair unbound.
Full o'er their Heads the swelling Bag he rent,
And all the Furies issued at the Vent.
Belinda burns with more than mortal Ire,
And fierce *Thalestris* fans the rising Fire.
O wretched Maid! she spread her Hands, and cry'd,

(while *Hampton*'s Ecchos, wretched Maid! reply'd)
Was it for this you took such constant Care
The *Bodkin*, *Comb*, and *Essence* to prepare;
For this your Locks in Paper-Durance bound,
For this with tort'ring Irons wreath'd around?

[35] 'Thalestris was Queen of the Amazons.

For this with Fillets strain'd your tender Head,
And bravely bore the double Loads of Lead? [36]
Gods! shall the Ravisher display your Hair,
While the Fops envy, and the Ladies stare!
Honour forbid! at whose unrival'd Shrine
Ease, Pleasure, Virtue, All, our Sex resign.
Methinks already I your Tears survey,
Already hear the horrid things they say,
Already see you a degraded Toast, [37]
And all your Honour in a Whisper lost!
How shall I, then, your helpless Fame defend?
'Twill then be Infamy to seem your Friend!
And shall this Prize, th' inestimable Prize,
Expos'd thro' Crystal to the gazing Eyes,
And heighten'd by the Diamond's circling Rays,
On that Rapacious Hand for ever blaze?
Sooner shall Grass in *Hide*-Park *Circus* grow,
And Wits take Lodgings in the Sound of *Bow*;
Sooner let Earth, Air, Sea, to *Chaos* fall,
Men, Monkies, Lap-dogs, Parrots, perish all!
     She said; then raging to *Sir Plume* repairs,
And bids her *Beau* demand the precious Hairs:
(*Sir Plume*, of *Amber Snuff-box* justly vain,
And the nice Conduct of a *clouded Cane*) [38]
With earnest Eyes, and round unthinking Face,
He first the Snuff-box open'd, then the Case,
And thus broke out—'My Lord, why, what the Devil?
Z—ds! damn the Lock! 'fore Gad, you must be civil!
Plague on't! 'tis past a Jest—nay prithee, Pox!
Give her the Hair'—he spoke, and rapp'd his Box.
     It grieves me much (reply'd the Peer again)
Who speaks so well shou'd ever speak in vain.
But by this Lock, this sacred Lock I swear,
(Which never more shall join its parted Hair,
Which never more its Honours shall renew,
Clipt from the lovely Head where late it grew)
That while my Nostrils draw the vital Air,
This Hand, which won it, shall for ever wear.
He spoke, and speaking, in proud Triumph spread

[36] The curling papers for ladies' hair were fastened with strips of pliant lead.
[37] as in drinking a toast
[38] with dark veins

The long-contended Honours of her Head.
　　But *Umbriel*, hateful *Gnome*! forbears not so;
He breaks the Vial whence the Sorrows flow.
Then see! the *Nymph* in beauteous Grief appears,
Her Eyes half-languishing, half-drown'd in Tears;
On her heav'd Bosom hung her drooping Head,
Which, with a Sigh, she rais'd; and thus she said.
　　For ever curs'd be this detested Day,
Which snatch'd my best, my fav'rite Curl away!
Happy! ah ten times happy, had I been,
If *Hampton-Court* these Eyes had never seen!
Yet am not I the first mistaken Maid,
By Love of *Courts* to num'rous Ills betray'd.
Oh had I rather un-admir'd remain'd
In some lone Isle, or distant *Northern* Land;
Where the gilt *Chariot* never marks the Way,
Where none learn Ombre, none e'er taste *Bohea*!
There kept my Charms conceal'd from mortal Eye,
Like Roses that in Desarts bloom and die.
What mov'd my Mind with youthful Lords to rome?
O had I stay'd, and said my Pray'rs at home!
'Twas this, the Morning *Omens* seem'd to tell;
Thrice from my trembling hand the *Patch-box* fell;
The tott'ring *China* shook without a Wind,
Nay, *Poll* sate mute, and *Shock* was most Unkind!
A *Sylph* too warn'd me of the Threats of Fate,
In mystic Visions, now believ'd too late!
See the poor Remnants of these slighted Hairs!
My hands shall rend what ev'n thy Rapine spares:
These, in two sable Ringlets taught to break,
Once gave new Beauties to the snowie Neck.
The Sister-Lock now sits uncouth, alone,
And in its Fellow's Fate foresees its own;
Uncurl'd it hangs, the fatal Sheers demands;
And tempts once more thy sacrilegious Hands.
Oh hadst thou, Cruel! been content to seize
Hairs less in sight, or any Hairs but these!

　　CANTO V
She said: the pitying Audience melt in Tears,
But *Fate* and *Jove* had stopp'd the *Baron*'s Ears.
In vain *Thalestris* with Reproach assails,
For who can move when fair *Belinda* fails?

Not half so fixt the *Trojan* cou'd remain,
While *Anna* begg'd and *Dido* rag'd in vain.
Then grave *Clarissa* graceful wav'd her Fan;
Silence ensu'd, and thus the Nymph began.

    Say, why are Beauties prais'd and honour'd most,
The wise Man's Passion, and the vain Man's Toast?
Why deck'd with all that Land and Sea afford,
Why Angels call'd, and Angel-like ador'd?
Why round our Coaches crowd the white-glov'd Beaus,
Why bows the Side-box from its inmost Rows?
How vain are all these Glories, all our Pains,
Unless good Sense preserve what Beauty gains:
That Men may say, when we the Front-box grace,
Behold the first in Virtue, as in Face!
Oh! if to dance all Night, and dress all Day,
Charm'd the Small-pox, or chas'd old Age away;
Who would not scorn what Huswife's Cares produce,
Or who would learn one earthly Thing of Use?
To patch, nay ogle, might become a Saint,
Nor could it sure be such a Sin to paint.
But since, alas! frail Beauty must decay,
Curl'd or uncurl'd, since Locks will turn to grey,
Since painted, or not painted, all shall fade,
And she who scorns a Man, must die a Maid;
What then remains, but well our Pow'r to use,
And keep good Humour still whate'er we lose?
And trust me, Dear! good Humour can prevail,
When Airs, and Flights, and Screams, and Scolding fail.
Beauties in vain their pretty Eyes may roll;
Charms strike the Sight, but Merit wins the Soul.

    So spoke the Dame, but no Applause ensu'd;
Belinda frown'd, *Thalestris* call'd her Prude.
To Arms, to Arms! the fierce Virago [39] cries,
And swift as Lightning to the Combate flies.
All side in Parties, and begin th' Attack;
Fans clap, Silks russle, and tough Whalebones crack;
Heroes' and Heroins' Shouts confus'dly rise,
And base, and treble Voices strike the Skies.
No common Weapons in their Hands are found,
Like Gods they fight, nor dread a mortal Wound.
So when bold Homer makes the Gods engage,

[39] a female warrior

And heav'nly Breasts with human Passions rage;
'Gainst *Pallas, Mars, Latona, Hermes* arms;
And all *Olympus* rings with Loud Alarms.
Jove's Thunder roars, Heav'n trembles all around;
Blue *Neptune* storms, the bellowing Deeps resound;
Earth shakes her nodding Tow'rs, the Ground Gives way;
And the pale Ghosts start at the Flash of Day!
    Triumphant *Umbriel* on a Sconce's Height
Clapt his glad Wings, and sate to view the Fight:
Propt on their Bodkin Spears, the Sprights survey
The growing Combat, or assist the Fray.
    While thro' the Press enrag'd *Thalestris* flies,
And scatters Deaths around from both her Eyes,
A *Beau* and *Witling* perish'd in the Throng,
One dy'd in *Metaphor*, and one in *Song.*
O *cruel Nymph/ a living Death I bear,*
Cry'd *Dapperwit,* and sunk beside his Chair.
A mournful Glance Sir *Fopling* upwards cast,
Those Eyes are made so killing—was his last:
Thus on *Meander's* flow'ry Margin lies
Th' expiring Swan, and as he sings he dies.
    When bold Sir *Plume* had drawn *Clarissa* down,
Chloe stept in, and kill'd him with a Frown;
She smil'd to see the doughty Hero slain,
But at her Smile, the Beau reviv'd again.
    Now *Jove* suspends his golden Scales in Air,
Weighs the Men's Wits against the Lady's Hair;
The doubtful Beam long nods from side to side;
At length the Wits mount up, the Hairs subside.
    See fierce *Belinda* on the *Baron* flies,
With more than usual Lightning in her Eyes;
Nor fear'd the Chief th' unequal Fight to try,
Who sought no more than on his Foe to die.
But this bold Lord, with manly Strength indu'd,
She with one Finger and a Thumb subdu'd:
Just where the Breath of Life his Nostrils drew,
A Charge of *Snuff* the wily Virgin threw;
The *Gnomes* direct, to ev'ry Atome just,
The pungent Grains of titillating Dust.
Sudden, with starting Tears each Eye o'erflows,
And the high Dome re-ecchoes to his Nose.
Now meet thy Fate, incens'd Belinda cry'd,
And drew a deadly Bodkin from her Side.

(The same, his ancient Personage to deck,
Her great great Grandsire wore about his Neck
In three *Seal-Rings*; which after, melted down,
Form'd a vast *Buckle* for his Widow's Gown:
Her infant Grandame's *Whistle* next it grew,
The *Bells* she gingled, and the *Whistle* blew;
Then in a *Bodkin* grac'd her Mother's Hairs,
Which long she wore, and now *Belinda* wears.)
  Boast not my Fall (he cry'd) insulting Foe!
Thou by some other shalt be laid as low.
Nor think, to die dejects my lofty Mind;
All that I dread, is leaving you behind!
Rather than so, ah let me still survive,
And burn in *Cupid's* Flames,—but burn alive.
  Restore the Lock! she cries; and all around
Restore the Lock! the vaulted Roofs rebound.
Not fierce *Othello* in so loud a Strain
Roar'd for the Handkerchief that caus'd his Pain.
But see how oft Ambitious Aims are cross'd,
And chiefs contend 'till all the Prize is lost!
The Lock, obtain'd with Guilt, and kept with Pain,
In ev'ry place is sought, but sought in vain:
With such a Prize no Mortal must be blest,
So Heav'n decrees! with Heav'n who can contest?
  Some thought it mounted to the Lunar Sphere,
Since all things lost on Earth, are treasur'd there.
There Heroes' Wits are kept in pondrous Vases,
And *Beaus'* in *Snuff-boxes* and *Tweezer-Cases*.
There broken Vows, and Death-bed Alms are found,
And Lovers' Hearts with Ends of Riband bound;
The Courtier's Promises, and Sick Man's Pray'rs,
The Smiles of Harlots, and the Tears of Heirs,
Cages for Gnats, and Chains to Yoak a Flea;
Dry'd Butterflies, and Tomes of Casuistry.
  But trust the Muse—she saw it upward rise,
Tho' mark'd by none but quick Poetic Eyes:
(So *Rome's* great Founder to the Heav'ns withdrew,
To *Proculus* alone confess'd in view.)
A sudden Star, it shot thro' liquid Air,
And drew behind a radiant *Trail of Hair*.
Not *Berenice's* Locks first rose so bright,
The Heav'ns bespangling with dishevel'd Light.
The *Sylphs* behold it kindling as it flies,

And pleas'd pursue its Progress thro' the Skies.
This the *Beau-monde* shall from the *Mall* [40] survey,
And hail with Musick its propitious Ray.
This, the blest Lover shall for *Venus* take,
And send up Vows from *Rosamonda*'s [41] Lake.
This *Partridge* [42] soon shall view in cloudless Skies,
When next he looks thro' Galilæ'o's Eyes;
And hence th' Egregious Wizard shall foredoom
The Fate of *Louis*, and the Fall of *Rome*.
    Then cease, bright Nymph! to mourn thy ravish'd Hair
Which adds new Glory to the shining Sphere!
Not all the Tresses that fair Head can boast
Shall draw such Envy as the Lock you lost.
For, after all the Murders of your Eye,
When, after Millions slain, your self shall die;
When those fair Suns shall sett, as sett they must,
And all those Tresses shall be laid in Dust;
This Lock, the Muse shall consecrate to Fame,
And mid'st the Stars inscribe *Belinda*'s Name!

[40] an enclosed walk in St. James's Park
[41] a pond in St. James's Park
[42] John Partridge was a ridiculous Stargazer; in his
Almanacks every year, he never fail'd to predict the
downfall of the Pope and the King of France, then at war
with the English.

Exploring the Metaphors

"The Rape of the Lock" contains a remarkable store of shrewd poetic strategy. To discuss in detail all the examples and varieties of metaphoric language Pope employs would take a book. Here are a few instances to demonstrate the range of his technique:

Irony "Here Thou, Great Anna [Queen Anne]! whom three Realms obey,/ Dost sometimes Counsel take—and sometimes *Tea*." The juxtaposition of counsel (X) and tea (Y) produces an amused vision of a world where the two virtually contradictory enterprises—taking tea and conducting the affairs of state—have equal importance.

Metaphor Spleen's bag, in which the Goddess of Spleen "collects the Force of Female Lungs,/ Sighs, Sobs, and Passions, and the War of Tongues." In these covert metaphors sighs, sobs, passions (X) are treated as if they were objects (Y) to make them seem foolish, among other things.

Image, personification "From silver Spouts the grateful Liquors glide." The image is also a covert metaphor of personification: Liquors (X) are personified as persons capable of gratitude (Y).

Pun, irony During the card game, before the Baron has performed his evil act, Pope writes: "On one nice *Trick* depends the gen'ral Fate." "Trick" refers to the jargon of the card game as well as, ironically, to the trick that is about to be played on Belinda over her favorite lock of hair.

Symbol, image, metaphor "Now *Jove* suspends his golden Scales in Air,/ Weighs the Men's Wits against the Lady's Hair." Jove holds up the scales symbolizing justice. Notice that the image of scales—with Belinda's lock on one side and "wits" on the other—is a description that can be visualized, except for the wits. The symbol-image functions as a satiric metaphor comparing the argument between the men and Belinda over the lock (X) to cosmic justice (Y).

Allusion, image The poem contains overt and covert allusions to classical epics and mythology. The covert allusions are interesting, though we may need a scholar to point some of them out to us—for example, where Pope describes Belinda's petticoat: "Tho' stiff with Hoops, and arm'd with Ribs of Whale./ Form a strong Line about the Silver Bound/ And guard the wide Circumference around." In this description Pope mimics Vulcan making Achilles' shield in the *Iliad*. The allusion is almost completely concealed, but it adds a dimension to the poem if you discover it—though the situation has plenty to offer even if you do not make that discovery.

As we can see, Pope spares no possible technique, and for all practical purposes his poem is inexhaustible.

1. What has the lock of hair become by the end of the poem? What kinds of meanings and associations are attached to it?
2. Consider any small or large section of the poem and its relation to the rest of the piece. As an example, you could consider what effect the ongoing pun on "ombre" has on the poem (ombre is the name of the card game and is also the French word for "shadow").
3. What effect do the rhyme and meter have in this poem? How do they add to the poem's tone?

Technical Notes
The poem is written in iambic pentameter, in HEROIC COUPLETS, which Pope made famous.

118 *Metaphor:* The Logic of Poetry

Chapter 3

The Poem As Metaphor: X/Y

You may have noticed that some poems not only contain metaphoric language but also seem to have a central metaphoric idea that is worked out over the entire poem. We looked at several such poems in Chapter 1, including "A Patch of Old Snow" and "The Pearl." In "A Patch of Old Snow," the main metaphor compares a patch of old snow (X) to a blown-away newspaper (Y). We might call this the CENTRAL METAPHORIC RELATIONSHIP. A secondary, or local metaphor, dirt on the snow equals newsprint, is connected to this.

Similarly, in Jonson's "Houre-glasse," the central metaphor is the lovers (X) compared to ashes in the glass (Y). This is supported by the local metaphor of the lover, who is (like) a "flie in a flame," as well as by images of ashes, cinders and atoms.

Clearly, delineating the central metaphor does not explicate the poem because it is precisely the details surrounding and amplifying the central relationship which bring it to life. But the central metaphoric relationship is the direction, the focus of interest and poetic action. It shapes the poem. Think, for instance, of "The Rape of the Lock," where the basic relationship involves juxtaposing London high society (X) with the world of the epic (Y). In the process of working this out, literally hundreds of images, local metaphors, puns, paradoxes, and other varieties of metaphoric language are developed, all connecting with the central metaphor and heightening its impact. You might even say that the various elements (distinct and evocative in themselves) are "spun like a web" around this center.

In this chapter we'll look at central metaphors which are X/Y relationships extended throughout a poem. This sort of relationship might work ironically, as with Whitman's "When I Heard the Learn'd Astronomer": the astronomer's theories (X) versus the reality of the universe (Y); paradoxically (as in "On Nothing"); or even in punning ("Subject: Object: Sentence"). In any case, the poems here have both X and Y terms that are stated or obvious, and the focus is on how the relationship is unfolded. Generally, the discussions and considerations in this and the following chapters will touch on only major points. You can investigate detailed aspects of tone and levels of meaning yourself.

The central metaphoric relationship here is stated in the first line, but turns instantly into amazing subtlety. The auctioneer with his cry of "Going, going, gone" (X) is being juxtaposed to parting (Y). But what exactly is the relationship of X to Y?

Emily Dickinson

THE AUCTIONEER OF PARTING

The Auctioneer of Parting
His "Going, going, gone"
Shouts even from the Crucifix,
And brings his Hammer down—
He only sells the Wilderness,
The prices of Despair
Range from a single human Heart
To Two—not any more—

Exploring the Metaphors

This little eight-line poem is packed with nuance.

1. Is the auctioneer (*a*) "selling" parting or (*b*) is parting itself selling something else? If you think it's *a*), then are there implicit local metaphors comparing parting to a "Wilderness"? If you think it's (*b*), then what is the something being compared to Wilderness? Could it be both (*a*) and (*b*)?
2. What are some of the connotations of "auctioneer" and how do they fit into your perception of this poem?
3. Note the biblical allusion-symbols in "Crucifix" and "Wilderness." How are these connected to the central metaphoric X/Y relationship of auctioneer/parting? How does Christ's "parting" relate to the last line?
4. What is the auctioneer bringing his hammer down like?

Technical Notes

Note the use of slant rhymes ("gone" and "down," "Despair" and "more"). The liberal use of dashes is characteristic of Dickinson's style. What function do you think they serve?

The central metaphoric relationship is stated in the title of this sixteenth-century poem. The distraught lover (X) is (like) a ship on a stormy sea (Y). The poem itself elaborates this comparison in evocative detail. *

Sir Thomas Wyatt
THE LOVER COMPARETH HIS STATE TO A SHIP IN PERILOUS STORM TOSSED ON THE SEA

My galley charged with forgetfulness
Through sharp seas in winter nights doth pass
'Tween Rock and Rock; and eke ° my enemy, alas,
That is my lord, steereth with cruelness.
And every oar a thought in readiness,
As though that death were light in such a case;
An endless wind doth tear the sail apace
Of forced sighs and trusty fearfulness.
A rain of tears, a cloud of dark disdain,
Have done the wearied cords great hinderance;
Wreathed with error and eke with ignorance.
The stars be hid that led me to this pain.
Drown'd is reason that should me consort,
And I remain, despairing of the port.

* This piece is a famous example of conceit.
° also

Exploring the Metaphors

1. Why is the poet's galley "charged with forgetfulness"? What does the word "charged" imply here?
2. What do the "sharp seas" and "winter nights" suggest to you in terms of the lover's state? Is each an X referring to some Y or Y's? What do the rocks suggest? The oars?

3. Who or what might the enemy be? Is the enemy also the Lord?

4. How do you explain the near paradox (ambiguity) in the line "As though that death were light in such a case"?

5. Consider the "endless wind" and "sail." Could they be X's with unstated Y's too? If so, what possible things could they refer to? What about the "wearied cords" in terms of the lover's state?

6. What kind of "error" could be involved in this state? What "ignorance"? What are the "stars" that led the lover to his "pain"? What is the port the narrator despairs of?

7. Could the lover be referring to his love for God too? Could you read this poem consistently as a religious poem?

8. In the original sixteenth-century spelling, the word which has been rendered here as "tears" (line nine) was "teris," suggesting a possible pun on "terrors." What effect would this pun have if instead of rain of tears, the line reads "reign of terrors"? Some texts of this poem also suggest that the word "oar" in the fourth line should be read "hour"? What effect would this have?

9. Can you really give specific answers to the above questions without limiting the poem? Can you experience and understand this piece without knowing what these things mean?

Notice Wyatt's striking use of local metaphors, all related to the central metaphor: the lover's state is (like) a ship on a stormy sea. Given this central comparison, every detail takes on metaphoric possibilities: the galley of forgetfulness; the oars (like) thoughts in readiness; the sea, rocks, wind, sails—every item brings new vision and focus. Are the rocks the lovers' quarrels? Desires? How is every oar a thought in readiness? Readiness for what—to move the galley further into these stormy metaphoric seas? The simple central comparison mysteriously fills out with connotation and nuance.

Interestingly, we are given no information about the love relationship, who the poet's lover is, or why he is in this "state." But we sense the reason for it out of our own experience of love. Can you see this? Can you feel how we seem to know, for example, what "ignorance," "cruelness," and "fearfulness" the narrator is talking about here?

Technical Notes

This piece is a PETRARCHAN SONNET written in iambic pentameter.

We have discussed how a poem can spin a complex web of association and meaning using metaphoric language. In Marvell's "On a Drop of Dew," though the central metaphoric idea is relatively simple (a drop of dew = the soul), the relationship is worked out in vivid detail, linking idea and image to make one of the richest, most intricate short poems in the language.

Andrew Marvell
ON A DROP OF DEW

See how the orient dew,
Shed from the bosom of the morn
Into the blowing roses,
Yet careless of its mansion new,
For the clear region where 'twas born,
Round in its self incloses;
And in its little globe's extent,
Frames as it can its native element.
How it the purple flower does slight,
Scarce touching where it lies,
But gazing back upon the skies,
Shines with a mournful light,
Like its own tear,
Because so long divided from the sphere.
Restless it rolls and unsecure,
Trembling lest it grow impure:
Till the warm sun pity its pain,
And to the skies exhale it back again.
So the soul, that drop, that ray
Of the clear fountain of Eternal Day,
Could it within the human flower be seen,
Rememb'ring still its former height,
Shuns the sweet leaves and blossoms green;
And, recollecting its own light,
Does, in its pure and circling thoughts, express
The greater heaven in an heaven less.
In how coy a figure wound,
Every way it turns away:
So the world excluding round,
Yet receiving in the Day.
Dark beneath, but bright above:
Here disdaining, there in love.
How loose and easy hence to go:
How girt and ready to ascend.
Moving but on a point below,
It all about does upward bend.
Such did the manna's sacred dew distill;
White, and entire, though congealed and chill.
Congealed on earth: but does, dissolving, run
Into the glories of th' Almighty Sun.

Exploring the Metaphors

If we paraphrased the drop-of-dew argument, we might write: "God and the soul are of one nature, though separated; therefore, the soul longs to return to God." But in metaphor this argument is transformed: The soul and its longing seem "real," palpable, irrefutable, or at least we have no desire to refute it. Could even an atheist fail to be affected, to react to this extremely sensual image? And if she could reject the argument, or what she might take for argument, that would still leave the substance of the poem to be experienced.

The accompanying diagram is an attempt to illustrate the remarkable interaction of terms in this poem. There are probably dozens of alternatives to this diagram, and it is far from complete, but it may help you visualize how we get so many meanings out of a poem, why poems seem so rich. Here we can see how virtually every detail in Marvell's piece extends the basic metaphoric relation (drop of dew = soul) and combines with other terms to create a web of meaning. It is not surprising that a poem like this stays unique and insightful reading after reading. On each approach to the piece we come in on a different strand, so to speak, and so our view of the whole looks different.

In the diagram only two of the terms ("self" and "sphere") have been connected up with others to which they relate. The terms in parentheses, like "mind," are ideas unstated but clearly implied by poetic context. As you see, the diagram is extremely dense with just two terms. Can you imagine what it would look like if all the terms were interconnected to reflect the complex pattern of metaphoric comparison, contrast, identity, and association in the poem? No logical presentation tied to its premises could develop this range of meaning.

1. Consider how the central metaphor (soul = drop of dew) relates to the other details in the poem. What is metaphorically associated, contrasted, compared, or identified with the drop of dew? What are the possible implications of these juxtapositions (for example, the image of the dewdrop as "Dark beneath, but bright above" or as "careless")?
2. The term "God" is never used in this poem. There is no bearded old man, flights of angels, or clouds here. What kind of picture do we have of where the soul comes from and where it goes?
3. What is the difference between the sense of the soul that you get from Marvell's poem and the *idea* of the soul you might get from theology?

Technical Notes

This poem interweaves lines of five distinct meters. Marvell has indicated them by indenting his lefthand margin. Starting with the lines beginning at the margin, these meters are (1) iambic pentameter, (2) iambic tetrameter, (3) TROCHAIC tetrameter, (4) iambic trimeter, and (5) iambic dimeter ("Like its own tear").

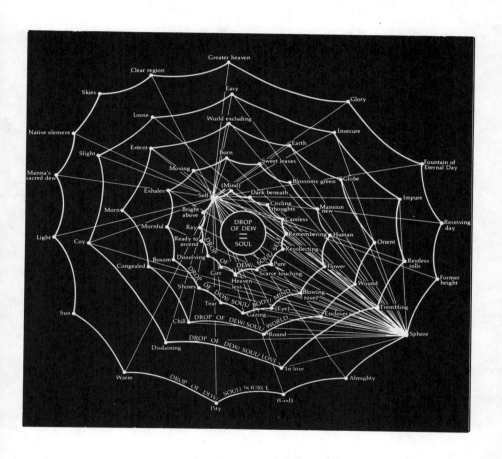

Compare *"On a Drop of Dew"* with the poem below, written at about the same period. Which do you think is more effective?

Sir John Davies

OF THE SOUL OF MAN AND THE IMMORTALITY THEREOF

O Light! (which mak'st the light, which mak'st the day;
Which sett'st the eye without, and mind within)
Lighten my spirit with one clear heavenly ray.
Which not to view itself doth first begin.

For her true form how can my spark discern?
Which, dim by nature, art did never clear;
When the great wits, of whom all skill we learn,
Are ignorant both what she is and where!

. . . .

Thou! that hast fashioned this soul of ours,
So that she is by double title Thine!
Thou only knowest her nature and her powers;
Her subtle form Thou only canst define!

To judge herself, she must herself transcend;
As greater circles comprehend the less:
But she wants power her own powers to extend;
As fettered men cannot their strength express.

But thou bright morning Star! Thou, rising Sun!
Which, in these later times, has brought to light
Those mysteries that, since the world begun,
Lay hid in darkness and eternal night!

Thou, like the sun, dost with indifferent ray
Into the palace and the cottage shine,
And showest the soul, both to the clerk and lay,
By the clear lamp of thy oracle divine!

This lamp, through all the regions of my brain,
Where my soul sits, doth spread such beams of grace,
As now, methinks, I do distinguish plain
Each subtle line of her immortal face!

Exploring the Metaphors

Davies's poem aims to inspire, and he certainly chose an inspiring subject—but his result inspires perhaps only drowsiness. There's nothing like the brightness and excitement we found in Marvell's piece. Not that Davies's poem is particularly "bad"—the point is that Marvell's metaphor is immediate, untheoretical, and independent of argument or systems of belief. Instead of statements, opinions, hopes, and ideas, Marvell presents the drop of dew, and the complex web spun around his gleaming globe has infinitely more power and reality than Davies's assertions and heartfelt piety.

1. Compare the tone of "On a Drop of Dew" with the tone of this poem. What is the difference? Can you account for it?
2. Consider Davies's use of local metaphor. Are Marvell's local metaphors more effective? What difference does Marvell's use of a central relationship make?
3. Do you think a poem's "truth" depends on whether you agree or disagree with its point of view?

What is the central metaphoric relationship in this poem by a famous nineteenth-century French poet?

Paul Verlaine
CLAIR DE LUNE
(Light of the Moon)

Your soul is the chosen landscape
Where charmed troubadors go,
Playing their lutes and dancing;
Beneath fantastic masks half-sad.

Singing in a minor key
Enchanted tales of love and pleasure,
Of happiness they can never quite believe,
Their song is dissolving in the light of the moon.

Pale light of the moon, so sad and lovely,
Makes birds dream in the trees,
And fountains sob with ecstasy,
Slender and wishful among statues of stone.

Translation from French by John Briggs

Exploring the Metaphors

Consider the details of Verlaine's landscape of the soul. What are some of the possibilities for the meaning (Y levels) in each of these details?

1. Who or what are the "charmed troubadors"?
2. Why are they "half-sad"?
3. Why do you think they are singing here in "a minor key" of "Enchanted tales of love and pleasure"?
4. Why is their song "dissolving in the light of the moon"?
5. What is the light of the moon metaphorically? Reality? Fantasy?
6. What are some of the implications of the last two lines ?

Here, as in Wyatt's poem, the complete metaphoric relationship is given in the title. But instead of the usual metaphor comparing an abstraction (time or the lover's state) to something concrete (a "wingèd chariot" or a ship on a stormy sea), here an abstraction is compared to an abstraction. See whether you can tell how the poet makes this difficult central comparison work.

W. H. Auden
LAW LIKE LOVE

[1]
Law, say the gardeners, is the sun,
Law is the one
All gardeners obey
To-morrow, yesterday, to-day.

[2]
Law is the wisdom of the old,
The impotent grandfathers shrilly scold;
The grandchildren put out a treble tongue,
Law is the senses of the young.

[3]
Law, says the priest with a priestly look,
Expounding to an unpriestly people,
Law is the words in my priestly book,
Law is my pulpit and my steeple.

[4]
Law, says the judge as he looks down his nose,
Speaking clearly and most severely,
Law is as I've told you before,
Law is as you know I suppose,
Law is but let me explain it once more,
Law is The Law.

[5]
Yet law-abiding scholars write:
Law is neither wrong nor right,
Law is only crimes
Punished by places and by times,
Law is the clothes men wear
Anytime, anywhere,
Law is Good morning and Good night,

[6]
Others say, Law is our Fate;
Others say, Law is our State;
Others say, others say
Law is no more
Law has gone away.

[7]
And always the loud angry crowd
Very angry and very loud
Law is We,
And always the soft idiot softly Me.

[8]
If we, dear, know we know no more
Than they about the law,
If I no more than you
Know what we should and should not do
Except that all agree
Gladly or miserably
That the law is
And that all know this,
If therefore thinking it absurd
To identify Law with some other word,
Unlike so many men
I cannot say Law is again,

No more than they can we suppress
The universal wish to guess
Or slip out of our own position
Into an unconcerned condition.
Although I can at least confine
Your vanity and mine
To stating timidly
A timid similarity,
We shall boast anyway:
Like love I say.

[9]
Like love we don't know where or why
Like love we can't compel or fly
Like love we often weep
Like love we seldom keep.

Exploring the Metaphors

Here Auden, like most poets before him, explores the issue of love. But after several centuries of literary convention, the traditional metaphors for love (metaphors usually made up of natural or literary-natural images like flowers, clouds, stars, and shepherds) have been pretty much worn out. In any case, writing in the age of science and the "death" of God, twentieth-century poets tend not to express romance in Marlowe's way; their tone is closer to Donne's or Marvell's: unsentimental, ironical, "logical." In fact, in this poem, when Auden talks about love, his voice almost suggests the sociologist—taking account of all points of view, looking at the question with an analytic, investigative eye. His (and our) metaphoric "leap," however, leaves all this intellectual machinery behind.

By itself, the comparison of law to love is interesting but pale. In fact law, like a pair of compasses or a technological discussion, seems a surprisingly dry and unpoetic thing to compare to love. But again, we find that the secondary relationships give force to the primary, or central, relationship.

First, notice that although the central comparison is of an abstraction with an abstraction, the poem does not lack concrete references: The "sun," "shrilly scold,"the "priestly look," "clothes men wear," "soft idiot," etc.

Second, having asserted that law is like love, Auden casts the entire poem (except for the last stanza) in terms of the law (X), which is not, in fact, the main subject. So there is a vision of law which simultaneously is a vision of his subject, love (Y). Since the unlike factor in this comparison is great, the author gains considerable distance on his subject. Recall how Marvell did this with a drop of dew. Here the distance gives the tone a touch of cynicism, as well as amplifying the poetic tension.

A simple way to follow how Auden works around his central metaphor is to examine the effect of local metaphor and image. A minute drama is enacted in each of the first seven stanzas, with characters speaking as priests, judges, children, and so on.

In the first stanza, instead of saying something like "law = eternal natural processes," the poet presents gardeners who talk about the sun. Can you grasp how this metaphoric image reaches beyond the statement underlying it (law equals = natural law)?

Similarly, in stanza two, instead of "law = experience" (whether of age or of the senses), grandfathers and children present a little enactment of the age-old conflict between generations. How does this reach past the more abstract statement underlying it? Can you connect with this?

In the third stanza law equals symbols; in the fourth, law equals itself; and stanza five offers us law as various customs, the product of social history.

In stanza six what the previous stanzas have been implying is focused: law equals whatever our opinion about the world is. Then stanza seven draws a kind of conclusion: law equals the ego, the self, self-interest, the "I." But, again, the dramatization—the crowd, the idiot—is clearly richer than the statement that law equals ego, the self, and so on.

In stanza eight, there is a sudden change of voice; after the caustic irony of the first half, a "dear" is being addressed, a reminder (in case we had forgotten) that the main term of the central metaphor is love. Perhaps we just now realize that this is in fact a love poem. The key line, in the eighth stanza, might be: "That the law is." On one level, law (or love) exists, but all efforts to define what it is are futile or, worse, involve us in the opinionated foolishness of the little characters which the poem mocks. So this "universal wish to guess" what law/love is leads to "an unconcerned condition," perhaps imagining we "know" what it is, having our petty opinions, avoiding the essentially unknowable dimensions of it.

Within this frame of reference, how do you understand the final stanza? Here is one approach: The law/love relationship plays on our assumptions that law is sound, fixed, understood, all worked out. Metaphoric tension reveals a mysterious dimension to law by exposing how the concept is entangled with conceit, egotism, and prejudice. The truth of law and love, the poem begins to reveal, is something other than this, though it includes it.

1. Most of the first seven stanzas involve the use of irony in the descriptions of the characters (the grandfathers, the priest, the scholars). What is the irony in each case, and how does it affect the overall tone of the poem?
2. In stanza five, what is the irony in the "law-abiding scholars" position? What new angle does the poet add with "Law is Good morning and Good night"? How do we use these terms ordinarily?

3. Consider the tone change in stanza eight. What factors account for this change?
4. What kinds of insight does this poem spark in you? Can you come up with angles of interpretation different from the one above?

Technical Notes

This poem is written in accentual meter, predominately four stresses to a line. It is a modern adaptation of the rhythm used in traditional nursery rhymes. (See also Blake's "Auguries of Innocence" on page 33.)

What is the central metaphoric relationship in this poem? Do you see anything particularly unusual about it?

Francesco Petrarca (Petrarch)
THE WHITENED, SPRUNG OLD MAN . . .

The whitened, sprung old man carries the pain
That has become himself and leaves his home
And bent in silence walks the bitter road
Leaving his family with their helpless love
And bears his last living days on the road to Rome;
With weak and delicate steps he goes
Alone with time and the hurt of a long life,
His will bent, strong but shaky as his stick.

In Rome he dreams of the image of God
And longs to see below what waits above;
Even the dead and clumsy picture of heaven
Quickens him more than all the breathing earth.
    This is how I look for you my love:
    Seeing in all other lovers the imitation of you.

Translation from Italian by Richard Monaco

Exploring the Metaphors

The old man dreaming of God (X) is compared to the lover dreaming of his love (Y). The metaphor is striking for several reasons:

(1) Fourteenth- and fifteenth-century poets often used love for a woman to illustrate love for God, but here the traditional comparison is reversed;

(2) there is a contrast between an old man and young lovers;

(3) most of the poem elaborates the image of the old man—the Y term appears only at the very end, in effect causing us to re-react to the poem and relate the earlier details to lovers.

This last effect is very strong. How is the old man's journey to Rome like a lover's yearning? The "bitter road," the "will bent, strong but shaky," "alone with time"—these certainly fit with the lovers' "state," but what happens when we try to superimpose the lover and his longing on the whole vivid picture of the old man? Is there some eerie vision of young love as old age, of fleshly desire as celestial longing? Do you somehow feel the two are the same?

1. Consider the local metaphor: will = stick. How is this metaphor connected to the central metaphoric relationship? For example, how do the words "strong" and "shaky" relate to the lover? Is there a sexual connotation too?
2. The image of the "bitter road" is actually a covert local metaphor. What are the X/Y terms of this metaphor?
3. Taking the "road to Rome" is an expression symbolically equivalent to traveling toward your ultimate objective or goal. ("All roads lead to Rome.") How does the symbolic road to Rome relate to the central metaphor here? What other associations can you make to Rome? Do you detect in this any religious associations?
4. Would the poem be as effective without the last two lines? Would the old man's journey still have metaphoric meaning?
5. Consider any of the other details of this poem in terms of the central metaphor.

Technical Notes

In the original Italian this is a sonnet, rhyming *a b b a a b b a c d e c d e*. This version of the sonnet was picked up by English RENAISSANCE poets (Wyatt among them), who popularized the form in our language.

The central metaphoric relationship of this poem might be stated as: the lover's emotional state (X) is (like) a businessman in financial trouble (Y). Here the central metaphor is not stated outright, as in the previous poems; still, it is clear enough.

Sir Philip Sidney
WITH WHAT SHARP CHECKS . . .

With what sharp checks I in myself am shent, °
When into Reason's audit I do go:
And by just counts myself a bankrupt know
Of all those goods, which heav'n to me hath lent:
Unable quite to pay even Nature's rent,
Which unto it by birthright I do owe:
And, which is worse, no good excuse can show,
But that my wealth I have most idly spent.
My youth doth waste, my knowledge brings forth toys,
My wit doth strive those passions to defend,
Which for reward spoil it with vain annoys.
I see my course to lose myself doth bend:
    I see and yet no greater sorrow take,
    Than that I lose no more for Stella's sake.

° punished

Exploring the Metaphors

Consider the possible levels of meaning in the details supporting Sidney's central metaphor here.

1. What is "Reason's audit"?
2. What are the "goods" which heaven has "lent" the narrator?
3. What is "Nature's rent"? (Note the possible pun.)
4. Why does knowledge bring forth "toys"?
5. In what ways could the narrator "lose" himself? What is the AMBIGUITY in the line "Than that I lose no more for Stella's sake"?

Richard Wilbur
THE WRITER

In her room at the top of the house
Where light breaks, and the windows are tossed with linden,
My daughter is writing a story.

I pause in the stairwell, hearing
From her shut door a commotion of typewriter-keys
Like a chain hauled over a gunwale.

Young as she is, the stuff
Of her life is a great cargo, and some of it heavy:
I wish her a lucky passage.

But now it is she who pauses,
As if to reject my thought and its easy figure.
A stillness greatens, in which

The whole house seems to be thinking,
And then she is at it again with a bunched clamor
Of strokes, and again is silent.

I remember the dazed starling
Which was trapped in that very room, two years ago;
How we stole in, lifted a sash

And retreated, not to affright it,
And how for a helpless hour, through the crack of the door,
We watched the sleek, wild, dark

And iridescent creature
Batter against the brilliance, drop like a glove
To the hard floor, or the desk-top,

And wait then, humped and bloody,
For the wits to try it again; and how our spirits
Rose when, suddenly sure,

It lifted off from a chair-back,
Beating a smooth course for the right window
And clearing the sill of the world.

It is always a matter, my darling,
Of life or death, as I had forgotten. I wish
What I wished you before, but harder.

Exploring the Metaphors

The first five stanzas present the situation in detail: The narrator's daughter is writing a story (X). The next five stanzas shift to the description of the starling (Y). The final stanza overtly ties the two together. Notice Wilbur's effective use of parallel details: the daughter clattering on the typewriter juxtaposed to the starling clashing against the window.

1. What are the terms of the central metaphor in this poem?
2. Consider the local metaphors in the first five stanzas. How do they relate to the central metaphoric idea, particularly the details of "passage"?
3. What does Wilbur's choice of a "starling" add to the implications of the poem? Could the word be a kind of pun?
4. What kinds of things might the bird itself mean in terms of the poem?
5. The opening image of light breaking at the top of the house and the windows "tossed with linden"—is this a covert metaphor for the writer's state of mind?
6. In the third stanza the voice of the poem makes a metaphor which is rejected in the next stanza. Why? Do you see that this rejected metaphor comes back to life in the last stanza? Can you give a reason for that?
7. The voice of the poem is writing a poem (the one we're reading) about his daughter's struggle to write. What ironies does this situation produce?

Technical Notes

The poem is written in accentual meter. Each stanza is composed of two three-stress lines with one five-stress line in the middle.

Can you see any similarity in approach between this Wyatt poem below and the Wilbur piece we just read? Consider it in detail.

Sir Thomas Wyatt

THE LOVER SHOWETH HOW HE IS FORSAKEN OF SUCH AS HE SOMETIME ENJOYED

They flee from me that sometime did me seek
With naked foot stalking in my chamber.
I have seen them gentle tame and meek
That now are wild and do not remember
That sometime they put themselves in danger
To take bread at my hand; and now they range
Basely [1] seeking with a continual change.

Thanked be fortune, it hath been otherwise
Twenty times better; but once in special,
In thine [2] array after a pleasant guise
When her loose gown from her shoulders did fall,
And she caught me in her arms long and small;
Therewithall sweetly did me kiss,
And softly said, "Dear heart, how like you this?"

It was no dream: I lay broad waking.
But all is turned thorough my gentleness
Into a strange fashion of forsaking;
And I have leave to go of her goodness,
And she also to use new fangledness.
But since that I so kindly am served,
I would fain know [3] what she hath deserved.

---

[1] In the original this word is "besely," suggesting a possible pun: basely and busily.
[2] "Thine" could also be "thin" array.
[3] like to know

In this piece the cause of grief is probed metaphorically. Can you see the stated central metaphoric relationship ?

Gerard Manley Hopkins
SPRING AND FALL:
To a Young Child

Márgarét, are you grieving
Over Goldengrove unleaving?
Leáves líke the things of man, you
With your fresh thoughts care for, can you?
Ah! ás the heart grows older
It will come to such sights colder
By and by, nor spare a sigh
Though worlds of wanwood leafmeal lie;
And yet you wíll weep and know why.
Now no matter, child, the name:
Sórrow's spríngs áre the same.
Nor mouth had, no nor mind, expressed
What heart heard of, ghost guessed:
It ís the blight man was born for,
It is Margaret you mourn for.

Exploring the Metaphors

1. What makes the word "blight" in the second-to-last line a particularly appropriate word choice?
2. In what ways does the last line relate to the rest of the poem?
3. What is the tone of the poem? How do you account for it?
4. Notice how Hopkins, in his eccentric style, compresses images. The bright, fall-leaved trees become "Goldengrove"; the pale, shattered autumn leaves become "wanwood leafmeal." Do you perceive metaphoric action here? It might be interesting to compare Hopkins with various Anglo-Saxon poets in this respect. See the definition of KENNINGS in the Glossary.

Technical Notes

Hopkins wrote poems in what he called SPRUNG RHYTHM. The accented syllables are an attempt to control our reading of the poem. The rhyming is in couplets, with one exception.

The next two poems have the same X terms and similar Y terms, but the poets'
choice of details (secondary relations) makes the pieces quite different in tone and
sense. Notice that Taylor extends his initial comparison in a manner reminiscent
of Marvell's "On A Drop of Dew."
*   As you read consider:*

1. How does each poet use the details of the spider and the spider web to further his
*   poem's meanings?*
2. What abstractions does each poet associate with the spider?
3. Do the different abstractions associated with the spider account for part of the
*   difference in tone between the two poems?*

Edward Taylor
UPON A SPIDER
CATCHING A FLY

Thou sorrow, venom elf:
    Is this thy play,
To spin a web out of thyself
    To catch a fly?
      For why?

I saw a pettish [1] wasp
    Fall foul therein,
Whom yet thy whorl-pins [2] did not clasp
    Lest he should fling
      His sting.

But as afraid, remote
    Didst stand hereat
And with thy little fingers stroke
    And gently tap
      His back.

Thus gently him didst treat
    Lest he should pet,
And in a froppish, [3] waspish heat
    Should greatly fret
      Thy net.

Whereas the silly fly,
    Caught by its leg
Thou by the throat tookst hastily
    And hind the head
      Bite dead.

This goes to pot, that not
    Nature doth call.
Strive not above what strength hath got
    Lest in the brawl
      Thou fall.

This fray seems thus to us.
    Hell's spider gets
His entrails spun to whip-cords thus,
    And wove to nets
      And sets.

To tangle Adam's race
　　In's strategems
To their destructions, spoiled, made base
　　By venom things,
　　　　Damned sins.

But mighty, gracious Lord
　　Communicate
Thy grace to break the cord, afford
　　Us glory's gate
　　　　And state.

We'll nightingale sing like
　　When perched on high
In glory's cage, thy glory, bright,
　　And thankfully,
　　　　For joy.

[1] peevish
[2] the flywheel on a spinning wheel;
indicates the spider's legs here
[3] fretful

Walt Whitman
A NOISELESS PATIENT SPIDER

A noiseless patient spider,
I mark'd where on a little promontory it stood isolated,
Mark'd how to explore the vacant vast surrounding,
It launch'd forth filament, filament, filament, out of itself,
Ever unreeling them, ever tirelessly speeding them.

And you O my soul where you stand,
Surrounded, detached, in measureless oceans of space,
Ceaselessly musing, venturing, throwing, seeking the spheres to connect them,

Till the bridge you will need be form'd, till the ductile anchor hold,
Till the gossamer thread you fling catch somewhere, O my soul.

144 *Metaphor:* The Logic of Poetry

Chapter 4

The Poem As Metaphor: X/Y's

Instead of a single central metaphoric relationship—a drop of dew (X) = the soul (Y)—each poem in this chapter has what we might call a METAPHORIC SUBJECT (X) which relates to several Y's—whether images, local metaphors, or ideas. Actually, we saw this type of poem in the first two chapters. Remember that in MacLeish's "Ars Poetica," the X term ("a poem") was identified, compared, contrasted, and associated with various specific items ("mute as a globed fruit," the feel of "old medallions to the thumb," the moon climbing through the trees), presenting a rich image and impression of poetic dynamics. Dorn's "Knowledge of Silence" (Chapter 2) is compared and associated with a museum, marble, the "sculpting mind," and other things, producing a comparable effect.

So, like the X/Y relationship just dealt with, the principle here is simple, though the result can be very complicated: the metaphoric subject (X) is related to various Y's in the poem. In the process, the X term gathers potency and weight. To judge the effectiveness of this technique, let's look at some examples. Once more, detailed interpretation is left to you.

This poem appears at first to state a straight X/Y identity in the title: the mind (X) is a enchanting thing (Y). But it turns out that "enchanting thing" is a launching pad for the poet to send up a whole fireworks display of Y's. The mind's enchantment becomes a central metaphoric subject, an X term around which are spun the dazzling Y's.

Marianne Moore
THE MIND IS AN
ENCHANTING THING

is an enchanted thing
  like the glaze on a
katydid-wing
      subdivided by sun
      till the nettings are legion.
Like Gieseking playing Scarlatti;[1]

like the apteryx-awl[2]
  as a beak, or the
kiwi's rain-shawl
      of haired feathers, the mind
      feeling its way as though blind,
walks along with its eyes to the ground.

It has memory's ear
  that can hear without
having to hear.
      Like the gyroscope's fall,
      truly unequivocal
because trued by regnant certainty,

it is a power of
  strong enchantment. It
is like the dove-
      neck animated by
      sun; it is memory's eye;
it's conscientious inconsistency.

It tears off the veil; tears
  the temptation, the
mist of the heart wears,
      from its eyes,—if the heart
      has a face; it takes apart
dejection. It's fire in the dove-neck's

iridescence, in the
inconsistencies
of Scarlatti.
Unconfusion submits
its confusion to proof; it's
not a Herod's oath that cannot change.

[1] Scarlatti was a seventeenth-century Italian composer;
Walter Gieseking was a well known concert pianist who
died in 1956.
[2] A kiwi is a flightless bird with a long slender beak.

Exploring the Metaphors

1. Notice that in the title the mind is an "enchanting thing" and in the first line the mind is an "enchanted thing." What meanings come out of this change in the verb form?
2. The enchantment quality of mind (X) is compared to a number of Y terms throughout the poem. Can you pick them out? What dimensions of mind and its enchantment are revealed by each of these Y's?
3. Notice how the metaphors build on each other. For instance, the mind (X) is first compared to a (Y) katydid-wing. Then the mind (X) is compared to a (Y) pianist playing Scarlatti. But the katydid-wing is itself also being compared to the pianist playing Scarlatti. Do you see how this multiplies the possibilities for nuance in the poet's quest for a picture of the enchantment of mind? What connotations of all these X and Y terms do you see? Do you see other metaphors building on each other? For instance notice how the kiwi metaphor turns into "memory's ear" and then into a "gyroscope's fall."
4. Are the lines about the "unequivocal" nature of mind ironic? Why? How does the notion of inconsistency (mentioned twice in the next few lines) fit here?
5. The final Y term involves a double negative and the allusion to "Herod's oath." Can you untangle this? How does it fit with the other Y terms like the "dove-neck," the "katydid-wing" and "Scarlatti"?
6. Note the poet's use of direct and slant rhymes and the pattern to the way the lines break. How does this fit with the central metaphor of the poem, for example the idea of "certainty" and "inconsistency"?
7. What picture of the central metaphoric subject, mind, do you have by the end of this poem?

Even a casual reading of this poem would probably reveal that it is much more than a vivid description of a bullfight. The bull and the fight are metaphorically exploring profound and complex territory.

W. S. Merwin
TORO

Black, black, the sheen of his back and shoulders
Blazing, his brawn and wide forehead plunging
On, on into wrath, hooves detonating the dust
Under his rushing darkness, the green and white
Streamers fixed in the hump of his anger rattling
And snapping behind like slaver from a mad mouth, and
The high-shaken lances of his tossing horns seeking
Bodies for shock, his wrath like a ghost seeking
Bodies to sink in, to house in, destruction to be wrought,
Out of the starving dark, daring headlong
The one-way doors of day, he hurls himself now
Into the orange light, and lunging down
Like judgment erupting or a dark planet he crashes
Across the spread glare and becomes the raging centre
Of these flickering faces ranged in rings, who thirst
For his darkness, who stare like blains
In the sun-blaze. They thought it was they
Who for their thirst's sake, and that their black fear might be
Loosed and defeated in the familiar light, conceived
A darkness and set him there. But all black
Is the abyss brooding, and he brings into the day
The one dark, that was there before the world was. Low
In his own shadow deep as a mountain he waited
Till they said, "Now we are all together
And seem brave in the light, let the challenging shadow
Show itself among us, now, that we may shame it,
Let there be dark." And he heard the first day
Of Creation banging on the barrier, and, ravenous,
His red eyes saw the light. And, look: he became
The black sun and burst among them, and the sun has horns
As the moon has, whereby all dawns shall be bloody
And all wests ripped with crimson! Bull. And legs,
Spoke-flashing of knees, even thunder of hooves seem as
    nothing
To pillar and propel that bulk and fury. His belly gulping
For breath sucks up and drops like a blast-shaken

4. The Poem As Metaphor: X/Y's 149

Floor; between his flanks censer and tassel
Of generation swing and lurch, and nothing in the profound world
Blares deep as now his maddened bellow. What torment is it
That baits him, that wrings forth this roar: for the men
Performing with bright darts are toys merely,
Masquers playing with emblems, signifying far off
The one faceless pain, momentary puppets
Of the infliction he tolls. The blood and burning
In his eyes are not blindness, but bring the world's rage
To be seen red as it is. And oh do not suppose
Because a thin blade may empty him suddenly
Of fury, and his black become the colour of quiet,
That it means that the known earth is broad world enough
To be his battling-ground. His death, though dedicated,
May end much, but will fulfill nothing; will be adequate
Neither to sate the size and lust of his fury
Nor to gather and bless with acceptable sacrifice
Those faces so small, so faint and far that still
They sit and sway in a world where such things
As danger are. But he, for all fear's reasons
Worshipful, slumps back into fear's secret   .
And abyss, more terrible, for his rage disdains now
All that they know of pain, and looks like infinite
Gentleness, waiting, forever patient,
Black, with long horns. What trouble is it
That baits them now, since the shape they made of their fear
Is dead? The light is different. And they are alone.

Exploring the Metaphors

First let's list some terms the poet relates to his central metaphoric subject (the bull) in the opening lines. The bull (X) is associated with or likened to (Y):

> wrath
> rushing darkness
> anger
> madness
> a ghost seeking bodies
> a ghost seeking destruction
> a product of the "starving dark"
> daring
> judgment
> a dark planet

a raging center
black fear
the abyss brooding
Dark, that was there before the world was

Do you see how the interaction of these terms resembles the relationships in "On a Drop of Dew"? By means of numerous associations the bull (and therefore the bullfight) gathers great significance.

Note that Merwin uses black and darkness as the bull's primary associations, playing off the connotations of anger, evil, mystery, and so on.

Compare this with Wallace Stevens's use of black in "Thirteen Ways of Looking at a Blackbird."

In "Toro" the drama of the bullfight becomes a drama of meaning. By the end of the poem, even the bull and audience itself are united in the "moment of truth" (the bull's death): it is "the shape they had made of their fear." With this audience-bull association in mind, go back and reread the poem and see how this adds a significant new dimension.

If the poet simply listed what his central metaphoric subject "meant," would there be such impact? Instead, we have a description, a story, or picture that is activated metaphorically by stress, context, and association and so extends past the literal level (things seen and heard) into deeper meanings. For example, the description of the bull lunging out of the chutes into the bullring "like judgment erupting or a dark planet" gives both a visual picture and a deeper response, something like "arrows of desire." We can imagine the bull lunging out of the ring, but the relation of this image to "judgment" we can "see" only with our *in*sight, our intuition.

1. Metaphorically, what reasons do you feel there are for holding this bullfight? Consider in particular the audience's relation to the bull.
2. Consider any of the local metaphors or images (such as "and his black become the colour of quiet") and observe its connection with the whole poem. What does it add to the bull's meaning?
3. Can you answer the poet's question about the bull: "What torment is it / That baits him, that wrings forth this roar?"
4. What levels of meaning do the last lines suggest?
5. What do you think the bull and the bullfight come to represent in this poem? Can you see several viable possibilities?
6. Describe the tone of this poem; consider especially the line beginning "And all wests ripped with crimson! Bull. . ."

Technical Notes

The poem is written in accentual pentameter (five strong stresses to the line).

152 *Metaphor:* The Logic of Poetry

In this poem a nineteenth-century Russian poet employs one of poetry's favorite metaphoric subjects, the natural image, a flower. Look for the Y's that are linked to this X.

Alexander Pushkin
THE FLOWER

A dead, pale flower falls,
forgotten, from a dusty book.
And so by a strange dream
my soul is filled.

When did this flower bloom? And where?
In what lost spring? Was it a familiar
or a stranger's hand which picked it?
Who pressed it in these pages here? And why?

Was it in memory of a tender meeting?
The token of a fatal parting?
Or memento of a lonely walk—in the silence
of the fields, or woody shade?

And is he still living?—And is she?
Together did they find their place?
Or were they lost, like love, like youth—
like this forgotten flower?

Translation from Russian

Exploring the Metaphors

1. What does the poet associate with the flower? What two abstractions are specifically identified with the flower? Are there also unstated abstractions the flower could imply?
2. What do you think the flower comes to mean? How?
3. Why does the narrator ask all these questions of the flower?
4. How would you describe the tone of this poem? Is it sentimental? What effect does the tone have on the meaning? How does the poet keep the poem from being a cliché, like a popular, sentimental song: "He loved her and now she's gone, and all that's left is this flower"?

Compare this poem with Merrill's "Laboratory Poem". What is the central subject in the Robhs piece? Is this also the central subject of Merrill's poem? How are the two different?

Dwight Robhs
SLICE OF LIFE
For Judy

1) each pair will share one frog apiece (lovers
touch hands at the dissecting tray: the tools
sharp, cool to the hand are oddly familiar)
2) turn to the ventral side

3) cut down from chin to groin (expose what beats,
bleeds, feels and fills; trace what delicate webs
shuddered with life—stopped—lovers risk unknitting)
4) when most vital substance is removed or when
(in short, when the heart is out of something
the tangle that's left is dead to the touch)
by dead is meant (this wonderful design
no longer works—fingers touch as if
untying—light, outside and in, includes them)
5) next notice the heart, expose it by lifting
aside (whatever conceals it: intimate
discovery gleams in feral light, almost
suggests the probe that skews the symmetry
of life's woven ease) 6) peel the nerves from flesh;
these stringy radial extensions (once told
cold from heat from pain) 7) cut

the cord below the medulla (striking
how, careful and gentle,

they pull the dead apart and call it
understanding life: a tangle of ends
fingers distinguish with some urgency)
8) turn to the dorsal side 9) now bend the skull
to the chest until you hear a snap,
then part the head from trunk—chip bone with care
or else the brain will smear (their fine fingers
untie the delicate knots of being:

call this understanding another's mind:
this head, in one sense, holds no secrets:
this kind of learning can be killing)
observe (it is all here)

sketch, make notes, measure, probe in detail
(this bloody lesson sprawls in the tray
naked in a way that lovers are not:
a fear persists for all their science;
the scalpels of knowledge feel familiar to hands
that discovered another's nakedness,
loosened and undressed the self, and knew
fear in carnal wisdom)

10) write a report (his hand in her webs
of hair weaves golden glints
as fingers ripple shine—electric light
hones the scalpel's edge with fire, she winces at
the light, perhaps at more: all myths of love
start with the fear of finding out too much:
Lamian terrors wake

at intimate moments—the stripped frog marks
off one extreme, lovers
the other, between them both the numbered
text explains what it can—
demanding lovers pull the live apart
understanding death.

Exploring the Metaphors

The central subject is the dissection, X. Notice all the Y terms associated, compared, contrasted with it, for example "lovers risk unknitting," "intimate discovery," "naked in a way that lovers are not," "scalpels of knowledge," "her webs of hair," and many others. In some cases when a term is juxtaposed to the central subject (e.g., "scalpels of knowledge," "lovers risk unknitting"), the metaphor created is explicit. In other cases it's implicit. For example, the phrase at the end of the third stanza, "once told cold from heat from pain" seems merely a description of the nerves. But in this metaphoric context "cold," "heat," and "pain" are Y terms related to the feelings of the lovers who are undergoing this metaphoric dissection.

1. The central metaphoric subject is the dissection; what's this poem really about?
2. What are some of the possible meanings that death takes on here? For example, does death have to do with a dissective way of living or looking at the world?
3. What is the tone of the numbered text? What kind of a contrast do you detect between the pure lyrical passages and the lines with numbers? How is this connected to the central subject?
4. Look at some of the images. For instance, why have the "delicate webs shuddered with life"? How do the images relate to the central subject?
5. How do the abstract statements, such as "a fear persists for all their science," relate to the central subject?

What is really the central metaphoric subject of this rather outlandishly humorous poem? Is it the girdle?

Edmund Waller
ON A GIRDLE

That which her slender waist confin'd,
Shall now my joyful temples bind:
No monarch but would give his crown,
His arms might do what this has done.

It was my heart's extremest sphere,
The pale which held that lovely deer.
My joy, my grief, my hope, my love,
Did all within this circle move!

A narrow compass! and yet there
Dwelt all that's good, and all that's fair:
Give me but what this riband bound,
Take all the rest the sun goes round.

Exploring the Metaphors

1. How many different circles do you see in the poem?
2. What different things are identified or associated with circles?
3. What is the effect of the poem?
4. What makes this poem funny?

Emily Dickinson
THERE'S A CERTAIN SLANT OF LIGHT

There's a certain slant of light,
On winter afternoons,
That oppresses, like the weight
Of cathedral tunes.

Heavenly hurt it gives us;
We can find no scar,
But internal difference
Where the meanings are.

None may teach it anything,
'Tis the seal, despair,—
An imperial affliction
Sent us of the air.

When it comes, the landscape listens,
Shadows hold their breath;
When it goes, 'tis like the distance
On the look of death.

Exploring the Metaphors

Several local metaphors are associated with the "slant of light" the central X term, which is (like) several Y's: oppression "like the weight of cathedral tunes," a "heavenly hurt," an "internal difference where the meanings are," a "seal," "despair," an "imperial affliction," something which makes landscape listen and "shadows hold their breath," and "the distance on the look of death."

Also consider the fact that the subject is light. Light has connotations of wisdom, God, reason, life, etc., and the poet plays off these. Moreover, we are dealing with a "slant" of light, and therefore an "angle" of wisdom, God, life, etc. What is it? Could we ever say for sure? For instance, why do the images and local metaphors paradoxically relate this light to experience usually associated with darkness, despair, affliction, death? How is this paradox resolved in the last two lines? Do you agree that the question of what the slant of light means is probably less important than our intuitive experience of the highly charged area of interplay between light and darkness "where the meanings are"?

1. Consider each of the local metaphors and images. How do they extend the meaning of the slant of light?
2. Is there a paradox in the phrase "heavenly hurt"? What are the levels of meaning here?
3. Consider the lines "when it comes, the landscape listens" and "when it goes, 'tis like the distance." These are the two longest lines in the poem. Do their length and sound bear any relation to their meaning? Is it possible to separate their length or sound from their meanings What would have been the effect on the entire poem if the poet had written as the last line, "when it goes, 'tis like the look of death"?
4. What do you feel the slant of light means in the poem—or can you say? Could it be read consistently as meaning love? Insight? The poem itself?

This poem is among the most quoted in English literary history and one of the most elusive. Its central metaphoric subject is obvious.

John Keats
ODE ON A GRECIAN URN

Thou still unravish'd bride of quietness,
   Thou foster-child of silence and slow time,
Sylvan historian, who canst thus express
   A flowery tale more sweetly than our rhyme.
What leaf-fring'd legend haunts about thy shape
   Of deities or mortals, or of both,
      In Tempe [1] or the dales of Arcady? [2]
What men or gods are these? What maidens loth?
What mad pursuit? What struggle to escape?
   What pipes and timbrels? What wild ecstasy?

Heard melodies are sweet, but those unheard
   Are sweeter; therefore, ye soft pipes, play on;
Not to the sensual ear, but, more endear'd,
   Pipe to the spirit ditties of no tone:
Fair youth, beneath the trees, thou canst not leave

Thy song, nor ever can those trees be bare;
　　Bold Lover, never, never canst thou kiss,
Though winning near the goal—yet, do not grieve;
　　She cannot fade, though thou hast not thy bliss,
　　For ever wilt thou love, and she be fair!

Ah, happy, happy boughs! that cannot shed
　　Your leaves, nor ever bid the Spring adieu;
And, happy melodist, unwearied,
　　For ever piping songs for ever new;
More happy love! more happy, happy love!
　　For ever warm and still to be enjoy'd,
　　　For ever panting, and for ever young;
All breathing human passion far above,
　　That leaves a heart high-sorrowful and cloy'd,
　　　A burning forehead, and a parching tongue.

Who are these coming to the sacrifice?
　　To what green altar, O mysterious priest,
Lead'st thou that heifer lowing at the skies,
　　And all her silken flanks with garlands drest?
What little town by river or sea shore,
　　Or mountain-built with peaceful citadel,
　　Is emptied of this folk, this pious morn?
And, little town, thy streets for evermore
　　Will silent be; and not a soul to tell
　　　Why thou art desolate, can e'er return.

O Attic shape! Fair attitude! with brede [3]
　　Of marble men and maidens overwrought,
With forest branches and the trodden weed;
　　Thou, silent form, dost tease us out of thought
As doth eternity: Cold Pastoral!
　　When old age shall this generation waste,
　　　Thou shalt remain, in midst of other woe
Than ours, a friend to man, to whom thou say'st,
　　"Beauty is truth, truth beauty,"—that is all
　　　Ye know on earth, and all ye need to know.

---

[1] a valley sacred to the Greek god Apollo
[2] a Greek pastoral district
[3] braid or embroidery, doubtless a pun

Exploring the Metaphors

Critics have been puzzled by the phrase "Beauty is truth, truth beauty." If you take it for itself, outside the poem's context, and think of it as having some general meaning, it seems a mere tautology, like saying "A = B, therefore B = A." Can we take this statement outside the poem? Is this just a vague, abstract, and unpoetic "idea"?

The central metaphoric subject (X) of the poem is the urn. The narrator associates it with various terms which not only describe the urn but also shape its meaning. For example, it is a "bride of quietness," a "Sylvan historian," a "fair attitude" (note the pun: attitude as a feeling about something and attitude as physical posture), a "Cold Pastoral," and a "friend to man," among other things. In addition, it expresses "a flowery tale," pipes "not to the sensual ear" but to "the spirit ditties of no tone," and teases "us out of thought as doth eternity."

Now, how does our statement about truth and beauty relate to all this and the urn? By the time we reach this statement, it is clearly possible to associate the urn with beauty. So on the metaphoric level we have: the urn (X) is (like) truth (Y). There is a recognizable metaphor.

Everything we know about the urn, all the complex meaning gathered through the four previous stanzas, is compressed into one line. What seems abstract is actually identified with a concrete image. If beauty is (like) the urn and if the urn pipes to the spirit and teases "us out of thought as doth eternity," then on one level is the concept that beauty (which cannot here be logically defined apart from the metaphoric context) takes us beyond thought to an intuition of truth, and this truth is (like) eternity—timeless, free from birth and death "for ever piping songs for ever new." So in the truth/beauty metaphor Keats is expressing the effect of poetry itself. We should not mistake it for some vague or general conclusion separable from the poem.

And this is but one aspect of the piece. Consider, as another way of getting into it, the contrast between the hot life depicted on the urn (X) and the cold pastoral—the "brede of marble men and maidens" (Y). What do we discover in this juxtaposition of art to life? How does it relate to the truth/beauty equation? The poem explores these and other profound territories not by logically playing to our "sensual" ear but by "piping," so to speak, metaphor to the spirit.

1. Consider the terms Keats uses to describe the urn ("unravished bride of quietness," "Sylvan historian," etc.). What does each add to the total meaning of the urn?
2. In what way is the scene depicted on the urn ironic? What levels of meaning does this irony add?
3. What does the progress of the description (from the first line to the last) tell you about the meaning of the urn? The psychology of the narrator? How does his mood change? What's the significance of describing scenes not on the urn?

4. Consider whether the progress of the description of the urn mirrors in some way the cloying passion of life which the urn figures are said to have escaped.

5. Why is the urn a "Cold Pastoral"? How does this phrase affect you, coming where it does? How does it relate to the truth/beauty metaphor?

6. Who is the "Ye" in the last line?

7. It's obvious how thought can be said to come and go, live and die. Is it possible, then, to think about a state untouched by living and dying? Why must we be teased "out of thought"? Can the logic of experience come to any conclusions here? How is Keats suggesting that the metaphoric experience of beauty/truth ceases when conclusions about beauty/truth are drawn?

Technical Notes

The poem is an ode in basic iambic meter, stanzas rhyming *a b a b c d e c d e.*

In a Greek myth, Queen Philomela sent her husband Tereus to bring her sister, Procne, for a visit. As soon as Tereus saw Procne, he desired her. His desires became desperate, and on the return voyage he carried her off. When Procne rejected him, he raped her, cut out her tongue, and returned home to Philomela with the lie that Procne had died during the voyage. Procne, however, wove the story of her outrage into a tapestry which she sent to Philomela, who rescued her. Then together they slew Procne's and Tereus's son and served him to his father as a stew. As a result of these pleasantries the gods pursued the trio and transformed Tereus into a hawk, Procne into a sparrow, and Philomela into a nightingale destined forever to sing and lament the tragedy.

This myth of the nightingale's origin fascinated poets for centuries, and the bird became a symbol of sorrow, grief, betrayal, immortality, and passion. In this piece, the nineteenth-century poet Matthew Arnold has structured this symbol as a metaphoric subject.

Matthew Arnold
PHILOMELA

Hark! ah, the nightingale—
The tawny-throated!
Hark, from that moonlit cedar what a burst!
What triumph! hark!—what pain!

O wanderer from a Grecian shore,

Still, after many years, in distant lands,
Still nourishing in thy bewilder'd brain
That wild, unquench'd, deep-sunken, old-world pain—
Say, will it never heal?
And can this fragrant lawn
With its cool trees, and night,
And the sweet, tranquil Thames,
And moonshine, and the dew,
To thy rack'd heart and brain
Afford no balm?
Dost thou to-night behold,
Here, through the moonlight on this English grass,
The unfriendly palace in the Thracian wild?
Dost thou again peruse
With hot cheeks, and sear'd eyes
The too clear web, and thy dumb sister's shame?
Dost thou once more assay
Thy flight, and feel come over thee,
Poor fugitive, the feathery change
Once more, and once more seem to make resound
With love and hate, triumph and agony,
Lone Daulis, and the high Cephissian vale? °
Listen, Eugenia—
How thick the bursts come crowding through the leaves!
Again—thou hearest?
Eternal passion!
Eternal pain!

° Locale in which the story of Philomela is said
to have taken place

Exploring the Metaphors

1. What does Arnold associate with the nightingale?
2. The nightingale is a symbol of sorrow, grief, immortality, etc. How does Arnold make this symbol metaphoric? That is, how does he go beyond the defined idea of the nightingale to make the bird mean something complex, multi-faceted, and indefinable?
3. Consider the tone in which the narrator addresses the nightingale. How does this contribute to the poem's levels of meaning?
4. How do the details of landscape add to the significance of the nightingale? Is there any comparison of landscapes here? For instance, how is the "Thracian wild" associated with "English grass"?

Judy Willington
THE RECLUSE

She sits embroidering them,
those spots of mind
where darkness kinks.
Her privacy, a quiet room
to pace in now the going's done.
Sewing empty flowers,
their outlines blooming,
threaded shaky as her pulse,
she senses how the outside evening deepens.
It is the hour women weep.
She adjusts her lamp and fixes tea;
a warm sip and she sighs out over silence.
Her eyes lightly close
on wallpaper ovals,
like the hoops of years,
vacant, trimmed with roses.
She circles round the rim of pain,
loops a stitch, mechanical,
and circles round again.

Exploring the Metaphors

1. The first Y term associated with the central subject is "spots of mind." These are then associated with "empty flowers." What are some of the implied meanings here?
2. The outlines of the flowers are "threaded shaky as her pulse." How does that add to the implications of the flowers and spots of mind?
3. The central subject of this poem is a recluse and there is some tension between inside and outside where "evening deepens." What is that tension?
4. Does "lamp" become metaphoric in this context?
5. What are the implications of the connection between the central subject, the recluse, and circles?
6. Do you see how the sewing metaphor is stitched all the way through the poem, tying together the individual Y terms?

164 *Metaphor:* The Logic of Poetry

Chapter 5

The Poem
As Metaphor: X/?

The poems in this chapter have one characteristic in common: The central subject (or situation) described by each is obviously meant to be taken metaphorically (that is, as an X), though the subject is not explicitly compared to anything. In order to get an idea of how this works, let's look at the Frost poem we referred to before.

Robert Frost
THE ROAD NOT TAKEN

Two roads diverged in a yellow wood,
And sorry I could not travel both
And be one traveler, long I stood
And looked down one as far as I could.
To where it bent in the undergrowth;

Then took the other, as just as fair,
And having perhaps the better claim,
Because it was grassy and wanted wear;
Though as for that, the passing there
Had worn them really about the same,

And both that morning equally lay
In leaves no step had trodden black.
Oh, I kept the first for another day!
Yet knowing how way leads on to way,
I doubted if I should ever come back.

I shall be telling this with a sigh
Somewhere ages and ages hence:
Two roads diverged in a wood, and I—
I took the one less traveled by,
And that has made all the difference.

Reading this poem literally (as many people have), we might conclude, as one student did, that "it's about a man who comes to a place where there are two roads; he can't decide which one to take, and so he takes the one that looks less used and he's glad." That is basically the story, the "plot." But if you don't see past that and go deeper, you stop short of the real experience. This issue is basic to a common misapprehension of poetry, that is, the idea that poetry is mainly a pretty description or a fancy way of expressing everyday adventures.

A superficial reading of the Frost piece leaves a superficial impression, just a pleasant description of the poet's feelings while taking a morning walk. This is a problem because it's easy to let Frost's simple diction beguile you into thinking he writes simple poems. Some imitators call him a nature poet who captures our open-air moods. But Frost's surface simplicity belies a subtle, sophisticated treatment of metaphor. "The Road Not Taken" turns out to be a complicated ironic statement.

Notice that there are none of the local metaphors or striking images we usually see in poetry. One reason for this is that Frost structures the entire situation to be metaphoric, to constitute an X referring to some unstated Y or Y's.

But how can we identify metaphor shorn of the usual poetic language? The poet does not provide the sort of direct statements or relationships we've been getting used to. He does not say "the road of time" or "two roads like life." Instead, we are given just a seemingly literal picture of a man choosing between two roads while taking a walk.

One way to grasp the metaphor is to "feel" what the tone stresses—to perceive how the narrator puts weight on the situation. Lines like "I took the one less traveled by,/ And that has made all the difference" tend to reveal the metaphoric intentions; once you are alert to this, it's quite easy to see. Anyone who wants to take this poem as mere mood and description still has to relate the last stanza to the body of the poem, and the great weight of these lines is absurd if the rest of the piece is seen only on a literal level: Why has a choice between two roads made "all the difference"? To what? What level connects with "ages and ages hence"? So metaphoric action takes place as soon as you become sensitive to the contrast between the clearly far-reaching conclusions of the last lines and the "simple" presentation of the opening stanzas.

The narrator's situation implies at least two abstract subjects (Y's). One we might call "decision making," and the other "human limitation"; that is, the narrator choosing between the roads discovers that he is limited, that he can take only one of the choices. This concrete situation allows Frost to explore these abstractions without ever seeming abstract. We cannot really take his remarks as advice or cracker-barrel philosophy, as if someone said, "You can never tell when you make a decision what's going to happen" or "You know, every time you make a decision you have to leave something behind." Yet, in a sense these statements are contained in the lines "And looked down one as far as I could" and "Yet knowing how way leads on to way/ I doubted if I should ever come back." These lines do not present philosophy, but description; so, as we have seen in other cases, in poetic context we experience certain philosophic implications, and the experience is very different from merely hearing about an idea.

In addition, the central metaphor permits many of the details of the concrete situation to become X's with unstated Y's. Consider, in this light, some questions about various images and statements in the poem:

1. Look at the images such as the "yellow wood," "leaves," "trodden black," and "undergrowth." What are some of the Y's you could connect with each of

these images in terms of decision making and human limitation?

2. The lines "Though as for that, the passing there/ Had worn them really about the same" are descriptive. Are they also metaphoric? How? Of what?

3. How does the title, "The Road Not Taken," add to the meaning of the poem?

4. Could the line "And that has made all the difference" be ironic? If so, how?

In examining the "undergrowth" detail, for example, do you encounter Y levels here? Without trying to specify them, can you feel, as a kind of effect of the context, the connotations of this image? If you do, it becomes clear that in understanding the central or primary metaphoric subject (in this case, the choice between roads), we become alert to deep implications of images, local metaphors, and statements.

Interestingly, the germinal idea behind Frost's poem is a cliché. "Being on the right road," "going down the road to salvation (or destruction)," "the fork in the road of life," and "the paths of life" are all standard versions of Frost's central metaphor. An insight becomes a cliché because at first we see some truth in it; then overuse deadens the impact. We specify a conclusion about what is meant, and insight is over; it stops stimulating new responses. Frost puts new life and depth into the cliché by presenting two specific roads. The secret here is that you experience the image of the roads first, and then the meanings, and that the meanings remain unstated. The reverse order would be hard to take—for example, "I've reached a fork in the road of life in a yellow wood, and sorry. . ."

In each of the following poems it's obvious (but not actually stated) that we are meant to take the entire poem as an X in relation to some Y or Y's. Usually there is a concrete subject or situation, like choosing between two roads, and we're implicitly asked to discover the abstraction or abstractions it evokes. We have already seen at least one poem of this type—Blake's "The Sick Rose" (page 70). It is certain that the rose relates to something (is meant metaphorically), though we are not openly told what. Can you find other poems of this type in earlier chapters?

Bear in mind that although we are dividing poems into categories (X/Y; X/ Y's; X/?), this is only for the purpose of getting into them. In fact, many pieces presented in one chapter could be discussed in another. Poems do not fit neatly into intellectual niches. For example, "Ode on a Grecian Urn" might be treated as a poem of X/Y form if we took the tack that the urn is (like) beauty and truth and then we related everything else in the piece around that central metaphor. Many poems may be subtle combinations of metaphoric strategies. Stevens's "Thirteen Ways of Looking at a Blackbird" is an X/Y's poem in that the blackbird as a central X term is put into various contexts where it becomes associated with situations and abstractions, Y terms: the oneness of men and women, "three minds," "the edge of one of many circles," for example. But in some cases the blackbird is treated as an X with an unstated Y, as in the opening scene where the eye of the blackbird is moving among "twenty snowy mountains." That stanza is pure description, yet we feel the weight of unstated meanings, as in "The Road Not Taken."

But the idea here is not to spend time trying to define or categorize poems; instead it is just to use these categories as a way of approaching given pieces. In the end, to experience poetry in a complete way, we must totally discard all the fragmentary and often distracting techniques we used to make a beginning. Once you have learned to swim, you no longer think about how to kick your legs or move your arms; you just swim.

*The wild swans in this delicate poem obviously have great meaning, and much of
the effect of the piece depends on that meaning remaining unstated and
mysterious.*
A. What abstractions do you see as Y levels for the swans (X)?
B. What relation does the narrator's age have to the significance of the swans?
C. How are the details of the description metaphoric?

William Butler Yeats
THE WILD SWANS AT COOLE

The trees are in their autumn beauty,
The woodland paths are dry,
Under the October twilight the water
Mirrors a still sky;
Upon the brimming water among the stones
Are nine-and-fifty swans.

The nineteenth autumn has come upon me
Since I first made my count;
I saw, before I had well finished,
All suddenly mount
And scatter wheeling in great broken rings
Upon their clamorous wings.

I have looked upon those brilliant creatures,
And now my heart is sore.
All's changed since I, hearing at twilight,
The first time on this shore,
The bell-beat of their wings above my head,
Trod with a lighter tread.

Unwearied still, lover by lover,
They paddle in the cold
Companionable streams or climb the air;
Their hearts have not grown old;
Passion or conquest, wander where they will,
Attend upon them still.

But now they drift on the still water,
Mysterious, beautiful;
Among what rushes will they build,
By what lake's edge or pool
Delight men's eyes when I awake some day
To find they have flown away?

Exploring the Metaphors

Like the poems in the last chapter, this poem's metaphoric subject (swans) associates with specific Y's (passion and conquest, for example), but the real significance of the birds remains unstated. What are the swans? Life? Youth? Art? Perfection? The soul? Each detail in the poem seems to add to the swans mystery and meaning.

In the first lines the swans float over water mirroring a "still sky" (sky = heaven?). Do the trees, paths, stones, and twilight here seem to have metaphoric potential? How about autumn itself?

Later, the swans "suddenly mount/ And scatter wheeling in great broken rings/ Upon their clamorous wings." Their action suggests some great significance: Why "clamorous wings," for example? What are they clamoring for? Could this refer to just the sound alone? The narrator says that when this happened, nineteen years earlier, he had been trying to count the swans when they flew away. Were they some portent, some omen he misread then but now seems dimly to grasp? A portent of what? Was the act of counting a hopeless attempt to bring a rational order to bear on what cannot be measured? Notice how we are forced to keep asking (without ever answering the question): What are the swans?

In the third stanza they are "brilliant creatures" exciting awareness of some change (apparently for the worse) that has taken place since the narrator first heard the "bell-beat of wings." Can we know whether it is an internal or external change? Can you see how the swans as lovers are somehow being subtly compared with human lovers and love? Why are the streams "cold/ Companionable"?

In the end, when the swans have flown, we're left with unanswered questions. The swans remain mysterious, unknown. In trying to relate to them and all the implications of their coming and going, their very being, the narrator has an indefinable yet profound experience. This may hold for us as well, but can it be talked about? Since metaphoric insight can only be evoked, never stated, the experience is somehow very private, isn't it? We can reason, discuss, and analyze, right to the threshold of poetic awareness, but once across it we come upon this mysterious silence that Yeats has gathered into the image of the swans.

1. In lines three and four of the last stanza, do you find that the natural images are metaphoric in the way Frost's roads are? How about other natural images throughout the piece?
2. The swans might represent (among other things) some permanent, natural perfection, some ideal form, that the speaker can keep in sight only for a time because they come and go beyond his control. Does that feeling touch your own life in some way?
3. Why does the speaker say, "when I awake someday"? Does he simply mean that

some morning they will be gone? Is this a literal sleep? Now, he says, the experience is with him; someday it will end. But what will he awaken to? Some realization? Or has he been asleep all along? Can we ever really come to a conclusion about this?

Technical Notes

The stanzas are SESTETS of *a a b b c c* rhyme. Iambic and ANAPESTIC feet predominate.

In this piece by Wyatt, unlike "The Lover Compareth His State . . ." poem we looked at in the last chapter, the poet does not tell us what the Υ term is. As you read, try to see how many things the deer in this piece might signify.

Sir Thomas Wyatt
WHOSO LIST TO HUNT

Whoso list [1] to hunt, I know where is an hind,[2]
But as for me, *helas*! I may no more.
The vain travail hath wearied me so sore,
I am of them that furthest come behind.
Yet may I, by no means, my wearied mind
Draw from the deer; but as she fleeth afore
Fainting I follow. I leave off therefore,
Since in a net I seek to hold the wind.
Who list her hunt, I put him out of doubt,
As well as I, may spend his time in vain;
And graven with diamonds in letters plain
There is written, her fair neck round about,
Noli me tangere,[3] for Caesar's I am,
And wild for to hold, though I seem tame.

[1] wishes, desires
[2] a doe
[3] Latin for "Do not touch me!"

Exploring the Metaphors

Your list of Y terms for this poem could include money, fame, success, a girlfriend, a boyfriend, good luck, youth, happiness, life. Any of these would make sense in terms of the poem. Many feel that because the poet was alleged to have had an affair with the Queen of England, the doe stands for this particular woman. But you can't prove that just by referring to the piece.

However, what if the poet had told us that the deer was something specific, the Queen or money, for example? Would the poem be as effective? You can see that equating chasing the deer to chasing money, for example, would reduce the piece to an aphorism: "Money is easy to chase but hard to catch," an opinion we might even argue over.

The reference to Caesar in the second-to-last line is an allusion to the point in the New Testament where Christ, when asked about paying taxes, responds: "Render therefore unto Caesar the things which are Caesar's; and unto God the things that are God's." In other words, Caesar's things are the things of this world, while God's are beyond it. So, on one level, chasing the deer is (like) chasing after the things of this world. But even this formulation misses something. Why?

Because the deer's meaning is unstated, mysterious, the poem engages us beyond the level of idea and opinion. We understand what it is to pursue things we want and can't have but continue to pursue. We don't simply identify this with some specific area of life (love, money, or whatever), but we seem to understand it in a profounder sense. Without the deer's mysterious quality, would such an understanding be possible?

1. How is the local metaphor "since in a net I seek to hold the wind" related to the central metaphoric subject?
2. Could "Caesar" be a reference to some specific king or prince of Wyatt's era? How would the poem read then? Consider the traditional laws about poaching the king's deer. How might this affect the poem's meaning?
3. Consider Wyatt's delicate use of detail: "Fainting I follow," "my wearied mind draw from the deer," and the last line. What sort of impression do you get from the tone of the narrator's pursuit of the deer?

Technical Notes

This is a variation of a Petrarchan sonnet. Iambic meter predominates.

The Kraken is the Scandinavian version of the sea dragon. What is Tennyson's Kraken? What are some of the possible abstractions (or Y terms) you could associate with it?

Alfred, Lord Tennyson
THE KRAKEN

Below the thunders of the upper deep;
Far, far beneath in the abysmal sea,
His ancient, dreamless, uninvaded sleep
The Kraken sleepeth: faintest sunlights flee
About his shadowy sides: above him swell
Huge sponges of millennial growth and height;
And far away into the sickly light,
From many a wondrous grot and secret cell
Unnumber'd and enormous polypi
Winnow with giant arms the slumbering green.
There hath he lain for ages and will lie
Battening° upon huge seaworms in his sleep,
Until the latter fire shall heat the deep;
Then once by man and angels to be seen,
In roaring he shall rise and on the surface die.

° feeding gluttonously and growing fat

As the title of this poem indicates, X is a road, but quite a different one from Robert Frost's. As you read this unusual contemporary piece, try to see how the poet gets his road to become intensely meaningful. Here again, as in the Yeats poem about swans, although specific things are associated with the subject, its essential significance remains unstated.

Richard Hugo
BLONDE ROAD

This road dips and climbs but never bends.
The line it finally is, strings far beyond
My sight, still the color of useless dirt.
Trees are a hundred greens in varying light
As sky breaks black on silver over and in

The sea. Not one home or car. No shacks
Abandoned to the storms. On one side,
Miles of high grass; on the other, weather
And the sea reflecting tons of a wild day.

The wind is from Malay. Tigers in the wind
Make lovers claw each other orange. Blonde
Dirt rises to recite the lies of summer
Before the wind goes north and cats rip
White holes in the sky. Fields are grim
And the birds along this road are always stone.

I planned to cheat the road with laughter.
Build a home no storm could crack
And sing my Fridays over centuries of water—
Once more, have me back, my awkward weather—
But the land is not for sale. Centuries
Are strung; a blonde road north and south
And no one will improve it with macadam.

The road is greased by wind. Sun has turned
The blonde dirt brown, the brown grass
Black and dark ideas of the ocean
Silver. Each month rolls along the road
With an hour's effort. Now the lovers
Can't recall each other or identify
That roar: the northern pain of tigers

I know that just a word I'll never have
Could make the brown road blonde again
And send the stone birds climbing to their names.

Exploring the Metaphors

1. What does the poet associate with the road and the landscape surrounding it?
   How are these things metaphoric? Is there any consistent quality to what is
   associated with the road?
2. How does "I planned to cheat the road with laughter" add to the meaning of
   the poet's road?
3. What is the relation of time (centuries, months) to the road?
4. If the poet had said "golden" road instead of "blonde" road, would the poem
   be easier to interpret? Why?

5. Can you see any tension between the blonde road (X) and homes, cars, and macadam (Y)? What is it? How does this tension relate to the "tigers" and "tons of a wild day"?
6. Why doesn't the narrator have the word that will "make the brown road blonde again"? Does this statement suggest that the road is ultimately an X with an unstated Y? Is the road suggesting time's passage, age, fate, etc.?

On the first reading, this may seem a difficult poem. Giving a logical interpretation would be a problem, but experiencing the piece involves simply perceiving that the road has hidden meaning, metaphoric implication, and so all the details (images, ideas, etc.) reflect and develop this meaning. The metaphoric tension tells us something. For example, look at the line (from stanza three) "And sing my Fridays over centuries of water." Notice how the word "Fridays" (like "leaven" in the Christ parable, Chapter 1) obviously means more than just a day of the week. It's much more effective than if the poet said, "And I sing my happiness over centuries of water." Fridays are the end of the workweek and therefore represent pleasure, relief, rest. And how is water like centuries?

In effect, the poem acts as a metaphoric puzzle, and as we try to solve it (perhaps asking ourselves: What is this road?), while we may get no specific answer, we make discoveries.

In this peculiarly mystifying poem the central metaphoric subject (yachts) leads us to find another principal metaphoric subject of almost equal weight. Can you find this second subject?

William Carlos Williams
THE YACHTS

[1]
contend in a sea which the land partly encloses
shielding them from the too heavy blows
of an ungoverned ocean which when it chooses

[2]
tortures the biggest hulls, the best man knows
to pit against its beatings, and sinks them pitilessly.
Mothlike in mists, scintillant in the minute

[3]
brilliance of cloudless days, with broad bellying sails
they glide to the wind tossing green water
from their sharp prows while over them the crew crawls

[4]
ant like, solicitously grooming them, releasing,
making fast as they turn, lean far over and having
caught the wind again, side by side, head for the mark.

[5]
In a well guarded arena of open water surrounded by
lesser and greater craft which, sycophant, lumbering
and flittering follow them, they appear youthful, rare

[6]
as the light of a happy eye, live with the grace
of all that in the mind is feckless, free and
naturally to be desired. Now the sea which holds them

[7]
is moody, lapping their glossy sides, as if feeling
for some slightest flaw but fails completely.
Today no race. Then the wind comes again. The yachts

[8]
move, jockeying for a start, the signal is set and they
are off. Now the waves strike at them but they are too
well made, they slip through, though they take in canvas.

[9]
Arms with hands grasping seek to clutch at the prows.
Bodies thrown recklessly in the way are cut aside.
It is a sea of faces about them in agony, in despair

[10]
until the horror of the race dawns staggering the mind,
the whole sea become an entanglement of watery bodies
lost to the world bearing what they cannot hold. Broken,

[11]
beaten, desolate, reaching from the dead to be taken up
they cry out, failing, failing! their cries rising
in waves still as the skillful yachts pass over.

Exploring the Metaphors

1. What qualities are associated with the yachts?
2. What happens to the sea in stanza nine? What new relationship is established?
3. What qualities are associated with the sea? How is the "ungoverned ocean" related to the "sea which the land partly encloses"? Are these metaphoric X's? For what unstated Y's?
4. What is the relationship between the yachts and the sea at the end of the poem?

We feel that the situation is metaphoric—that the dramatic little yacht race refers to other things.

In stanzas three through six, the yachts personify sleek, skillful, clever people. In stanza seven the description of the sea as "moody," and "feeling for some slightest flaw" in the boats, introduces a sinister tone. The ominous feeling in the first two stanzas suggests that the sea will ultimately master these delicate craft. Stanza eight supports this idea. But suddenly in the ninth stanza the sea itself is mastered. The surreal personification in which waves become the hands and arms of drowning people shifts our focus from the yachts to the sea they "pass over."

So we find ourselves (as in previous poems) with more questions than answers about what the yachts and the sea are expressing. These questions are not imposed on the poem (to promote some specific point of view) but, rather, arise naturally out of it.

The voice of the narrator of the poem on the next page is a young girl who has been buried alive beside her dead father. The situation becomes a metaphoric X with unstated Y's. What is this situation like?

Anne Sexton
THE MOSS OF HIS SKIN

"Young girls in old Arabia were often buried alive
next to their dead fathers, apparently as sacrifice
to the goddesses of the tribes..." Harold Feldman,
"Children of the Desert," Psychoanalysis and
Psychoanalytic Review, *Fall 1958.*

It was only important
to smile and hold still,
to lie down beside him
and to rest awhile,
to be folded up together
as if we were silk,
to sink from the eyes of mother
and not to talk.
The black room took us
like a cave or a mouth
or an indoor belly.
I held my breath
and daddy was there,
his thumbs, his fat skull,
his teeth, his hair growing
like a field or a shawl.
I lay by the moss
of his skin until
it grew strange. My sisters
will never know that I fall
out of myself and pretend
that Allah will not see
how I hold my daddy
like an old stone tree.

Exploring the Metaphors

1. Why does the narrator say that "it was only important to smile and hold still"?
2. Is it possible for a daughter to feel buried alive with her father while he remains living and above ground? How might the poem reflect this?
3. The father's skin is evidently growing mossy with decay, but the last lines describe the narrator clinging to her father as if she were moss. What do you make of this?
4. Certain images in the poem might be seen as allusions to ideas in psychoanalytic theory, for example the idea of the Oedipus complex. Do you see that? Do you think the poet's treatment of these ideas is ironic? Is there irony in the line "I lay by the moss of his skin until it grew strange."
5. Is strangeness part of the metaphor here? How is it connected to moss?

The next poem appears to be a description of a person walking across a winter landscape. The last sentence suggests, but does not quite reveal, the unstated Y.

William Cassegrain
LUCID PRODIGY IN SNOW
For Joe LaRocca

Winter buries things. . . World a generality of snow, I
hike across the strangely frozen landscape   Icebound
lake lies absolute and still   Air seems airless   Far
off trees look stark
           Across this abstract land I find a buried
stream   A pool of ice   where wind has blown a
fragment's clearness   (view another world)
           Evening settles dim and cold   Long
winds stir   flakes upon the silent desolation   swirl
Across the darkened snow land I retreat   Know
a secret fear that bends me homeward   Know
the wind that blows this cosmic snow   Has blown
through all dark space

Exploring the Metaphors

1. The narrator or voice of the poem finds a piece of clear ice on a stream and this seems to bring about some transformation in his experience. What do you think the transformation is? What has happened?
2. What is the narrator's "secret fear"?

Technical Notes

This poem is set up in a text block to look like a paragraph, which makes it a PROSE POEM. But it's poetry, all right. One clue is that the language is basically iambic meter. Another is that the poet has taken care to create spaces and line breaks within the poem.

The next two poems are among the most famous in the English language. They are very different poems in tone and subject matter, but they have in common that they create an intense, mysterious X. In the first poem, the X is a tiger; in the second it is a loving yet merciless lady. What Y possibilities do you see for the X metaphoric subject in each of these poems? In other words: What is the tiger? Who is the lady? Could any answer be conclusive? Why not?

William Blake
THE TIGER

Tiger! Tiger! burning bright
In the forests of the night,
What immortal hand or eye
Could frame thy fearful symmetry?

In what distant deeps or skies
Burnt the fire of thine eyes?
On what wings dare he aspire?
What the hand dare seize the fire?

And what shoulder, and what art,
Could twist the sinews of thy heart?
And when thy heart began to beat,
What dread hand? and what dread feet?

What the hammer? what the chain?
In what furnace was thy brain?
What the anvil? what dread grasp
Dare its deadly terrors clasp?

When the stars threw down their spears,
And water'd heaven with their tears,
Did he smile his work to see?
Did he who made the Lamb make thee?

Tiger! Tiger! burning bright
In the forests of the night,
What immortal hand or eye,
Dare frame thy fearful symmetry?

5. The Poem As Metaphor: X/? 181

John Keats
LA BELLE DAME SANS MERCI

O what can ail thee, knight-at-arms,
    Alone and palely loitering?
The sedge has wither'd from the lake,
    And no birds sing.

O what can ail thee, knight-at-arms,
    So haggard and so woe-begone?
The squirrel's granary is full,
    And the harvest's done.

I see a lily on thy brow
    With anguish moist and fever dew
And on thy cheeks a fading rose
    Fast withereth too.

I met a lady in the meads,
    Full beautiful—a faery's child,
Her hair was long, her foot was light,
    And her eyes were wild.

I made a garland for her head,
    And bracelets too, and fragrant zone;
She look'd at me as she did love,
    And made sweet moan.

I set her on my pacing steed,
    And nothing else saw all day long,
For sidelong would she bend, and sing
    A faery's song.

She found me roots of relish sweet,
    And honey wild, and manna dew,
And sure in language strange she said,
    "I love thee true."

She took me to her elfin grot,
    And there she wept, and sigh'd full sore,
And there I shut her wild wild eyes
    With kisses four.

And there she lullèd me asleep
    And there I dream'd—Ah! woe betide!
The latest dream I ever dream'd
    On the cold hill side.

I saw pale kings, and princes too,
    Pale warriors, death-pale were they all
They cried—"La belle Dame sans Merci
    Hath thee in thrall!"

I saw their starved lips in the gloam
    With horrid warning gapèd wide,
And I awoke and found me here
    On the cold hill's side.

And this is why I sojourn here
    Alone and palely loitering
Though the sedge is wither'd from the lake,
    And no birds sing.

Technical Notes

Keats's poem is written in BALLAD STANZAS.

Metaphor: The Logic of Poetry

Chapter 6

Metaphor in Poetic Argument and Description

In this chapter we'll concentrate on two interesting aspects of poetry: (1) poets promoting points of view or causes, making arguments (subtle or obvious), then using logic or rhetoric; and (2) poets (often the same ones) describing objects and events without appearing to present more than an image. In both cases the metaphoric activity may seem to be suppressed or may only seem to serve the poet's point of view. But can poetry really be limited in this way? We have seen that without metaphoric action, a poem is a dead thing, and most of the pieces in this chapter will strike you as very much alive. Actually, as we'll discover, there is no contradiction, but finding out why there isn't one takes alertness and extreme sensitivity to tone.

We've seen that poems cannot be reduced to simple, "logical" statements, but what do we do when the poet seems to want only (or mainly) to convince us of something? For example:

John Donne
CONFINED LOVE

Some man unworthy to be possessor
Of old or new love, himself being false or weak,
Thought his pain and shame would be less,
If on womankind he might his anger wreak,
And thence a law did grow,
One might but one man know;
But are other creatures so?

Are sun, moon, or stars by law forbidden,
To smile where they list, or lend away their light?
Are birds divorced, or are they chidden
If they leave their mate and lie abroad a-night?
Beasts do no jointures lose
Though they new lovers choose,
But we are made worse than those.

Who e'er rigg'd fair ships to lie in harbors,
And not to seek new lands, or not to deal with all?
Or built fair houses, set trees and arbors,
Only to lock up, or else to let them fall?
Good is not good unless
A thousand it possess,
But doth waste with greediness.

Since logic ordinarily serves its premise (which is usually a theory or opinion), opinion is really the issue here, not the logical presentation. Opinion is a matter of conditioning: If we are taught (from our early years) certain principles, ethics, moral codes, and ways of looking at the world, then most of us take these things we have heard over and over for granted; they become part of our environment, and we forget that they may not be truths but habits. Even many so-called facts turn out to be opinion—scientific facts which have to be revised as new information becomes available, political facts that shift continually, and so on. In other words, we structure our lives, we define our very selves, on sets of opinions (our own and other people's) about what we like and dislike, what's good and bad, what's real and unreal, what's logical and illogical. We have observed that effective poems go deeper than these essentially mechanical reactions to life, that metaphor can free the mind (even if only for a moment) from the closed circle of opinion.

Donne, in the poem above, has done something we all do in conversations, speeches, essays, and textbook writing: He has taken one point of view and set it against another in order to demonstrate that what he thinks is "logical." In the poem, at least, it's amusing.

The first lines amount to an idle thought in the vein of: "I'd like to find the one who started all this!" Donne then presents this as a premise: If you believe it, then the rest will follow. Notice that there is no metaphoric activity at all in stanza one—just the open presentation of a point of view that some weak fellow once must have established the convention that women should be faithful to one man.

In stanzas two and three we have metaphors and personifications. Look closely at them. To undercut traditional Western moral attitudes toward marriage and monogamy, the poet sets a contrary opinion and illustrates it with local images and metaphors. Considered as an idea, his is clearly no better than the one he opposes. If you agree with him, you like it; if you don't, you don't. You may think your reasons for agreeing or disagreeing are profound, but that's your opinion. So the "argument" in a poem is of little consequence. The poet may be serious or not (which you might get from the tone), but what of it? Nevertheless, are there deeper, "opinionless" insights here, despite the propaganda? Surely something happens to the way we see ourselves and our mating habits as a result of human love and rituals (X) being contrasted with the ways of animals (Y). Obviously, this comparison is not an opinion, despite the fact that Donne arranges it to serve (or seem to serve) his purposes. Try going into the poem from this angle. Look at the last three lines. What is being said about love apart from (even if including) sexuality? Are the metaphors really limited by the "logic" of the argument? Notice the little shock you get with the word "greediness."

Perhaps you see an irony here, that it is greedy to love only one, but also greedy to want to love more than one. The two opposing opinions in stanzas one and two are brought together poetically in this word, which propels us beyond them.

A number of poems in this chapter involve propaganda in poetry. They seem to promote a slant on life by means of rhetoric (strong, expressive, or hypnotic phrases and literary devices), a form of logic, emotional appeals, or, more frequently, rhetorical description. We'll try to see whether the experience of poetry spills over the boundaries of a poet's intellectual intentions. Other poems here might seem to be just descriptions of moments of intense emotion or beauty, descriptions of the narrator's feelings (point of view) about something, or stories with vivid scenes.

Naturally, there is no hard-and-fast division between poems in this chapter and those in previous ones. If you look back at "Ode on a Grecian Urn," you will discover that Keats used arguments; Frost's "The Road Not Taken" is mainly descriptive. But here we'll examine poems where the metaphoric relationships are more fragmented or are harder to see, either because they are obscured by the argument or because they are worked into a picture or story.

Bear in mind that if a statement works poetically, it will reach beyond mere description and transcend opinion. Metaphoric action creates new relationships that take the mind beyond itself, and this cannot be achieved by simply stringing out dead images and putting "like" between them. The action of poetry cannot be expressed mechanically or through some system or other, and no system "proves" a poem poetic; we have to be able to experience it ourselves to find the poetry out.

As you read this piece, you will observe that the poet is insisting on a certain point of view and is slanting his rhetorical description of life to that end. Unlike the Donne poem given at the beginning of the chapter, Ginsberg's does not openly present an argument.

Allen Ginsberg
DEATH ON ALL FRONTS
"The Planet Is Finished"

A new moon looks down on our sick sweet planet
Orion's chased the Immovable Bear halfway across the sky
from winter to winter. I wake, earlier in bed, fly corpses
cover gas lit sheets, my head aches, left temple
brain fibre throbbing for Death I Created on all Fronts.
Poisoned rats in the Chickenhouse and myriad lice
Sprayed with white arsenics filtering to the brook, City
   Cockroaches
stomped on Country kitchen floors. No babies for me.
Cut earth boys & girl hordes by half & breathe free
say Revolutionary expert Computers:
Half the blue globe's germ population's more than enough,
keep the cloudy lung from stinking pneumonia.
I called in Exterminator Who soaked the Wall floor with
bed-bug death-oil: Who'll soak my brain with death-oil
I wake before dawn, dreading my wooden possessions,
my gnostic books, my loud mouth, old loves silent, charms
turned to image money, my body sexless fat, Father dying,
Earth Cities poisoned at war, my art hopeless—
Mind fragmented—and still abstract—Pain in
left temple living death—

Sept. 26, 1969

Exploring the Metaphors

   The force of this piece is rhetorical: it is emotionally intense, in places almost an outcry, hammering its points over and over without pretending to be logical. The speaker says, in effect: "This is me, I'm important, I feel this, I'm suffering, look at this!" There is a tone of violent sincerity. In fact, doesn't the very intensity of the piece tend to obscure the opinions underlying it? Donne pretends to argue us into taking his viewpoint, but here we are being pulled toward identifying ourselves with the author's voice. Let's write a counter poem:

LIFE EVERYWHERE!
The earth is reborn!

The full moon smiles on our vital world;
Aries has swayed across the sky,
Spring after spring. I get up early
Body light, head clear, my forehead
Tingling for life around me, everywhere.
The chickens gurgle and flap, the morning
Insects buzz, the country stirs.
My children wake, I feel the love in things
Today, lover and children waking
like the sun
All around the world.

I'm up before dawn anticipating
The rich air, my seeing, touching again,
My body part of the hush of life
And holiness of taking breath again,
Mind feeling the wholeness alive,
About to live.

One poet says he is depressed; the other is happy. One says the world is dreadful—too many people in it, bad air, ecology gone to hell and the other feels things couldn't be nicer. Now, opinions about experience, which we can hear on television, read in the papers, and so on, obviously don't trigger the shock of poetry in us. Never mind which piece we happen to prefer reading (our opinion); rather, consider whether insisting on suffering or claiming to be in ecstasy makes something true. Poems are not important or unimportant because of their points of view or subject matter. To like or dislike a poem for its ideas is no indication of the quality of its poetry. For example, noticing that we are poisoning our air isn't an insight. So where does the poet take us? Is there a deeper level?

The piece is essentially built on metaphoric associations: rats and cockroaches (X) with babies and "boys & girl hordes" (Y); bedbugs (X) with the mind (Y); and then insects (implicitly) with all mankind. As a result of these interrelations, is there a surprise, a discovery about the self or the world?

1. How does the use of technological and nonliterary images affect the tone (for example, "death-oil")?
2. In the last lines the poet lists reasons why he is so unhappy. Could you paraphrase this without losing the impact?

Yamanoue Okura

ON THE INSECURITY
OF HUMAN LIFE

We are adrift in this world.
The days, months, years slip past
Like a rapid stream that draws us to oblivion,
Swirled in our private eddies and pain.
Girls, wrists braceleted in exotic stones,
Join hands and dance away their youth.
Time is their dance. And soon their smooth black hair,
Is white as the breaking waves,
And on their tender faces
Cruel age has appeared.

Boys play and take up swords
And hunting bows,
And ride fast horses in pride.
But can their world for a moment remain? . . .
He opens the door,
Where a girl sleeps,
Makes his way in the darkness to her side.
Her arm on the pillow.
Touches the cold stones of her bracelet.
How soon he will be old
and neglected . . .
All this change we resent—
But it is useless.
Bitterly, we long to be the rock,
Enduring and secure
against the tides.
But a man in the river of time
Is in the current and must flow with it, inevitably,
Toward the sea . . .

Rendition from Japanese

Exploring the Metaphors

In common with the Ginsberg piece, this poem is telling us that things are dark. The tone is not cheerful. Like Ginsberg, Okura selects his images and shapes his material to support his views. He does not try to "prove" that the lot of human beings is hopeless; he simply describes and focuses on the process of decay and death. The essential difference (other than the obvious ones of style and period) seems to be that the contemporary piece is an openly subjective interior monologue, whereas this poem strikes us as somehow *objective* in treatment. If we tried to write a counter poem here, how would it be done? Ginsberg presented "ugly" images so we could respond with "pretty" images. Here, since the facts of human mutability (whether pretty or ugly) are beyond dispute, the only change we could make would be in mood: "I love the awareness that I'm dying moment to moment; I'm delighted to be passing away from this world," or some such.

The poem culminates in a pair of metaphors that go beyond the attitude of despair or depression into a final mood of *reflection*. And there is something hinted at here which goes deeper than our egocentric fears and doubts. There is a sense of the cosmic. In a way, the poet puts an end to his own despairing tone; not that he becomes joyful, but there is a mood of reflection which is insight, which is simply "seeing"—which is metaphoric, poetic action. This cannot be countered because the opposite of it is dullness, *un*reflection. So the poem has extended past any limited personal viewpoint toward what we might call an "experience of truth": not what we think or believe, but what we seem to *know*.

1. This poem contains many descriptive passages. What is their prime function?
2. The three lines that open the second section are a description. Do you think the poet really means just to talk about boys playing? Do they constitute an X as well? If so, what are the Y levels? What other descriptive passages in the poem operate in this way?
3. How do the last lines relate to the rest of the poem?

Like the Okura piece, this one begins in description and moves toward the insights of a reflective mood. Can you spot the underlying point of view (opinion) here? Does this opinion transcend itself in the poem? If so, how?

Matthew Arnold
DOVER BEACH

The sea is calm to-night.
The tide is full, the moon lies fair
Upon the straits;—on the French coast, the light
Gleams, and is gone, the cliffs of England stand,

Glimmering and vast, out in the tranquil bay.
Come to the window, sweet is the night-air!
Only, from the lone line of spray
Where the sea meets the moon-blanch'd sand,
Listen! you hear the grating roar
Of pebbles which the waves draw back, and fling,
At their return, up the high strand,°
Begin, and cease, and then again begin,
With tremulous cadence slow, and bring
The eternal note of sadness in.
Sophocles long ago
Heard it on the Aegean, and it brought
Into his mind the turbid ebb and flow
Of human misery; we
Find also in the sound a thought,
Hearing it by this distant northern sea.

The Sea of Faith
Was once, too, at the full, and round earth's shore
Lay like the folds of a bright girdle furl'd,
But now I only hear
Its melancholy, long, withdrawing roar,
Retreating to the breath
Of the night-wind down the vast edges drear
And naked shingles of the world.

Ah, love, let us be true
To one another! for the world, which seems
To lie before us like a land of dreams,
So various, so beautiful, so new,
Hath really neither joy, nor love, nor light,
Nor certitude, nor peace, nor help for pain;
And we are here as on a darkling plain
Swept with confused alarms of struggle and flight,
Where ignorant armies clash by night.

° shore

Exploring the Metaphors

1. The sea (X) the poet describes in stanza one is compared to the "Sea of Faith"
(Y). Are the other things in the poem described and then compared in open
metaphor this way?

2. Do metaphors develop by context in the first section of the poem? That is, do individual images like "pebbles" in the first stanza take on metaphoric significance? How? If pebble is X, what is the Y or Y's it is being associated with?
3. Are those images (in the first section) metaphoric for you until you have read "eternal note of sadness" or "Sea of Faith," for example?

Reading this poem twice might be a good idea. It seems to be one sustained image, doesn't it?

Arthur Rimbaud
LE DORMEUR DU VAL
(The Sleeper in the Valley)

The lush, green landscape is breached by a silver river,
Which glides through a tangled meadow,
Glinting in the sunlight beneath lordly crags,
Filling the little valley with the scintillance of afternoon.

A young soldier, open-mouthed, without his hat,
Rests his head in the cool blue grass,
Sleeps, sprawled palely in this herbal bed,
Where sunlight spills through shifting clouds.

His feet stretched out in flowers, he sleeps,
Uncertainty in his smile, like a child who is ill.
Nature cradles him warmly; he is cold.

The fragrances of afternoon do not awaken him.
Hand on his chest, in sunlight, he sleeps tranquilly.
His right side is breached by two red holes.

Translation from French by John Briggs

Exploring the Metaphors

1. Is this poem metaphoric? If so, how?
2. Do you think the poem is actually making a very subtle argument against war?

The metaphors in the third stanza intensify the description, but there is really no *overt* metaphoric action and no apparent central metaphoric relation or unstated metaphor (as in "The Road Not Taken"). Can you see what this piece has in common with Whitman's "When I Heard the Learn'd Astronomer"? A scene is painted with smells and sights; the landscape is almost tangible. Then, like the astronomer piece, the poem becomes violently poetic at the end. The contrast, the raw irony, ignites the metaphor. Remove the last line, and you have the image of a pleasant afternoon and a sketch of a sleeping, if somewhat ambiguous, man. Add the line, and the reader is surprised into insight.

Technical Notes

The poem in the original French is a sonnet.

This poem also seems to be pure description, but the tone of the description makes the piece more than just a portrait of the narrator's "last duchess."

Robert Browning
MY LAST DUCHESS
Ferrara

That's my last Duchess painted on the wall,
Looking as if she were alive. I call
That piece a wonder, now: Fra Pandolf's hands
Worked busily a day, and there she stands.
Will't please you sit and look at her? I said
"Fra Pandolf" by design, for never read
Strangers like you that pictured countenance,
The depth and passion of its earnest glance,
But to myself they turned (since none puts by
The curtain I have drawn for you, but I)
And seemed as they would ask me, if they durst,
How such a glance came there; so, not the first
Are you to turn and ask thus. Sir, 'twas not
Her husband's presence only, called that spot
Of joy into the Duchess' cheek: perhaps
Fra Pandolf chanced to say "Her mantle laps
Over my Lady's wrist too much," or "Paint
Must never hope to reproduce the faint
Half-flush that dies along her throat": such stuff

Was courtesy, she thought, and cause enough
For calling up that spot of joy. She had
A heart—how shall I say?—too soon made glad,
Too easily impressed; she liked whate'er
She looked on, and her looks went everywhere.
Sir, 'twas all one! My favour at her breast,
The dropping of the daylight in the West,
The bough of cherries some officious fool
Broke in the orchard for her, the white mule
She rode with round the terrace—all and each
Would draw from her alike the approving speech,
Or blush, at least. She thanked men,—good! but thanked
Somehow—I know not how—as if she ranked
My gift of a nine-hundred-years-old name
With anybody's gift. Who'd stoop to blame
This sort of trifling? Even had you skill
In speech—(which I have not)—to make your will
Quite clear to such an one, and say "Just this
Or that in you disgusts me; here you miss,
Or there exceed the mark"—and if she let
Herself be lessoned so, nor plainly set
Her wits to yours, forsooth, and made excuse,
—E'en then would be some stooping, and I choose
Never to stoop. Oh, Sir, she smiled, no doubt
Whene'er I passed her; but who passed without
Much the same smile? This grew; I gave commands;
Then all smiles stopped together. There she stands
As if alive. Will't please you rise? We'll meet
The company below, then. I repeat,
The Count your master's known munificence
Is ample warrant that no just pretence
Of mine for dowry will be disallowed;
Though his fair daughter's self, as I avowed
At starting, is my object. Nay, we'll go
Together down, Sir. Notice Neptune, tho',
Taming a sea-horse, thought a rarity,
Which Claus of Innsbruck cast in bronze for me!

Exploring the Metaphors

Critics call this type of poem a DRAMATIC MONOLOGUE; i.e., the narrator is talking to someone whose voice we don't hear but who is obviously there. The poem seems to be all description. Is it metaphoric? Consider:

A. What sort of woman is revealed by the narrator's description?
B. What is revealed about the narrator's relationship to his late wife?

The satiric tone is crucial to perceiving the overall point of view, the poet's opinion, here: The duke is talking about his last wife to an agent of the count (father of his future wife), and through his description he reveals himself as self-important, haughty, unfeeling. It is implied (through the irony) that his former duchess was in fact quite the reverse: modest, democratic, sensitive, full of spirit and freedom. There is a feeling that what the duke could not do to her in life (restrain her) he did after death by framing her portrait, finally stilling, fixing her, possessing her as an object of art. This obviously touches on the profound question of controlling another person and its effects.

Consider the rich levels of metaphoric irony here: The duke (often himself ironic) talks about the duchess, and yet the tone of the poem subtly (and ironically) shows him up without a single external comment (it is all his voice), so that his criticisms of his wife actually work as praise.

1. Do you see a subtle hint that the duke thought his wife unfaithful in the lines "not/ Her husband's presence only, called that spot/ Of joy" and "Fra Pandolf's hands/ Worked busily a day, and there she stands." "Fra" means "brother." Is this perhaps an ironic word choice?
2. Some readers have felt that the duke actually killed his wife. Can you find any evidence to support that view? Could he have killed her, but not literally?
3. Why do you think "as if . . . alive" is said twice?
4. The duke tells the silent listener, first, that he is certain he will get a dowry because the count is known to be generous; then he adds that of course the daughter herself is his real object. What does this suggest about the duke?
5. Why does the duke keep the painting covered so that no one but himself can look at it? What does this tell us about his relationship to the last duchess?
6. Everything is set up here so that we hear nothing but the duke's point of view. How does the poem transcend his opinions? Most important, how does it transcend even the poet's obvious satiric attitude? Look at the last two lines in particular. On one level the duke is referring to another of his possessions. But how does this relate to the duchess on other levels? What is the significance of the fact that it is a sea horse?
7. Compare the last lines here with the "twist" ending of the Rimbaud poem. Have they some effects in common?

Technical Notes

The poem is in heroic couplets; it does not maintain a regular adherence to END-STOPPED lines.

If you didn't know that the poet is referring to famous battles, would this poem make much sense?

Carl Sandburg
GRASS

Pile the bodies high at Austerlitz and Waterloo.
Shovel them under and let me work—
        I am the grass; I cover all.

And pile them high at Gettysburg
And pile them high at Ypres and Verdun.
Shovel them under and let me work.
Two years, ten years, and passengers ask the conductor:
        What place is this?
        Where are we now?

        I am the grass.
        Let me work.

Exploring the Metaphors

Note that the juxtaposition of grass (X) with various bloody battlefields (Y) is really what keeps this from becoming a simple prose statement.

1. Can you see the structure of the implied arguments here? Can you tell what the poet for and against ?
2. What are the levels of meaning in the line "Let me work"?

Technical Notes

The poem is in free verse.

Does this poem involve (like the Okura and Arnold poems) a reflective mood? Or is it (like the Browning poem) ironic description? Is this piece metaphoric at all?

Alexander Blok

THE NIGHT, A STREET

The night, a street, a pharmacy, a lamp,
a light cast, dead and meaningless.
Even if you live for another quarter century,
it will be like this.
There is no way out.
You will die. And it will begin again.
Everything will be repeated, as before:
The night, cold ripples on the dark canal,
the pharmacy, the street,
the lamp.
              Translation from Russian

Exploring the Metaphors

You might say that on the surface, this piece is all statement (opinion) and description. There is no argument or intense rhetoric. The speaker says, "This is how life is. Period."

But can you see an implicit metaphor where the street, pharmacy, lamp—the whole landscape—are (like) a prison of some kind, or a sort of cosmic treadmill where you go round and round without getting anywhere?

As before, it makes no difference whether we agree or disagree with the statements: Maybe things *will* change; maybe we could see meaning in the light, maybe "it" will be nothing at all like this again. The point is that the speaker's whole "dead" vision acts as an X to contrast Y, the living world which we conceive of as changing and meaningful. Through this contrast we may grasp something of deadness, narrowness, repeating patterns imposed on our life or underlying it. Thus we may suddenly confront our familiar world with new (perhaps frightened) awareness.

1. What do you think the "it" is in the sixth line? What is the effect of placing the statement, "And it will begin again" after the statement "You will die"? Is the poet espousing reincarnation?
2. How is the statement "Everything will be repeated" reinforced by the very structure of the poem? In what sense will everything "be repeated"? What is the effect of the added image at the end, "cold ripples on the dark canal"?
3. "Night" is a loaded word. Is it being used as an X here? What are some of the possible Y's?

Metaphor: The Logic of Poetry

Basically, the following two poems are not making arguments or promoting points of view with their descriptions. About all they are "selling" is mood. We will be looking to see how they extend past their moods into metaphoric discovery.

John Keats
TO AUTUMN

Season of mists and mellow fruitfulness,
  Close bosom-friend of the maturing sun;
Conspiring with him how to load and bless
  With fruit the vines that round the thatch-eaves run;
To bend with apples the moss'd cottage trees,
  And fill all fruit with ripeness to the core;
    To swell the gourd, and plump the hazel shells
  With a sweet kernel; to set budding more,
And still more, later flowers for the bees,
Until they think warm days will never cease,
  For Summer has o'er-brimmed their clammy cells.

Who hath not seen thee oft amid thy store?
  Sometimes whoever seeks abroad may find
Thee sitting careless on a granary floor,
  Thy hair soft-lifted by the winnowing wind;
Or on a half-reap'd furrow sound asleep,
  Drows'd with the fume of poppies, while thy hook
    Spares the next swath and all its twinèd flowers:
And sometimes like a gleaner thou dost keep
  Steady thy laden head across a brook;
  Or by a cider-press, with patient look,
    Thou watchest the last oozings hours by hours.

Where are the songs of Spring? Aye, where are they?
  Think not of them, thou hast thy music too,—
While barrèd clouds bloom the soft-dying day,
  And touch the stubble-plains with rosy hue;
Then in a wailful choir the small gnats mourn
  Among the river sallows, borne aloft
    Or sinking as the light wind lives or dies;
And full-grown lambs loud bleat from hilly bourn;
  Hedge-crickets sing; and now with treble soft
The red-breast whistles from a garden-croft;
  And gathering swallows twitter in the skies.

6. Metaphor in Poetic Argument and Description 201

Dwight Robbs
TO AUTUMN

Countless sparrows riot in the trees,
The air stirs dryly and the landscape stiffens,
Thinned woods fill with shadow and I feel
The tears of another century rise
And stop—And I know why they wept
Or said they wept: it takes you as the wind
Unwinds a shape in the dark leaves, sparrows
Stutter in the sky . . .

You want to cry:
"These sensations dim and drum in me,
The bones of life now show beneath the skin
And shadows like the footfalls of centuries
Stalk through the woods and stalk across my lawn. . ."

You know it was all real: priapic
Shelley wasted with abstract love, and Keats
Ached his gleaming, shadowed head and saw
The mournful body of the season move
Like mist across the fields of all his days . . .

The sparrows wheel and gust through crinkly air
And scatter; darkness fills the woods in
As gleaming silence fills me—The fluent
Raptures of old grief are stuttered now . . .
You see the form of Autumn stir and stride
And tangle through the shadows with her scythe
And hear it sweep and whisper like the wind
That starts and gusts through the stunned leaves.

Exploring the Metaphors

Keats's poem (which obviously came first) lushly describes autumn scenes and heaps natural image upon natural image until we think he'll never cease. There are several metaphoric levels here: First, the opening stanza, with many images of ripeness and fullness, sets up a contrast with the last half of the second stanza, where overripeness is about to be cut into by the winter edge of autumn. So possibly autumn is an X for a very traditional Y: human life, labor, approaching

202 *Metaphor:* The Logic of Poetry

death. Expressions like "maturing sun" reinforce this idea. Second, the personification of autumn certainly (as in Keats's "Ode on Melancholy") sets up a basic
comparison between human characteristics and the ways of nature. Where
autumn is "conspiring" with the sun or where "small gnats mourn," human
behavior is being grafted onto, or interpreted into, nature.

But the unique thing here is that the mood of the piece seems to overwhelm
our usual associations. Despite the metaphoric relations, description dominates
to the end, and what we are most taken with is the richness and intensity of image.
So, third, on a deeper level, this poem presents an experience of autumn and
compares this essence, this life, this intensity of beauty in itself(X) to the fact that
it is passing, dying moment to moment(Y)—in short, beauty (X) is contrasted to
time (Y) (remember that time's symbol is the scythe), a sense of eternal now
against eternal passing away. The piece is really not a description of a scene; rather,
it is an experience of mood, and more than mood. All these images are used to
evoke a state that is indescribable. This is the action of metaphor.

The second piece, while complete in itself, uses the Keats poem as a frame of
reference. Robhs has played off the tone, keying his conception to the scythe, the
sense of winter and death. One of the subjects of his poem is Keats's life and times
and philosophy of poetry. The personification of Autumn and the metaphor of
human life as (like) a season both appear explicitly in the metaphoric image "The
bones of life now show beneath the skin." It's useful to see the vast difference in
mood of the two poems, despite the fact that the second piece is consciously
related to the first. They both reflect similar feelings and perceptions, but in the
second poem description is much more openly metaphoric.

1. In Robhs's poem, the speaker is saying that Romantic poetry (critics consider
   Keats a Romantic poet) is a moment of nostalgia for him. What is he implicitly
   contrasting this Romantic feeling with?
2. Why does Robhs's speaker say, "Or said they wept"? What does this reveal
   about his attitude toward Keats?
3. How deeply do the two moods contrast? Which poem seems to have greater
   "distance" from the subject matter? How does this affect the tone?
4. Consider how both poems slant their moods by choice of image and diction:
   birds "riot" in one and "twitter" in the other, for instance.
5. Is the cider press (in the Keats poem) a metaphor? What are its Y levels?
6. What other metaphoric aspects do you see in these pieces?

Technical Notes

The Keats poem is in iambic pentameter. The Robhs poem uses iambic feet
with more variation and a pentameter background.

William Blake
NEVER SEEK TO TELL
THY LOVE

Never seek to tell thy love
Love that never told can be;
For the gentle wind does move
Silently, invisibly.

I told my love, I told my love,
I told her all my heart,
Trembling, cold, in ghastly fears—
Ah, she doth depart.

Soon as she was gone from me
A traveller came by
Silently, invisibly—
O, was no deny.

Exploring the Metaphors

This poem is a LYRIC, that is, it sounds like a song. You might say that the first two lines are imperative opinion, and the next two a statement—description of wind. Notice that the first two are an X, the second two their Y: Love is implicitly compared to the "gentle wind," and a causal relation between them is suggested by juxtaposition.

Notice the pattern in the three stanzas: (1) Don't tell / the wind is silent; (2) I told / she departed; (3) she was gone / the invisible traveler came.

1. Wind (X) is (like) traveler (Y). Blake describes the traveler and the wind. Do you have a sense of what they refer to?
2. Does the description of the traveler actually describe anything at all? Is it completely metaphoric?

Meng Chiao
SADNESS OF THE GORGES

Looking up from the gorges the sky winds like a thread;
Down the steep slope cords of water twist.
Sunlight on a tilt sprays the rims; by night
The moon spreads ghostlight like silver dew.
The bases vibrate to unceasing waves.
Centuries of shadow frozen in the depths
Stunned by a needle of light . . . another . . .
These long rays tilt past noon down into darkness . . .
At the most deadly twists white water raves
Like the drool of brute and naked appetite.
Treeroots stitch and knot through crumbled coffins,
And dangle the unstrung skeletons upright
As if they were just setting out in life . . .
The bony branches bare and white with frost
Tune the wind to clear and distant notes
That grieve harmoniously everywhere.

The guts of the exile shrivel, boil and burn
In the water and fire of his life;
Life spun out like the finest thread . . .
The rising road is bordered by the hand rope
Frail hands clutch at.
When he offers his silver tears to the spirits of the stream
Those ghosts gather, shimmer there . . .

Rendition from Chinese by Richard Monaco

Exploring the Metaphors

1. When you finish the poem, consider whether you would call the first four lines
pure description setting the scene, or do you feel there has been metaphoric
"action" created by the context? If so, what, specifically, is this action?
2. Are the individual images (description) in the poem metaphoric? What kinds
of connotations emerge from the images, what meanings?

Alfred, Lord Tennyson
THE LADY OF SHALOTT

PART I
On either side of the river lie
Long fields of barley and of rye,
That clothe the wold and meet the sky;
And thro' the field the road runs by
    To many-tower'd Camelot;
And up and down the people go,
Gazing where the lilies blow
Round an island there below,
    The island of Shalott.

Willows whiten, aspens quiver,
Little breezes dusk and shiver
Thro' the wave that runs forever
By the island in the river
    Flowing down to Camelot.
Four grey walls, and four grey towers,
Overlook a space of flowers,
And the silent isle imbowers
    The Lady of Shalott.

By the margin, willow-veil'd,
Slide the heavy barges trail'd
By slow horses; and unhail'd
    The shallop'[1] flitteth silken-sail'd
    Skimming down to Camelot:
But who hath seen her wave her hand?
Or at the casement seen her stand?
Or is she known in all the land,
    The Lady of Shalott?

Only reapers, reaping early
In among the bearded barley,
Hear a song that echoes cheerly
From the river winding clearly,

[1] a small, light boat

6. Metaphor in Poetic Argument and Description **207**

Down to tower'd Camelot:
And by the moon the reaper weary,
Piling sheaves in uplands airy,
Listening, whispers, "'Tis the fairy
    Lady of Shalott."

PART II
There she weaves by night and day
A magic web with colours gay.
She has heard a whisper say,
A curse is on her if she stay
    To look down to Camelot.
She knows not what the curse may be,
And so she weaveth steadily,
And little other care hath she,
    The Lady of Shalott.

And moving thro' a mirror clear
That hangs before her all the year,
Shadows of the world appear.
    There she sees the highway near
Winding down to Camelot:
There the river eddy whirls,
And there the surly village-churls,[2]
And the red cloaks of market girls,
    Pass onward from Shalott.

Sometimes a troop of damsels glad,
An abbot on an ambling pad,
Sometimes a curly shepherd-lad,
Or long-hair'd page in crimson clad,
    Goes by to tower'd Camelot;
And sometimes thro' the mirror blue
The knights come riding two and two;
She hath no loyal knight and true,
    The Lady of Shalott.

But in her web she still delights
To weave the mirror's magic sights,
For often thro' the silent nights
A funeral, with plumes and lights
    And music, went to Camelot:

---

[2] medieval peasant

Or when the moon was overhead,
Came two young lovers lately wed;
"I am half sick of shadows," said
    The Lady of Shalott.

PART III
A bow-shot from her bower-eaves,
He rode between the barley-sheaves,
The sun came dazzling thro' the leaves,
And flamed upon the brazen greaves [3]
    Of bold Sir Lancelot.
A red-cross knight forever kneel'd
To a lady in his shield,
That sparkled on the yellow field,
    Beside remote Shalott.

The gemmy bridle glitter'd free,
Like to some branch of stars we see
Hung in the golden Galaxy.
The bridle bells rang merrily
        As he rode down to Camelot:
And from his blazon'd baldric [4] slung
A mighty silver bugle hung,
And as he rode his armour rung,
    Beside remote Shalott.

All in the blue unclouded weather
Thick-jewell'd shone the saddle-leather,
The helmet and the helmet-feather
Burn'd like one burning flame together,
        As he rode down to Camelot.
As often thro' the purple night,
Below the starry clusters bright,
Some bearded meteor trailing light,
    Moves over still Shalott.

His broad clear brow in sunlight glow'd;
On burnish'd hooves his war-horse strode;
From underneath his helmet flow'd
His coal-black curls as on he rode,
        As he rode down to Camelot.

[3] part of a knight's armour
[4] belt supporting a sword

From the bank and from the river
He flash'd into the crystal mirror,
"Tirra lirra," by the river
      Sang Sir Lancelot.

She left the web, she left the loom,
She made three paces thro' the room,
She saw the water-lily bloom,
She saw the helmet and the plume,
      She look'd down to Camelot.
Out flew the web and floated wide;
The mirror crack'd from side to side;
"The curse is come upon me," cried
      The Lady of Shalott.

PART IV
In the stormy east-wind straining,
The pale yellow woods were waning,
The broad stream in his banks complaining,
Heavily the low sky raining,
      Over tower'd Camelot;
Down she came and found a boat
Beneath a willow left afloat,
And round about the prow she wrote
      The Lady of Shalott.

And down the river's dim expanse
Like some bold seer in a trance,
Seeing all his own mischance—
With a glassy countenance
      Did she look to Camelot.
And at the closing of the day
She loosed the chain, and down she lay;
The broad stream bore her far away,
      The Lady of Shalott.

Lying, robed in snowy white,
That loosely flew to left and right—
The leaves upon her falling light—
Thro' the noises of the night
      She floated down to Camelot:
And as the boat-head wound along
The willowy hills and fields among,

They heard her singing her last song,
    The Lady of Shalott.

Heard a carol, mournful, holy,
Chanted loudly, chanted lowly,
Till her blood was frozen slowly,
And her eyes were darken'd wholly,
    Turn'd to tower'd Camelot.
For ere she reach'd upon the tide
The first house by the water-side,
Singing in her song she died,
    The Lady of Shalott.

Under tower and balcony,
By garden-wall and gallery,
A gleaming shape she floated by,
Dead-pale between the houses high,
    Silent into Camelot.
Out upon the wharfs they came,
Knight and burgher, lord and dame,
And round the prow they read her name,
    The Lady of Shalott.

Who is this? and what is here?
And in the lighted palace near
Died the sound of royal cheer;
And they cross'd themselves for fear,
    All the knights at Camelot:
But Lancelot mused a little space;
He said, "she has a lovely face;
God in his mercy lend her grace,
    The Lady of Shalott."

Exploring the Metaphors

1. How do local metaphors add to the intensity? Do they add *levels* to the story?
2. Consider the story as description: Is it, in itself, acting metaphorically? Is the story an X for which you can discover possible Y's? For example, who or what is the Lady of Shalott metaphorically?
3. This piece has layers of literary irony—irony upon irony. Can you peel some of these layers back? For example, do you see the irony that a woman who wants to join the "real world" ends up floating down to the mythical, fictional kingdom of Camelot?

6. Metaphor in Poetic Argument and Description   **211**

Metaphor: The Logic of Poetry

Chapter 7

Dense, Subtle, and Complex Metaphor

Many of the poems we'll treat in this chapter will seem the reverse of those in the last, where we had to discover the metaphor in apparently artless description and expository argument. Here the elements of scene, time, place, and logic will frequently seem lost in a storm of metaphors, abstract images, symbols, and allusions. In the following poems things may get very complex, but there is nothing essentially new. In previous chapters we've seen basic techniques; here the techniques are pushed to extremes. The trick here will be to spot the poet's particular strategy of making metaphor.

First we'll have to penetrate the abstractions—the dense, perhaps confusing, and ambiguous images. Collections of words that don't mean anything, don't get at anything, certainly aren't poetic. Unless we can *find* the X/Y, we might only be able to say, "That was a strange sentence," or something to that effect. People sometimes claim to like a certain poem but, when pressed, admit that they have no idea what it's about, except they think "the images are interesting." Unless the poet is trying to make poetic relationships to understand something, (s)he is babbling like anyone else who makes no sense. As we hope you've seen throughout this book, poets are not mad people exempted from having to be coherent. In fact, the reverse is true: When poets and readers leave (even for the space of a single poem) the safety of their habits and daily "logic," they have to be especially keen and alert, and their intellect has to function smoothly right up to where intuition, insight, truth, or whatever we call it takes over. Without discoverable order there is no metaphoric action and, as a result, there is no poetry. So working with the subtleties and complexities of technique is the real problem here, not the question of what these poems mean. Poetry is insight and insight isn't "hard" or "easy"; it simply is. Once the technique is grasped, then insight can manifest.

The complex, far-reaching imagery in this contemporary love poem is structured partly by a central metaphoric relationship along the lines of: the speaker's love (X) is (like) the world, the universe (Y).

Stanley Kunitz

THE SCIENCE OF THE NIGHT

I touch you in the night, whose gift was you,
My careless sprawler,
And I touch you cold, unstirring, star-bemused,
That are become the land of your self-strangeness.
What long seduction of the bone has led you
Down the imploring roads I cannot take
Into the arms of ghosts I never knew,
Leaving my manhood on a rumpled field
To guard you where you lie so deep
In absent-mindedness,
Caught in the calcium snows of sleep?

And even should I track you to your birth
Through all the cities of your mortal trial,
As in my jealous thought I try to do,
You would escape me—from the brink of earth
Take off to where the lawless auroras run,
You with your wild and metaphysic heart.
My touch is on you, who are light-years gone.
We are not souls but systems, and we move
In clouds of our unknowing
                              like great nebulae.
Our very motives swirl and have their start
With father lion and with mother crab.
Dreamer, my own lost rib,
Whose planetary dust is blowing
Past archipelagoes of myth and light,

What far Magellans are you mistress of
To whom you speed the pleasure of your art?
As through a glass that magnifies my loss
I see the lines of your spectrum shifting red,
The universe expanding, thinning out,
Our worlds flying, oh flying, fast apart.

From hooded powers and from abstract flight
I summon you, your person and your pride.
Fall to me now from outer space,
Still fastened desperately to my side;
Through gulfs of streaming air
Bring me the mornings of the milky ways
Down to my threshold in your drowsy eyes;
And by the virtue of your honeyed word
Restore the liquid language of the moon,
That in gold mines of secrecy you delve.
Awake!
            My whirling hands stay at the noon,
Each cell within my body holds a heart
And all my hearts in unison strike twelve.

Exploring the Metaphors

The scene: The male speaker is in bed beside his companion, reflecting on the gulfs between people. The poem is a TROPE, that is, it takes this idea into the realm of metaphoric language. Overall, the central relationship is worked out straightforwardly, but certain metaphoric twists and turns are especially dense and subtle.

First, notice that the "you" of lines three and four is identified with "the land of your self-strangeness." This makes "you" an X term compared to the Y's "land" and "self-strangeness." So the speaker's lover is like an isolated world, "star-bemused." Another identification is also suggested: land (the earth, the world) with the heavens (stars). (This central relationship will be amplified in stanza two.) The rest of stanza one is clear enough metaphorically, though dense with connotations. Consider what the lines beginning "What long seduction of the bone" might mean. Among other things, is the bone identified as the body? (Technically this kind of identification is called SYNECDOCHE.) Is the poet suggesting that the body essentially isolates us from one another? How does this connect with "the calcium snows of sleep"? Note that calcium is an interesting case of natural, nonliterary imagery. What is the effect on tone of this and technological expressions like "spectrum shifting red" later on?

In stanza two the speaker considers tracking his lover through the "land" (which is herself, her "self-strangeness"), but he sees she would escape him "from the brink of earth" where she becomes identified with the vast, intergalactic universe. Covertly, inner space is identified with outer, and the central relationship of lover as world/universe continues to unfold. With "metaphysic" the poet makes a direct reference to Donne and the metaphysical poets of the seventeenth century, and from here on he superimposes aspects of their metaphoric techniques onto his poem.

"We are not souls but systems" in the comparison to "great nebulae" expresses the mysterious motions and complexities of human personality and motive, and "systems," applied to stars, becomes a pun on human systems of thought, habit and behavior. So star systems (X) are associated with human systems (Y). "Father lion" and "mother crab" refer, among other things, to the astrological signs Leo (the lion) and Cancer (the crab). Astrologers say that Leo is ruled by the sun (which gives life to the soul as well as to our solar system) and that Cancer is ruled by the moon (which shapes form and personality).

"My own lost rib" is an allusion obviously comparing the speaker's lover with

Eve, who was formed from Adam's rib. In the next line, what is the lover's "planetary dust" like? Can you untangle this complex metaphor? Scientists have speculated that suns and world systems are formed from interstellar dust and, conversely, that this substance is the remains of novas, exploded stars. What are the "archipelagoes of myth and light"? Are her imaginations, mysteries, understandings, and dreams all possible Y terms here? The very swirlings of her "dust" are identified with "art." Why? Do you see any irony in identifying her with dust?

In the next lines the poet compares his vision of his companion to looking through a telescope ("that magnifies my loss"), revealing, once more, how far she is from him and how beautiful: He sees "the lines of [her] spectrum shifting red."

If you recall, in the Donne "Valediction," we noticed a similar "impossible" distance between the associated terms. Astronomers say that the most distant stars are moving the fastest and therefore their light (seen through a spectroscope) shifts toward the red end of the visible spectrum. So the poet is saying that his lover is moving far away from him. What else do you get from "red"? In terms of the next two lines, what other levels work here?

In stanza four the narrator calls her back, again playing on the paradox that she is infinitely far away and yet right beside him. He sees the whole universe of her, and in her, and the resulting metaphoric tension has enormous suggestive power.

1. In stanza four how might "language of the moon" relate to "gold mines of secrecy"? Gold is the color of the sun. Is there a connection? What else?
2. Examine the images in the last stanza. How are they connected to those in the previous five stanzas?
3. On one level, the last two lines are a way for the narrator to say he loves his lover with his entire being. How does the metaphor tie clocks in with the poem as a whole?

Technical Notes

Most of the lines are iambic pentameter, linked—often distantly—by exact and slant rhymes.

In this poem there is no scene or story, as in the previous three pieces. The framework of the piece (in the sense that scene and story are frameworks) is a structure of ideas about philosophy and religion. Concepts are personified and given concrete terms, and as you can see immediately, the poem extends far beyond its ideas. Images become metaphorically rich with meanings. It is worthwhile to read the poem rather slowly, letting the compact associations work on you.

Andrew Marvell
A DIALOGUE BETWEEN THE SOUL AND BODY

SOUL
O who shall, from this dungeon, raise
A soul enslaved so many ways?
With bolts of bones, that fettered stands
In feet; and manacled in hands:
Here blinded with an eye; and there

Deaf with the drumming of an ear:
A soul hung up, as 'twere, in chains
Of nerves, and arteries, and veins:
Tortured, besides each other part,
In a vain head, and double heart.

BODY
O who shall me deliver whole,
From bonds of this tyrannic soul?
Which stretched upright, impales me so,
That mine own precipice I go;
And warms and moves this needless frame
(A fever could but do the same);
And, wanting where its spite to try,
Has made me live to let me die:
A body that could never rest,
Since this ill spirit it possest.

SOUL
What magic could me thus confine
Within another's grief to pine?
Where whatsoever it complain,
I feel, that cannot feel, the pain.
And all my care itself employs,
That to preserve, which me destroys:
Constrained not only to endure
Diseases, but, what's worse, the cure:
And ready oft the port to gain,
Am shipwrecked into health again.

BODY
But physic yet could never reach
The maladies thou me dost teach:
Whom first the cramp of hope does tear;
And then the palsy shakes of fear:
The pestilence of love does heat;
Or hatred's hidden ulcer eat:
Joy's cheerful madness does perplex;
Or sorrow's other madness vex:
Which knowledge forces me to know;
And memory will not forgo.
What but a soul could have the wit
To build me up for sin so fit?
So architects do square and hew,
Green trees that in the forest grew.

7. Dense, Subtle, and Complex Metaphor 219

Exploring the Metaphors

The metaphors here are dense, and so it might help if we untied a few of the "knotty" places. Step by step, let's look over this dialogue.

First, bones, which are *within* the flesh, are identified as "bolts." We think of bolts and bars around the *outside* of something, a prison or jail. Great metaphoric tension results from this paradox. At this stage, you should be able to grasp these metaphors fairly quickly, though the last two lines of the first stanza might puzzle you briefly. First, untangle the diction: Besides the body being a torture (for the soul), the "vain head" (a reference, perhaps, to foolish, useless, or egotistical thinking, dreams, ideals) makes things worse. Unscrambled, we can say: "The soul is tortured by being *within* a 'vain head.'" In "double heart" there may be a specific philosophic reference to Plato, but what can we get directly from this image? Double-dealing? Deceiving? Dualistic feelings? What about the physical details of the heart?

The next stanza takes up the body's point of view. Why is the soul "stretched upright"? This is a dense metaphor. On one level, the soul points upward, heavenward, is "upright" in every sense of the word. The body, being animalistic, wants to crawl. Since human beings "stretched" up by the soul are compelled to move upright, unlike the animals we alone are in danger of falling. Falling is an implied term of "precipice," suggesting the fall from grace, falling low. The soul's effect is then compared to a fever, and the rest is obvious. In lines one and two of the third stanza there is a minor case of complex diction (the soul is the body's grief); in lines four, six, and seven there are several (sometimes humorous) paradoxes.

The last four lines of the final stanza are worth extra care. In effect, the soul (X) is blamed for making sin possible and so is compared to architects (Y). As well as standing for the soul, might architects also refer to something else? Can you see what it might be?

1. Does the final couplet really seem intended to win the body's argument? Does squaring and hewing suggest, perhaps, a valid and necessary purpose? Why does the poet say "green trees"? What does green suggest in this context? Why is the soul said to be the cause of sin here?
2. In the last four lines of stanza three, why is the "cure" so troublesome to the soul? What does the "port" refer to?
3. Consider the extent to which this poem goes beyond its structure of ideas. Does it convey a sense of truth to you even though you might disagree or find irrelevant its specific ideas of sin? Can you account for this? How do the metaphors go beyond the notion of sin?

Technical Notes

The poem is written in iambic tetrameter. The rhyme scheme is *a a b b c c*, etc.

As in the Marvell poem, it is partly the old-fashioned diction that gives this piece a difficult look.

Sir Philip Sidney

WHEN FAR-SPENT NIGHT

When far-spent night persuades each mortal eye,
To whom nor art nor nature granted light,
To lay his then mark-wanting shafts of sight,
Clos'd with their quivers, in sleep's armory;
With windows ope then most my mind doth lie,
Viewing the shape of darkness and delight,
Takes in that sad hue which the inward night
Of his maz'd powers keeps perfect harmony;
But when birds charm, and that sweet air which is
Morn's messenger, with rose enamel'd skies,
Calls each wight ° to salute the flower of bliss,
In tomb of lids then buried are mine eyes,
    Forc'd by their lord, who is asham'd to find
    Such light in sense, with such a darken'd mind.

° creature

Exploring the Metaphors

In stanza one, "mark-wanting" means arrows lacking a mark or target. Eyes are compared to these arrows, and they are stored in "sleep's armory." In stanza two, "with windows ope" (the mind is covertly compared to a house), the narrator takes in dreams ("the shape of darkness"), the sad color and harmony of "inward night," the order of the "maz'd" (tangled, confused) dreams and visions. He is saying that in sleep, the pattern of dreaming moves in its own order, independent of consciousness.

In stanza three the narrator calls the sun "the flower of bliss." "Inward night" implies, among other things, a relationship between night and darkness as *ignorance*, ignorance of truth. The sun then suggests Y's referring to "enlightenment," heaven—and the whole poem gains a new unified level of metaphoric connections. Compare this with the Marvell piece we just went through. Look at "In tomb of lids." The body is again being represented as prisonlike. The flesh itself is cutting off the direct sight of the rising sun (God, truth, bliss, love—recall

7. Dense, Subtle, and Complex Metaphor **221**

"Almighty Sun" in "On a Drop of Dew"). But the flesh is "forc'd by their lord."
On *one* level, "such light in sense" could be interpreted to mean that the senses (eyes) perceive the sunlight and waken to it—that the senses are illuminated—but that the mind remains dark to the reality *behind* this light.

1. Why is "their lord" ashamed?
2. Is sleep here being identified with death? Is the coming of morning referred to in the poem a hint at resurrection? Can you work out a death and resurrection scheme here?
3. Does the poem have a strong effect even in a direct way without reference to the subtle levels of meaning we touched on above?
4. What are the ironies in this piece?

Technical Notes

The poem is a sonnet with an octave, sestet and couplet. The rhyme scheme is *a b b a a b b a c d c d e e*.

In this poem we have a dramatic human situation expressed in a metaphoric scene. Notice how the elements of the physical picture of a beach are tied to abstractions.

Judy Willington
WHAT EXISTS

A tidal wave of thought breaks,
rolls in foaming sequences.
Weary mind exhausted on the shore,
lid flipped partway open
admits an astral breeze.

Sharp-jointed, crystallized

senses glint like faces lit by dark,
rocks and stars tumbling me together.
I'm getting there, I say, repeat
until the words lie flat on the pale beach.

Dunes catapult time
through dark, glittering grasses
along a ridge of hill,
inundating memories, clung to in the vast night
under the white pebble of a moon.

Exploring the Metaphors

Thought is (like) a wave; onshore, the narrator is out of water (thought). What are the "lid" and the "astral breeze"? Notice the dead metaphor revived: "lid flipped partway open" suggests a touch of madness (the expression "flipped her lid").

Thought is exhausted, and with the narrator in an unusual mental state, the "astral breeze" blows in.

"Astral" suggests stars, but also refers to the spirit, the soul, or astral body, and is perhaps partly representative of the nuances of feeling and emotion. So a spiritual insight, vision, or state of some kind occurred after the speaker was hurled free of thought. But it is only a breeze, not a wind; just a hint.

In stanza two, the senses are sharp but altered and "glint like faces." The speaker is in a chaotic environment. The last four lines in this stanza are densely metaphoric. Can you work out the relationships?

In the last stanza, time is flung, as thoughts were in stanza one. The initial metaphor has been extended and altered. The speaker is drowned and tossed again; even on the "beach" memories (which are thoughts) are being inundated by time. The cosmic scope of all this is emphasized by the "white pebble of a moon."

1. Consider the phrase "rolls in foaming sequences." What does it suggest?
2. Look at the images of the poem, like "pale beach" and "moon." Are these X's with several Y levels ?
3. How does the "pebble of a moon" relate to the "crystallized senses like faces" and the rocks and stars in the second stanza?

Here we have an unusual dramatic contemplation of death. Instead of a scene, as in the last poem, the narrator arranges his metaphors around a mood.

W. S. Merwin
FOR THE ANNIVERSARY
OF MY DEATH

Every year without knowing it I have passed the day
When the last fires will wave to me
And the silence will set out
Tireless traveller
Like the beam of a lightless star

Then I will no longer
Find myself in life as in a strange garment
Surprised at the earth
And the love of one woman
And the shamelessness of men
As today writing after three days of rain
Hearing the wren sing and the falling cease
And bowing not knowing to what

Exploring the Metaphors

1. The poem is based on the idea that we can have an anniversary for something that lies in the future. Is this logically possible? On one level, since the date of death is unknown, does this have the effect of making this anniversary (and death) always there?
2. Silence is compared to a "tireless traveller" and to the paradoxical "beam of a lightless star." What is the effect of these comparisons?
3. In the second stanza the poet compares his life to a "strange garment." What or who, then, wears this garment, do you think? Is this a modern version of the old soul-body relation we saw in the Marvell dialogue and other poems?
4. At the end of the poem the narrator is struck by a suggestive natural event ("Hearing the wren sing and the falling cease"). Why does he bow "not knowing to what"?

The poem on the next page pictures something we have probably all seen and experienced. Can you find the metaphoric threads here? They are subtly buried in what otherwise seems mere description. The hidden metaphoric X's here are qualities rather than objects.

Denise Levertov
MERRITT PARKWAY

As if it were
forever that they move, that we
keep moving—

Under a wan sky where
as the lights went on a star
        pierced the haze and now
follows steadily
        a constant
above our six lanes
the dreamlike continuum . . .

And the people—ourselves!
        the humans from inside the
cars, apparent
only at gasoline stops
                unsure,
        eyeing each other

                drink coffee hastily at the
                slot machines and hurry
        back to the cars
                vanish
                into them forever, to
                keep moving—

Houses now and then beyond the
sealed road, the trees / trees, bushes
passing by, passing
        the cars that
                keep moving ahead of

        us, past us, pressing behind us
                and
                over left, those that come
                        toward us shining too brightly
        moving relentlessly

                in six lanes, gliding
        north and south, speeding with
        a slurred sound—

Exploring the Metaphors

1. How many things can you discover here that are "sealed" in or isolated in some
way? What associations does this suggest?

2. How many things can you find that relate to "continuum," that is, things that go on and on? What are the implications of this?
3. How are the things that are sealed connected with things in continuum?

As we have said, you must grasp a poem's own peculiar "logic" or order to experience it. You have to orient yourself in the work's "environment" before you can go beyond anything and discover metaphoric richness. Try doing that here.

Wallace Stevens
THE SENSE OF THE SLEIGHT-OF-HAND MAN

One's grand flights, one's Sunday baths,
One's tootings at the weddings of the soul
Occur as they occur. So bluish clouds
Occurred above the empty house and the leaves
Of the rhododendrons rattled their gold,
As if someone lived there. Such floods of white
Came bursting from the clouds. So the wind
Threw its contorted strength around the sky.

Could you have said the bluejay suddenly
Would swoop to earth? It is a wheel, the rays
Around the sun. The wheel survives the myths.
The fire eye in the clouds survives the gods.
To think of a dove with an eye of grenadine
And pines that are cornets, so it occurs,
And a little island full of geese and stars:
It may be that the ignorant man, alone,
Has any chance to mate his life with life
That is the sensual, pearly spouse, the life
That is fluent in even the wintriest bronze.

Exploring the Metaphors

Let's move carefully through this piece and uncover its structure. First, we quickly see that there is no story here and no argument, as in the Marvell dialogue. The structure is built instead on *concepts* that are animated and given form as vivid, natural images. Although these images may be private symbols, let's suppose there is no way to be sure of this and treat the poem on its immediate metaphoric level.

The poem opens with a cascade of comparisons: "grand flights" to "Sunday baths" to "tootings at the weddings of the soul." "Grand flights" suggests an exceptional state but is tempered with possible irony. Can you see that? Thus flights of imagination, intuition, vision—or whatever—are linked with the most mundane of activities, and then both of these are linked with a slightly sarcastic statement about some kind of spiritual marriage. What kind of wedding might this be? To "toot" suggests the colloquial "blowing your own horn." The poet says these three things (grand flights, baths, and tootings) "occur as they occur," they are what they are, and happen as they happen. Taken as a unit, these three terms become an X added to "so bluish clouds/ Occurred" (Y). So these occurrences are (like) the unpremeditated, natural, somehow inevitable appearance of clouds (a sense of inscrutable cosmic order?).

In lines four to six the leaves are rattling around the empty house. This natural image is associated metaphorically with "as if someone lived there." Why? Leaves move in the wind whether or not someone holds a lease. A subtle irony directs the reader: A human *pretension* (X) that events in the world somehow depend on us observing them happen is set against the fact that the universe goes on all by itself (Y). The house is empty and the occupants may be dead for all we know, but the clouds swell and fill, the flowers move. Nature has taken no notice of human coming and going. Would it be at all consistent with the tone and direction of this piece to imagine that the motions suggest life and someone moving around the grounds? Why "gold" leaves? Look at the images in the last three lines of stanza one. What do they add to the concepts already developed?

So far the poem suggests concepts of transience and the incomprehensible process of reality, which might seem random to our eyes, such as the Bluejay "suddenly" swooping to earth. Following this image is a symbol, operating as a metaphor: the wheel. The sun is compared to a wheel, and the shape and function of a wheel generate a host of metaphoric implications: endless turning (as in the expression, the sun "wheels" through the sky); a circle (which has no beginning); the wheel of fortune; *samskara*, the Hindu wheel of birth and death, being and decay; and so on. This wheel, we are told "survives the myths": The pure fact of the sun and its motion marking off time and the seasons outlasts all human stories about it, all human theories and imaginings, perhaps humanity itself. Notice that the irony is unrelenting all through the piece. From the "fire eye" Stevens shifts (and makes an implicit comparison) to the dove's eye. Now one of the poet's imaginative "flights" or "tootings" occurs. Why "pines," "cornets," and the "little island"?

The structure is finally delineated completely in the last four lines: The "ignorant man"—(ignorant of what?) without ideas, theories, or imaginings, and living the rhythm of reality without imposing on it—perhaps can "mate his life with life," unite with the actual flux and flow of existence and become one with the fierce sun and occurring clouds. Recall here "weddings of the soul." The "sensual, pearly spouse" intensely personifies a way of living which is finally said, in effect, to flow smoothly and easily in even the coldest moments.

1. What might "bronze" imply here? A work of art?
2. Linking pines with cornets results in a metaphor which connects with "tootings." How? Why do you think the poet wants to make this connection?
3. Do you think the "ignorant man" is really meant to be considered ignorant? In what sense is he ignorant, then? Is there irony here as well?
4. What levels might the empty house signify?
5. Is the one who thinks of the dove and pines, the "ignorant man," or is he being ironically contrasted with him?
6. The poet, when he imagines cornets, etc., is "tooting" himself. Does Stevens suggest that the poet goes *beyond* imagination in making his metaphors and that he contacts the reality where life can "mate" with life? Then why should the poet be the "ignorant man"?
7. Who is the "sleight-of-hand man"? Could it be the poet? How does the poem suggest this? In the title, does "sense" suggest meaning, intelligence, or perceptions? All three? How about "sense" as in "sense of humor"?

Technical Notes

The poem is written in free verse; internal and slant rhymes are used.

This poem seems a musing interior monologue in which statements of mundane facts are mixed with sudden, vivid imaginings. The difficulty is seeing how these are related.

John Berryman
DREAM SONG 176

All that hair flashing over the Atlantic,
Henry's girl's gone. She'll find Paris a sweet place
as many times he did.
She's there now, having left yesterday. I held
her cousin's hand, all innocence, on the climb to the tower.

Her cousin is if possible more beautiful than she is.

All over the world grades are being turned in,
and isn't that a truly gloomy thought.
All over the world.
It's June, God help us, when the sight we fought
clears. One day when I take my sock
off the skin will come with it

and I'll run blood, horrible on the floor
the streaming blood reminds me of my love
Wolves run in & out
take wolves, but terrible enough
I am dreaming of my love's hair & all her front teeth are false
as were my anti-hopes.

Exploring the Metaphors

The hair in the first line stands for the whole girl (see synecdoche in the Glossary). She has flown to Paris. The first nine lines of the poem contain personal, rather pedestrian comments on life: Henry liked Paris; his girl will like it; the speaker was out with her beautiful cousin; all over the world semesters are ending. Then, "God help us, when the sight we fought clears." Here, implicitly, all the trivial events of life (X) are being metaphorically juxtaposed to sight (Y). As we have seen in many poems, sight suggests such things as knowing, illumination, and realization.

1. In stanza two another mundane image, "When I take my sock off," becomes a metaphor of death (among other things); how is this put in an X/Y relationship with "my love"?
2. Can you see how the image of wolves is made a covert metaphor? What do these sudden, savage animals of death (and sexuality) suggest? It's very unspecific, but can you feel the violent shift of tone in the poem?
3. Can you unscramble the diction in the last two lines? Is the poet really Henry here? How would that interpretation alter "dreaming of my love's hair"? In these two lines notice the contrast of hair (X) to false teeth (Y)—the illusions of the world versus the ugly truth. Does the "sight" of these things suggest death? Why does the poet say "anti-hopes"? Resistance to hope? Hope *reversed* suggests despair. Would "as were my despairs" work here?

Read this poem over a few times. Try to become aware of the abbreviated references in scene and story, oblique allusions, and compressed and submerged metaphor at work here.

We have to be careful not to read too much into a poem of this type. We want to grapple with the levels that are "logically" there, and we need to discover the piece's internal order.

Robert Lowell

THE DEATH OF THE SHERIFF

"Forsitan et Priami Fuerint Quae Fata,
Requiras?" [1]
NOLI ME TANGERE [2]

We park and stare. A full sky of the stars
Wheels from the pumpkin setting of the moon
And sparks the windows of the yellow farm
Where the red-flanneled madmen look through bars
At windmills thrashing snowflakes by an arm
Of the Atlantic. Soon
The undertaker who collects antiques
Will let his motor idle at the door
And set his pine-box on the parlor floor.
Our homicidal sheriff howled for weeks;
We kiss. The State had reasons: on the whole,
It acted out of kindness when it locked

Its servant in this place and had him watched
Until an ordered darkness left his soul
A *tabula rasa*; when the Angel knocked
The sheriff laid his notched
Revolver on the table for the guest.
Night draws us closer in its bearskin wrap
And our loved sightless smother feels the tap
Of the blind stars descending to the west
To lay the Devil in the pit our hands
Are draining like a windmill. Who'll atone
For the unsearchable quicksilver heart
Where spiders stare their eyes out at their own
Spitting and knotted likeness? We must start:
Our aunt, his mother, stands
Singing *O Rock of Ages*, as the light
Wanderers show a man with a white cane
Who comes to take the coffin in his wain,[3]
The thirsty Dipper on the arc of night.

[1] "No doubt you'll have me tell how Priam met his fate?"
[2] Do not touch me.
[3] wagon; also, another name for the Big Dipper

Exploring the Metaphors

Where is the poem set? What is the locale? We have the outdoors, nighttime,
a farm or farm area, a state institution for the criminally insane ("red-flannelled
madmen"; "the State had reasons. . .had him watched"; "homicidal sheriff"). If
the poet just presented the facts of the case here as a story, wouldn't the very
impact of the abstract vision be vitiated?

What is the story, if any? Are there two lovers? A brother and sister? In any case,
one, possibly both, is cousin to the dead sheriff ("our aunt, his mother"); the two
have driven up to witness the undertaker's removal of the body. They sit and
watch. They kiss.

The poem takes this experience as a central metaphoric subject and (1) makes
literary, religious, and classical allusions to add dimensions to it; (2) intensifies
everything by surprising turns and contrasts of local metaphor; and (3) leaves out
literal connections, thereby forcing us immediately to the metaphoric level.

Without trying to be exhaustive, let's look at some of the ways the metaphors
connect with the basic "plot." They have parked. "A full sky of the stars" is a
slightly fresher way of saying "a sky full of stars," which is an obvious cliché. This
way Lowell's line suggests that the sky somehow belongs to the stars. The stars
are wheeling, moving against the "pumpkin setting of the moon." The moon is

being compared to a pumpkin. Why? This suggests autumn for one thing—pumpkins in the field, the yellowish color of the moon seen in the northern latitudes around Indian summer. Perhaps you also feel secondary implications of jack-o'lanterns, the grotesque, Halloween, witches, and darkness. The farm (yellow too) is illuminated, and the madmen look "at windmills thrashing snowflakes" near an extension of the ocean. Why windmills? They might imply flailing aimlessly in circles as a connection to the madmen and various general human states of flailing aimlessly in circles and/or a possible literary reference to Don Quixote, a "madman" himself. Then why "snowflakes"?

The undertaker who "collects antiques" (possible ironic humor) arrives. The couple kisses (in what sense?), and the speaker reflects. What is the tone of this reflection? How does he seem to feel about the "State"? Is "State" metaphoric? A pun? What is the "ordered darkness"? Death? If so, what about death? *Tabula rasa* means a void, a clean slate, and so, doubtless, death has wiped the sheriff's slate clean. At birth one's mind is said to be a *tabula rasa*. By context the Angel is probably the Angel of Death. Why has the poet introduced this image? The man died—why say that death "knocked" and that the sheriff put his gun on the table? Next, night is compared to a "bearskin wrap," suggesting heaviness and intimacy, and the two are deep in this "loved sightless smother" of close darkness, which may be a version of death too. But what other meanings does this image suggest? This "sightless smother feels the tap." Do the stars now seem to have something to do with the process of time and death? If the "sightless smother" is not a state of dying, then the stars "tap" it with time, which is here the mallet of death on one level, or the tap of a blind person's cane. Is it that we love our darkness, our blindness to reality? Of course, as often before, there is no hope of a simple answer and no need for one. The windmill image returns (as the stars just did), and we have to deal with "the Devil." There are various possible levels: the mythical Devil, the devil in ourselves, sex, and the "fall" of man, perhaps the sheriff as a devil. Remember, the windmill thrashes snow but cannot get a grip on anything, and so maybe we are "laying" him in the pit (the grave? our own darkness?) and yet another bit of life is "draining" from us. But is it possible to work *too* hard with these lines?

Next we see that the heart cannot be searched or held (like quicksilver). How about the spiders here? What do they represent? The devil again? The ego? You can't reduce the line to a statement, obviously. Notice "atone," for instance. The number of possibilities is large. Work through the last lines of this poem yourself.

Like many modern poems, the surface continuity here is broken up. If we couldn't piece together this continuity in some way, do you think the poem would work metaphorically?

1. Why do you think the Dipper is "thirsty"? Who is the man with the white cane? What is the connection to "the tap of the blind stars" earlier? What is the significance of the sheriff's mother singing *O Rock of Ages*?

2. When you know what the Latin title and epigraph mean, does that help you make contact with the poem?
3. Why might the poet have called the stars "light wanderers"? Has another Y meaning for them been suggested here? What have the stars been compared to throughout the piece?
4. What have the windmills been associated with?
5. What is the significance of the fact that a sheriff is the subject of this poem?

Technical Notes

All but three of the lines are iambic pentameter. Rhyme: *a b c a c b d e e d.*

You may read this poem, enjoy the images going by, and wonder what the poet is talking about. The poem is extremely dense, strewn with private symbols, and intensely oblique. But there is no technique here that we have not experienced before. Metaphor is pressed against metaphor, and for the piece to work on us effectively, we have to orient ourselves within the poem's structure. Read the work through more than once and try to perceive the "logic," the order.

William Butler Yeats
BYZANTIUM

The unpurged images of day recede;
The Emperor's drunken soldiery are abed;
Night resonance recedes, night-walkers' song
After great cathedral gong;
A starlit or a moonlit dome disdains
All that man is,
All mere complexities,
The fury and the mire of human veins.

Before me floats an image, man or shade,
Shade more than man, more image than a shade;
For Hades' bobbin bound in mummy-cloth
May unwind the winding path;
A mouth that has no moisture and no breath
Breathless mouths may summon;

I hail the superhuman,
I call it death-in-life and life-in-death.

Miracle, bird or golden handiwork,
More miracle than bird or handiwork,
Planted on the star-lit golden bough,
Can like the cocks of Hades crow,
Or, by the moon embittered, scorn aloud
In glory of changeless metal
Common bird or petal
And all complexities of mire or blood.

At midnight on the Emperor's pavement flit
Flames that no faggot feeds, nor steel has lit,
Nor storm disturbs, flames begotten of flame,
Where blood-begotten spirits come
And all complexities of fury leave,
Dying into a dance,
An agony of trance,
An agony of flame that cannot singe a sleeve.

Astraddle on the dolphin's mire and blood,
Spirit after spirit! The smithies break the flood,
The golden smithies of the Emperor!
Marbles of the dancing floor
Break bitter furies of complexity,
Those images that yet
Fresh images beget,
That dolphin-torn, that gong-tormented sea.

Exploring the Metaphors

First, we must consider the title. As mentioned before (page 53), "Byzantium" had special significance for Yeats. Without getting into that, however, the poem itself suggests a kind of fantasy scene: golden towers, exotic works of art, fantastic beings and creatures.

It is night. The "images of day recede," but, "unpurged," they still haunt the scene. Day and night are opposed, and we sense that each has a meaning, although perhaps these meanings never become completely clear; however, we get some idea of them just from everything that is associated with night. Day is obviously not the time when the visions in the poem manifest. Night might have something to do with a visionary consciousness which day tends to blot out. So the images "recede," and night subtleties begin. First, the "Emperor's drunken soldiery" are retired. They are not part of the time of the shadows, the time of the less "realistic" perceptions of things. Now we hear the "nightwalkers' song." Who are the night-walkers? Perhaps poets as well as anyone else who moves and "sings" in the mysterious "night" of visionary consciousness .

"A starlit or a moonlit dome" is an X term seeking Y's and is contrasted with "all that man is." A dome is an artifact, a kind of work of art, and seems meant to *symbolize* something as well as suggesting levels of purity and beauty. In any case, we certainly can find Y relationships from the context of the comparison to man: man (really, man and woman) is "merely" complex; human blood is (like) raging mud. Passion is "fury," and "mire" is thick and dull and touches on human impermanence, decay, the very substance of earth. The starlit dome is (like) something pure, calm, lasting in its perfect simplicity, "disdaining" the limitations of flesh.

In stanza two the speaker, within this night environment, sees an image before him, a man or the shade of a man—not a man of blood and mire, but possibly that which is left when the body (the earthly) falls away. The speaker adds that it is "more image than a shade"—a pure form. (Note how this relates to the dome in stanza one.) So this image is not even necessarily distilled from man (as a shade would be), but somehow was never a part of earth or day.

Already we begin to see that Yeats, in this sense, is working out a familiar structure: the spirit versus flesh contrast we have seen so much of. His structural elaborations happen to be so dense and evocative that the basic contrast is overwhelmed occasionally (at the same time there is constant, tantalizing metaphoric tension and suggestion), but this fundamental structure is always there, providing a track through the complex poetic territory.

Notice how Yeats adds metaphoric life to the allusion, Hades: He speaks of the "bobbin" of Hades, a bobbin that is (like) something characteristic of, or deriving from, Hades. This wild bobbin winds and unwinds the "mummy-cloth" thread— thus disentangles some entanglement and opens up some (visionary) path. Where might this path go? Can you follow possible Y terms here? All this seems to metaphorically express the spiritual deadness in human physical life, mind, and "day" vision of the world.

The next statement in the stanza may suggest someone in a kind of trance, a breathless yogic state of spiritual perception in which a "breathless mouth" can call up the "image," the thing "superhuman," neither dead nor alive: the eternal vision beyond what lives and dies.

In stanza three, can you see how the "miracle, bird or golden handiwork" is related to the "image" of stanza two and the "dome" of the first stanza? This bird image can crow "like the cocks of Hades" (mystery, death, the classical underworld, reflecting back to the previous stanza) and, when "by the moon embittered," can mock the "complexities of mire and blood," of physical existence. So the body-soul contrast is still being extended and explored.

In the fourth stanza the symbolic hour of midnight arrives. Strange fires burn with paradoxical heatless flames that are self-sustaining, feeding on no substance. Now "blood-begotten [mortal] spirits come" and leave their "complexities of fury" (mortality) behind. In other words, during that trance with "breathless" mouth, the pure, timefree, immortal spirit leaves all the misery and confusion and comes to the heatless, imperishable flame, the visionary fire. What does the "dance" suggest to you here?

In stanza five the dolphin ° is a symbol acting metaphorically. It rides the waves of the sea— of what? The flood is obviously a metaphor for something here. If it were a literal sea, the poem would suddenly seem flat and meaningless. Clearly the dolphin's "mire and blood" refers to the physical world again. The spirits ride them through waters that the "golden smithies" *break*. The smiths connect with the creation of the "miracle, bird or golden handiwork" (and the dome). What else might they suggest? They are breaking the furious sea. Waves break, of course, but we associate smiths with pounding on anvils, and so the two meanings are united. Are they freeing men's souls from mire and complexity by smiting the flood, breaking it down in some way the way a smith breaks down and reshapes a piece of metal? The "marbles of the dancing floor" (where the trance/dance takes place) suggest more handiwork. In stanza four, where we had "Dying into a dance," dance implied harmonious, unified motion, and, in context, cosmic harmonies. Now the images (marbles) that are associated with the dance (and so with cosmic simplicity, perfection) are breaking (up) the mortal furies. With the line "Fresh images beget," the images that stream from images, the smiths, the marbles—all are affecting or transforming the bitter "complexity." Perhaps at the end we experience the sea in association with a vision of all life, the whole motion of worldly existence—all the complex turmoil being torn by the dolphins, their flesh, their "mire and blood," as the spirits (aspiration, perfection, simplicity?) ride them on and on, the whole unimaginable image shuddering from the spiritual ringing of the gong. (Recall the "great cathedral gong" in stanza one.)

To repeat, this is one way of relating to this piece. No structural examination or explication can paraphrase this poem any more than it can paraphrase or reduce any metaphoric insight into ordinary language. Here we have tried to indicate an expeditionary track through the often bewildering density. We have purposely avoided discussing Yeats's private symbols since any poem first has to be dealt with as it stands. We first have to establish a frame of reference, something the intellect can get a grip on; otherwise, the images are wasted, in a way, and the

° In a Greek legend, Arion was saved from drowning by a dolphin.

mind beats its wings in a vacuum. Extraordinary images without familiar connections have no metaphoric impact.

1. Can you provide alternative levels to the ones mentioned above for the major images in this poem: the "image," the bird, dolphins, smiths?
2. In stanza one, why does the speaker say "unpurged" images? What is implied about these images?
3. What are the levels in "moon embittered" in stanza three? The moon is often associated with mutability, change. How does this relate here?
4. What are other levels in the "marbles of the dancing floor"? Why do they break the misery of mortality ("bitter furies of complexity")? How are they associated with the images of the bird, the gong? What do you think *are* the "bitter furies of complexity"?
5. Trace the development and relationships established by any image in the poem. Can you come up with a different track from the one we followed above? What new meanings do you find?
6. Why do you think Yeats is so concerned with "image" in this poem? Does the word "image" become a metaphor itself?
7. This poem, with all its meaning and insight, comes close to incoherence. Perhaps by considering how this piece finds its order, you may come upon a new understanding of the nature of poetry itself.

Metaphor: The Logic of Poetry

Chapter 8

The Poem Itself

How do we tell a good poem from a bad one, the great from the mediocre? Do kinds of metaphor make the difference? Does relative complexity or subtlety of technique make a "better" poem? How can we tell? Or *can* we tell?

It's human to want to evaluate, to judge, to be able to say what's good and what's not—to want to have "good taste." But can there be a formula for determining what good poetry is? Isn't every reader different so that what affects one may leave another cold? If we like the poet's viewpoint or sentiments or find that she is expressing thoughts or feelings we have had ourselves, won't we decide her poem is "great" because we identify with it? Won't someone else not identify with it, thus igniting a conflict of taste. To try to answer some of these questions, consider this famous poem by an early twentieth-century writer, Joyce Kilmer. What do you think of it?

TREES
I think that I shall never see
A poem lovely as a tree.

A tree whose hungry mouth is pressed
Against the earth's sweet flowing breast;

A tree that looks to God all day,
And lifts her leafy arms to pray;

A tree that may in summer wear
A nest of robins in her hair;

Upon whose bosom snow has lain;
Who intimately lives with rain.

Poems are made by fools like me,
But only God can make a tree.

Though many people like it, "Trees" has become a classic example of a "bad" poem. But how do we decide this? Critics, to support their distaste for the piece, point to logical inconsistencies in the metaphors: In stanza two the tree is a babe at the breast; in stanza three its branches are a girl's arms praying; in stanza four the branches are transformed into hair; and in stanza five the tree grows a bosom. Is consistency the key to excellence? Yes, the metaphors in "Trees" are inconsistent, but countless poems that critics consider outstanding also develop "illogical," inconsistent metaphors. Donne's "A Valediction: Forbidding Mourning," for instance, compares the souls of lovers to dying men, beaten gold, and a pair of compasses, and yet the poem is not now criticized for this.

The real problem with "Trees" is less obvious; it's a question of seeing that the metaphors are basically presenting opinion, propaganda, and little else. The speaker says, in effect, "I want to prove to you that trees are lovely, and so I'll compare them to things I'm sure you believe are lovely: a girl praying, babies, and bosoms"—reminiscent of the politician insisting that he's as American as the flag. Since most people already feel that trees are lovely, there is no real contrast between the X and Y terms. The metaphors are dead; they are just description or analogy, as if somebody had asked "What does a tree look like?" and the speaker had answered, "Like a girl lifting her arms to pray," and so on. And straining to make his point, the poet has rendered the images (tree as a mouth, hair full of birds) slightly grotesque. Since we *discover* nothing, we simply have description and opinion *disguised* as metaphor. Though the piece is printed as a poem, its contextual effect is more like that of an advertisement for God, trees, and beauty.

Further, as we have seen, the outlandish, inconsistent metaphors of a Donne or Stevens function within a framework of tonal consistency. Their poems are marked by playfulness, irony, and the uncovering of deep levels of meaning. Once you become aware that the tone of "Trees" is deadly serious and lyrical, but that the levels are shallow, doesn't the verse seem silly?

As we have frequently observed, if a poem is just a fancy way of telling us what somebody believes, imagines, feels, or wishes were true, then there is no metaphoric experience, no insight. Remember "Ode on Melancholy" (page 20). Keats's poem wasn't trying to make us feel depressed or react sentimentally the way a romance, sob story or soap opera might; rather, it focused on *seeing* melancholy, on providing an insight into it. Understanding the difference here may be very important to discrimination.

Obviously, some of the poems in this text go deeper than others. But how do we tell? Something isn't true just because lots of people (textbook writers, teachers, critics) think so, or false because they don't. Historically, generations of critics and students have often ignored or damned poets that later generations praised, and have praised what later generations found foolish or dull. Possibly this happens because time effaces the ideas, beliefs, and issues once considered important, thus leaving the poem itself. Poems that managed to go beyond the prejudices and issues of the day toward some profound intensity or metaphoric truth have endured, while others, however popular or important they may have seemed at the time, have faded away. This is as true of simple lyrics as it is of monumental epics.

So if there is no formula and no authority—and if even our personal opinions are suspect—what are we to do? First of all (we hope), we are investigating poetry not in order to pass judgment but rather to understand, to experience insight and depth. We want to discriminate only in order to further those aims. It has been said the best poems can be read repeatedly without going stale. Though our opinions and feelings change over the years, some poems stay new because they obviously do have great depth. Trying to develop taste by memorizing the opinions of "authorities" makes us secondhand as human beings and as readers. We don't have to do that when we can develop our own awareness and understanding. If we do, we won't need theories because we can see for ourselves. Only then can we answer the ancient question of why we should read poetry at all, what makes it worth the effort—because the answer lies in our own experience of the insight, awareness, clarity, depth, and truth that a poem has to offer.

A metaphor cannot work for us unless we first know what the terms mean. "My luve is like a red, red rose," says nothing if we don't know what a rose is. As we've seen, various poems require us to bring varying amounts of connotative and denotative knowledge to them if we expect to move into metaphoric understanding. In some pieces we had to have an idea of what certain allusions referred to. In "Science of the Night," for example, knowing something about astronomy and astrology added depth to the poem. But can we say that "Byzantium" is a better poem than "The Road Not Taken" just because Yeats's technique is more complex or claim that Frost's piece wins out by virtue of being more straightforward? Then what about "Trees"? Regardless of what techniques are used to evoke it, poetic insight is clearly a common denominator of good poems. We can debate stylistics, aesthetics, and all like issues (which have their importance), but either we experience insight or we don't. There's no way to argue it into or out of existence. And insight is something we must always find on our own.

In this text we have divided poetry into categories so that the reader could become familiar with metaphoric language; however, at this point bear in mind that these are imposed categories and should dissolve on contact with an actual poem. We should not mistake a finger for the thing it is pointing at. Every poem is a unique union of subject matter and metaphoric technique and has (except in rare cases) to be understood as complete in itself, whether it employs local metaphor, a central metaphoric relationship, metaphoric subject, metaphoric image, argument, irony, paradox, symbol, or whatever. No matter what method is used, the result, as we have seen, stands outside anything we can say about it.

And there is really no system for getting this. If we have missed the poem's flow and magic, any interpretations we could make become empty, conditioned responses, and we simply impose our ideas and desires on the work and perceive nothing from it. Since that "state of intuitive perception of truth" is what we are actually after, in the following chapter there are no categories, and you will have to read each poem here in its own unique terms. In a few cases we'll suggest some strategies for getting into the piece and some things to consider.

With this poem, take the flower as the X term and see how it unfolds into the Y terms "suicide" and "for the sake of all the dead."

Muriel Rukeyser
THE POWER OF SUICIDE

The potflower on the windowsill says to me
In words that are green-edged red leaves:
Flower   flower   flower   flower
Today for the sake of all the dead   Burst into flower.

The poet e.e. cummings liked to make poetry by playing visual and grammatic games with the English language. Do you see any such games here? How do they fit with the central metaphor? You may also want to investigate the tone of the last three lines.

e.e. cummings
BUFFALO BILL'S

Buffalo Bill's
defunct
            who use to
            ride a watersmooth-silver
                                    stallion
and break onetwothreefourfive pigeonsjustlike that
                                                Jesus

he was a handsome man
                        and what i want to know is
how do you like your blueeyed boy
Mister Death

Try seeing this poem in terms of the subliminal metaphoric relationship between two X's, time and friendship, and a Y, financial transactions.

William Shakespeare
WHEN TO THE SESSIONS

When to the sessions of sweet silent thought
I summon up remembrance of things past,
I sigh the lack of many a thing I sought,
And with old woes new wail my dear time's waste:
Then can I drown an eye, unused to flow,
For precious friends hid in death's dateless night,
And weep afresh love's long since cancelled woe,
And moan the expense of many a vanished sight:
Then can I grieve at grievances foregone,
And heavily from woe to woe tell o'er
The sad account of fore-bemoanèd moan,
Which I new pay as if not paid before.
    But if the while I think on thee, dear friend,
    All losses are restored and sorrows end.

In this poem, the situation of the mower and every detail of that situation are metaphoric; some of the metaphors are explicit, others covert.

Andrew Marvell
DAMON THE MOWER

Hark how the Mower Damon sung,
With love of Juliana stung!
While everything did seem to paint
The scene more fit for his complaint:
Like her fair eyes the day was fair;
But scorching like his am'rous care:
Sharp like his scythe his sorrow was,
And withered like his hopes the grass.

"Oh what unusual heats are here,
Which thus our sunburned meadows sear!
The grasshopper its pipe gives o'er;
And hamstringed frogs can dance no more:
But in the brook the green frog wades;
And grasshoppers seek out the shades.
Only the snake, that kept within,
Now glitters in its second skin.

"This heat the sun could never raise,
Nor Dog Star [1] so inflames the days.
It from an higher beauty grow'th,
Which burns the fields and mower both:
Which made the Dog, and makes the sun
Hotter than his own Phaëton.[2]
Not July causeth these extremes,
But Juliana's scorching beams.

"Tell me where I may pass the fires
Of the hot day, or hot desires.
To what cool cave shall I descend,
Or to what gelid fountain bend?
Alas! I look for ease in vain,
When remedies themselves complain:
No moisture but my tears do rest,
Nor cold but in her icy breast.

"How long wilt thou, fair Shepherdess,
Esteem me, and my presents less?
To thee the harmless snake I bring,
Disarmed of its teeth and sting:
To thee chameleons changing hue,
And oak leaves tipped with honey dew.
Yet thou, ungrateful, hast not sought
Nor what they are, nor who them brought.

"I am the Mower Damon, known
Through all the meadows I have mown.
On me the morn her dew distills
Before her darling daffodils:
And, if at noon my toil me heat,
The sun himself licks off my sweat:
While, going home, the evening sweet
In cowslip-water bathes my feet.

"What though the piping shepherd stock
The plains with an unnumbered flock,
This scythe of mine discovers wide
More ground than all his sheep do hide.
With this the golden fleece [3] I shear
Of all these closes every year.
And though in wool more poor than they,
Yet am I richer far in hay.

"Nor am I so deformed to sight,
If in my scythe I looked right;
In which I see my picture done,
As in a crescent moon the sun.
The deathless fairies take me oft
To lead them in their dances soft;
And, when I tune myself to sing,
About me they contract their ring.

"How happy might I still have mowed,
Had not Love here his thistles sowed!
But now I all the day complain,
Joining my labor to my pain;
And with my scythe cut down the grass,

Yet still my grief is where it was:
But, when the iron blunter grows,
Sighing I whet my scythe and woes."

While thus he threw his elbow round,
Depopulating all the ground,
And, with his whistling scythe, does cut
Each stroke between the earth and root,
The edged steel by careless chance
Did into his own ankle glance;
And there among the grass fell down,
By his own scythe, the mower mown.

"Alas!" said he,"these hurts are slight
To those that die by Love's despite.
With shepherd's-purse, and clown's-all-heal,
The blood I staunch, and would I seal.
Only for him no cure is found,
Whom Juliana's eyes do wound.
'Tis death alone that this must do:
For Death, thou art a Mower too."

[1] Sirius, associates with summer heat
[2] mythic charioteer of the sun
[3] allusion to the legend of Jason's
search for the golden fleece

Exploring the Metaphors

1. Consider the first stanza. How does this set up the central metaphoric situation and prepare us to see all that follows it in metaphoric terms?
2. Consider any image or local metaphor and its implications in terms of the entire piece. For example, in the second-to-last stanza, when Damon throws "his elbow round,/ Depopulating all the ground," metaphorically what is he cutting down—in addition to himself, that is? Are several answers are possible?
3. Metaphorically, what is Damon doing when he mows?
4. Is the snake a symbol? How is it being used metaphorically here?
5. What is the relation of death as a mower to Damon as a mower? What is the relation of death to Damon's desire for Juliana?

This poem has a point to make. What is it? Does the poem go beyond its point?
Notice, for example, what happens at the end of the second stanza.

Langston Hughes
AS I GREW OLDER

It was a long time ago.
I have almost forgotten my dream.
But it was there then,
In front of me,
Bright like a sun—
My dream.

And then the wall rose,
Rose slowly,
Slowly,
Between me and my dream.
Rose slowly, slowly,
Dimming,
Hiding,
The light of my dream.
Rose until it touched the sky—
The wall.

Shadow.
I am black.

I lie down in the shadow.
No longer the light of my dream before me,
Above me.
Only the thick wall.
Only the shadow.
My hands!
My dark hands!
Break through the wall!
Find my dream!
Help me to shatter this darkness,
To smash this night,
To break this shadow
Into a thousand lights of sun,
Into a thousand whirling dreams
Of sun!

Following are two English RENAISSANCE period translations of a poem by the Italian poet Petrarch. Which do you think is more effective? Why?

Henry Howard, Earl of Surrey
LOVE THAT DOTH REIGN

Love that doth reign and live within my thought,
And built his seat within my captive breast,
Clad in the arms wherein with me he fought,
Oft in my face he doth his banner rest.
But she that taught me love and suffer pain,
My doubtful hope and eke my hot desire
With shamefast look to shadow and refrain,
Her smiling grace converteth straight to ire,
And coward Love, then, to the heart space
Taketh his flight, where he doth lurk and plain
His purpose lost, and dare not show his face.
For my lord's guilt thus faultless bide I pain;
    Yet from my lord shall not my foot remove:
    Sweet is death that taketh end by love.

Sir Thomas Wyatt
THE LONG LOVE

The long love, that in my thought doth harbor
And in mine heart doth keep his residence,
Into my face presseth with both pretence,
And therein campeth, spreading his banner,
She that learneth to love and suffer,
And wills that my trust and lust's negligence
Be reined by reason, shame, and reverence,
With his hardiness taketh displeasure.
Wherewithall, unto the heart's forest he fleeth,
Leaving his enterprise with pain and cry;
And there him hideth and not appeareth.
What may I do when my master feareth
    But in the field with him to live and die?
    For good is the life ending faithfully.

What do the sailboat and the voyage become in this poem? How is the sailboat related to the poem itself ("this virgin verse")? What is the significance of the greeting at the end?

Stéphane Mallarmé
SALUTE

This froth, this virgin verse
is nothing but a cup
of the foamfar sea,
full of bubbles and mermaids.

We sail, O my various friends,
I on the deck, you at the prow
that crashes through the waves
like stormblasts and winters.

Across these rolling waters
blue drunkenness invades us,
as, braving all dangers,

we make this solitary greeting:
to sea and to sky, we show all
the white care of our sail.

Translation from French by John Briggs

The oral culture of many native peoples around the world is steeped in a poetry which is also religion. Compare this metaphor from the Bushman people with the metaphor by Goethe, a famous 19th century poet of our Western culture.

RE-BIRTH

A PRAYER TO THE NEW MOON
RELATED BY DAI-KWAIN

Young moon, take my face up yonder,
give back to me your face up there,
take away this pain.

Give me your face, small moon,
that dies, and when you die
living, you return again.
When we see you, and no more we see you
you lie down to sleep and come again.
Give me that I shall be like you
this joy that you possess forever
yonder with you, that living you come back
when we did not see you there.

Once when your child the hare
cried to you, his mother, not to let him die
you told us too that when we died
     we should return again.
          Bushman Prayer; c. after W.H.I. Bleek

Johann Wolfgang von Goethe
GESANG DER GEISTER ÜBER
DAN WASSERN

The soul
moves like water:
falls from above,
dissolves, rises,
thickens and falls,
again and again
without end.

Pure water
falls from the peak
where rock is sleek
sprays into cloud
sways and fills
streams smoothly on
within its mists
with slight sounds
moving away
into the valley deeps.

Where rocks
block flow it breaks
foams and spatters
down to the dark.

In lowland meadows
gently becoming
a still lake
it gleams deep and full of stars.

Wind like a lover
flows with and mixes
self with the other
loving in waves.

Human soul
you are water!
Human fate
you are wind!

Rendition from German by Richard Monaco

This poem is descriptive. The central metaphoric relation is in the fourth and fifth lines. How is it worked out? Consider the comparison in the last line very carefully, i.e., "mighty heart."

William Wordsworth
COMPOSED UPON WESTMINSTER BRIDGE
September 3, 1802

Earth has not anything to show more fair:
Dull would he be of soul who could pass by
A sight so touching in its majesty:
This City now doth, like a garment, wear
The beauty of the morning; silent, bare,
Ships, towers, domes, theatres, and temples lie
Open unto the fields, and to the sky;
All bright and glittering in the smokeless air.
Never did sun more beautifully steep
In his first splendour, valley, rock, or hill;
Ne'er saw I, never felt, a calm so deep!
The river glideth at his own sweet will:
Dear God! the very houses seem asleep;
And all that mighty heart is lying still!

Poets have said that there are only a few essential metaphors, but endless ways to unfold them. In the previous two poems we saw central metaphors involving the moon and water, images that turn up as terms in countless poems around the world. In the next two poems, poets from different centuries employ another popular metaphoric term: a mirror. But notice how each poet uses the popular mirror image to create a unique metaphorical statement. What is that statement in each case, and how does the mirror serve it?

John Donne
THE BROKEN HEART

He is starke mad, who ever sayes,
    That he hath been in love an houre,
Yet not that love so soone decayes,
    But that it can tenne in lesse space devour;
Who will beleeve mee if I sweare
That I have had the plague a yeare?
    Who would not laugh at mee, if I should say,
    I saw a flaske of powder burne a day?

Ah, what a trifle is a heart,
    If once into loves hands it come!
All other griefes allow a part
    To other griefes, and aske themselves but some;
They come to us, but us Love draws,
Hee swallows us, and never chawes:
    By him, as by chain'd shot, whole rankes doe dye,
    He is the tyran° Pike, our hearts the Frye.

If 'twere not so, what did become
    Of my heart, when I first saw thee?
I brought a heart into the roome,
    But from the roome, I carried none with mee:
If it had gone to thee, I know
Mine would have taught thine heart to show
    More pitty unto mee: but Love, alas,
    At one first blow did shiver it as glasse.

Yet nothing can to nothing fall,
    Nor any place be empty quite,
Therefore I thinke my breast hath all
    Those peeces still, though they be not unite;
And now as broken glasses show

A hundred lesser faces, so
     My ragges of heart can like, wish, and adore,
     But after one such love, can love no more.

° tyrant

Sylvia Plath
MIRROR

I am silver and exact, I have no preconceptions.
Whatever I see I swallow immediately
Just as it is, unmisted by love or dislike.
I am not cruel, only truthful—
The eye of a little god, four-cornered.
Most of the time, I meditate on the opposite wall.
It is pink, with speckles. I have looked at it so long
I think it is part of my heart. But it flickers.
Faces and darkness separate us over and over.

Now I am a lake. A woman bends over me,
Searching my reaches for what she really is.
Then she turns to those liars, the candles or the moon.
I see her back, and reflect it faithfully.
She rewards me with tears and an agitation of hands.
I am important to her. She comes and goes.
Each morning it is her face that replaces the darkness.
In me she has drowned a young girl, and in me an old woman
Rises toward her day after day, like a terrible fish.

Metaphor As The Logic of Poetry

Our world is various, complex, often frightening and awe inspiring, a kaleidoscope of perceptions and response. A form of order is imposed on this by means of human language and logic. With language and logic we make categories: "That's a man," "She's Russian," "They're socialists." Or, "This is desire," "That's a fear." We say, "I believe these things but not those," "I like this and hate that," and so on. In effect, we normally use our words and our logic to define, limit or break up the continuous flow of experience and organize it, sort it out, come to conclusions. This process involves constructing and interpreting around ourselves a familiar environment—and so breaking up our perceptions and the things perceived, our ideas and feelings, and organizing them according to their similarities, contrasts, causes, and effects. In short, it involves trying to make everything *known*.

As we have observed before, often in trying to make everything fit our "knowledge," we say that we are being logical when in fact we are simply promoting a belief—for example the famous syllogism: all men are mortal, Socrates is a man; therefore, Socrates is mortal. Obviously though this is logical, we are called upon first to agree with the premise. But how can anybody actually prove it? Maybe a nonmortal human exists somewhere; in fact, many believe that spiritually we are *all* nonmortal. However, in the syllogism this possibility is excluded, and we accept the statement. Notice that the logical form of the statement does not make it true.

We say we *know* something when we can fit it into our system; if it won't fit, we say it's *un*known, which clearly doesn't mean it's *unreal*. For instance, scientists say they do not fully understand the behavior of subatomic particles; the particles react in a way inconsistent with classical logic, and the reason for this is essentially unknown.

As we have seen, the logic of poetry, which is metaphor, works another way—in some respects, the opposite way:

1. Poetic metaphor acts to unify experience rather than to fragment it; it joins unlike things (X's and Y's) rather than separating them into categories. Logic tells us that an arrow is one thing, and a desire another. In the metaphor "Bring me my arrows of Desire," the two are united.

2. Metaphor makes use of similarities and contrasts, and sometimes even cause and effect, but never within a systematic framework. Can you see, for example, the difference between the logical contrast, "a pear is not an apple," and Stevens's metaphoric contrast, "pears are not viols, nudes or bottles"? Or think of Blake's "Auguries of Innocence" (page 33): "Each outcry from the hunted Hare / A fibre from the Brain does tear." This metaphor has a cause and effect form, but is it really an attempt at logic? The metaphoric relationship between X and Y is not predictable, not the result of theory. It's always unexpected.

3. Poetic metaphor does not aim at making something known, but at the *experience of the unknown*. Generally, we quickly lose interest in the familiar, the known, things fixed in categories, while what is unknown has vitality, spontaneity; it demands attention. Notice that working logically, when we haven't seen something before, we move to identify it with what we know. So the new rapidly and continuously becomes the old. We feel something and instantly say, "What am I feeling—love, fear, desire?" We look for a name, a familiar category, which defines and limits the experience. In poetry, however, we discover relationships like "arrows of Desire" which aim at the unlimited dimension of experience.

Poetic metaphor combines definitions, categories in new ways in order to express and evoke experiences we cannot pin down. Words in their customary usage point at things, feelings, ideas, but in metaphor there is no "thing." There is only discovery. And this kind of discovery does not end with a conclusion we can file away in a system or a notebook and forget, because it exists only in the experience of it. So we can't say we know poetry. We write it, talk about it, react to it, but what is poetic (as any poet will affirm) has to be continually rediscovered.

In Greek the word logic comes from a root word that means the art of speaking and reasoning. The word logos in Greek meant the creative word, the word by which inward thought is expressed, the word by which the whole is expressed. Logic governs the outward world of categories and knowledge; logos—or poetry—governs the inward world of wholeness and implication. In metaphor, which is the logic of poetry, the two worlds come together.

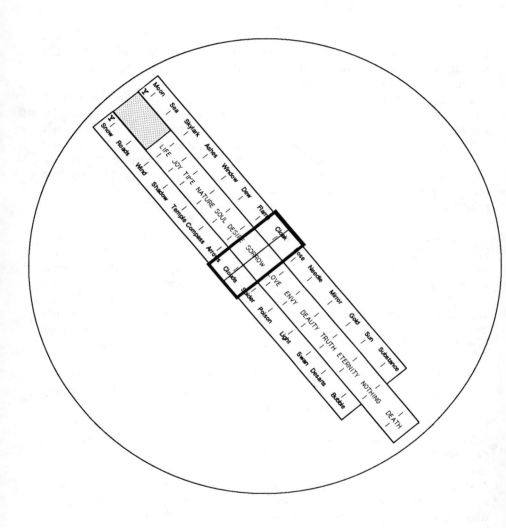

Glossary

ABSTRACT—Abstract terms are general terms—"hope," "joy," "love," "time," "beauty," "death." They are idea words. See CONCRETE.

ACCENT—A stressed syllable in a line of poetry.

ACCENTUAL VERSE METER—Lines measured by a regular pattern of stresses rather than, for example, a rigid pattern of metric feet.

AESTHETIC DISTANCE—The poet presents his subject without the reader's feeling the intrusion of the poet's personality or opinion.

ALEXANDRINE—A line of poetry consisting of six IAMBIC feet. The standard line in classical French poetry.

ALLEGORY—In order to make a thesis or doctrine interesting, an allegory sets up characters or images to represent concepts, moral qualities, or abstractions on a one-to-one basis. Generally, there is no unlike factor and little or no nuance in an allegory.

ALLITERATION—Repetition of the initial or stressed consonants: "The soup bubbling on the back of the stove / The stone staring into the sun" (Philip Levine's "How Much Can It Hurt?", page 41).

ALLUSION—Literary reference to a person, place, or event. See Chapter 2 (page 50).

AMBIGUITY—The assigning of two or more meanings relevant to a word, phrase, or poem, a characteristic of metaphoric language. In everyday language and expository prose ambiguity is considered a fault and results in a lack of clarity. In poetry, paradoxically, ambiguity often produces clarity and is considered a virtue. See CONNOTATION and METAPHOR.

ANAPEST (ANAPESTIC)—A metric foot with two unstressed syllables followed by a stressed syllable (x x ') .

ANTISTROPHE—See ODE.

APOSTROPHE—The author addressing an absent person, an abstraction, or an inanimate entity. Pope apostrophizes Queen Anne in "The Rape of the Lock": "Here Thou, Great *Anna*! whom three realms obey. . . "

ASSOCIATION (METAPHORIC)—One kind of metaphoric (X/Y) juxtaposition as defined by this text. See JUXTAPOSITION. See Chapter 1 (pages 4-5).

ASSONANCE—The repetition of a similar vowel sound, particularly in stressed syllables: "Our blood ref*u*sing to breathe, ref*u*sing to sleep / Asking the wo*u*nded m*oo*n" (Philip Levine's "How Much Can It Hurt?", page 41).

ATMOSPHERE—The mood of a poem: happy, sad, portentous, etc. See TONE.

AUGUSTAN AGE—Originally, the literary era of the classical poets Virgil, Horace, and Ovid under the Roman Emperor Augustus. Later writers applied the phrase Augustan Age to the first forty-five years of the eighteenth century, the period of Pope and Swift. See NEOCLASSIC PERIOD.

BALLAD (BALLAD STANZA)—A song which tells a story. The formal ballad stanza is a quatrain with alternating four- and three- stress lines and *a b c b* rhyme. Many ballads, both formal and informal, employ repeating lines, called REFRAINS: "And last year's snows, where are they?" (page 43).

BLANK VERSE—Unrhymed lines of iambic pentameter.

BURLESQUE—The generic term for literary forms (such as parody, caricature, travesty, satire, and lampoon) in which actions, people, or other literary works are made to seem ridiculous. Pope's "The Rape of the Lock" (page 94) is a burlesque.

CAESURA—A pause within a line of verse, e.g., from "The Rape of the Lock": "There lay three Garters, half a pair of Gloves."

CANTO—A division of a poem comparable to a chapter in a prose work.

CARICATURE—The exaggeration of a prominent feature of a character or person for the purpose of making him appear ridiculous. In Pope's "The Rape of the Lock" Sir Plume is cariactured as a man "with earnest eyes, and round unthinking face."

CAROLINE PERIOD—The period of the reign of Charles I (1625-1649)—the time of the English civil war. Herrick, Suckling, and Lovelace were poets of the period, called Cavalier poets.

CATALEXIS—The omission of final unaccented syllables in a line of verse.

CAVALIER POETS—See CAROLINE PERIOD.

CENTRAL METAPHORIC RELATIONSHIP—A metaphoric X/Y relationship worked out over an entire poem, as in Auden's "Law like Love" (page 130). See Chapter 3 (page 120).

CENTRAL METAPHORIC SUBJECT—A metaphoric X associated either with *a*) various Y's in a poem or *b*) some unstated Y's: *a*) Dickinson's "There's a Certain Slant of Light" (page 157) and *b*) Frost's "The Road Not Taken" (page 166). See Chapter 4 (page 146) and Chapter 5 (page 166).

CHIASMUS—A reversal in the order of words in two phrases that would otherwise be parallel, for example, Pope's comment on the fate of coquettes: "A fop their passion, but their prize a sot," from Pope's "The Rape of the Lock" (page 94).

CLASSICAL—Usually used in reference to the literature of the Greeks and Romans. Homer, Virgil and Horace are called classical poets.

CLICHÉ—An expression or idea that was once fresh but has lost its freshness through overuse: "Follow that road through life," for example. A good poet can revive a cliché and give it new meaning, as Frost does in "The Road Not Taken" (page 166).

COMPARISON (METAPHORIC)—A kind of metaphoric juxtaposition as defined by this text. See JUXTAPOSITION. See Chapter 1 (page 4).

CONCEIT—A metaphor linking two strikingly dissimilar things, as where Donne in "A Valediction: Forbidding Mourning" compares compasses to lovers' souls (see footnote, page 85).

CONCRETE—Concrete terms name specific instances or objects—roses, grapes, a lover waving good-bye, a boat race. See ABSTRACT.

CONNOTATION—A meaning that is suggested or implied by a word. For example, the word "owl" might connote death, night, darkness, and mystery, or, alternately, wisdom, in another context. See DENOTATION and Chapter 1 (page 21).

CONSONANCE—The repetition of consonants with changes in intervening vowels, for example, love-live, linger-longer.

CONTEXT—The situation in which a statement or set of statements is made. See Chapter 2 (pages 50-52).

CONVENTIONAL IMAGE—An image used frequently in literature. See page 50.

COUPLET—Two lines of poetry, usually rhymed: "A poem should be palpable and mute/ As a globed fruit," from MacLeish's "Ars Poetica" (page 9).

CRITICISM—The discussion, analysis, comparison, and evaluation of literary works.

DACTYL (DACTYLIC)—A metric foot with a stressed syllable followed by two unstressed syllables (' x x).

DEAD METAPHOR—A metaphor that has been so overused it is no longer recognized as a metaphor, for example "the eye of a needle." See Chapter 1 (page 3).

DENOTATION—The definition of a word: the thing it specifically refers to. For example, the word "owl" denotes a species of bird. See CONNOTATION.

DICTION—The vocabulary (slang, formal, standard, etc.) used in a literary work—the choice of words. See Chapter 2 (page 48).

DIDACTIC—The purpose of a didactic work is to teach something: a moral view, a world view, a doctrine. A good didactic poem must have something more, however, otherwise, when the moral or doctrine becomes passé, the poem falls into oblivion. See Chapter 8 (page 240).

DIMETER—A line consisting of two metric feet.

DIRGE—A poem expressing grief over a death. Dirges are usually short and often sung.

DISTANCE—See AESTHETIC DISTANCE.

DOGGEREL—A clumsily written verse, usually sing-songy. See "Poetry and Melancholy" (page 24).

DRAMATIC MONOLOGUE—In a dramatic monologue a single character speaks to one or more people who are not heard in the poem but who are obviously an audience. Robert Browning popularized the dramatic monologue. See Browning's "My Last Duchess" (page 195).

DREAM VISION—In this species of poem the narrator says he falls asleep and dreams. What he dreams is the material of the poem. This form was particularly popular in the Middle Ages. Dante's "Divine Comedy" is a dream vision.

ECLOGUE—A poem about shepherds or rural life. See the shepherd poems (page 89).

ELEGY—A formal poem in lament of a dead person. In the sixteenth and seventeenth centuries, the term "elegy" also meant any poem of serious meditation, such as Donne's "A Valediction: Forbidding Mourning," (page 82).

ELISION—A poetic contraction such as "ne'er" for "never," or "'tween" for "between."

ELIZABETHAN AGE—The era of the reign of Queen Elizabeth (1558-1603). It is considered to have been the greatest period of English literature because it was the time of Shakespeare, Marlowe, Jonson, Spenser, and Sidney.

END RHYME—Rhyming words at the end of lines of verse. See also INTERNAL RHYME. Examples of end-rhymed poems are Pope's "The Rape of the Lock," MacLeish's "Ars Poetica," and Keats's "Ode on Melancholy."

END-STOPPED LINE—A line of verse which ends with the completion of a grammatical unit, especially a clause or sentence.

ENJAMBEMENT—The continuation, without pause, of a phrase from one line of verse to the next. Also called a run-on line.

EPIC—A long poem about a heroic character.

EPIGRAM—A short poem, usually with a surprising turn of thought.

EPITHALAMION—A poem in celebration of a marriage.

EPODE—See ode.

EXACT RHYME—"white" and "night" are in exact rhyme.

FALLING METER—The TROCHEE and the DACTYL are falling meters.

FEMININE ENDING—A line of verse with an extra, unstressed syllable at the end.

FIGURATIVE LANGUAGE—Metaphoric language. See CONCEIT, HYPERBOLE, IMAGE, IRONY, LITERAL, METAPHOR, METONYMY, OXYMORON, PARADOX, PERSONIFICATION, PUN, SIMILE, TENOR AND VEHICLE, and TROPE.

FOOT—A unit of alternation of stressed and unstressed syllables in a line of poetry. There are five basic metric feet: IAMBIC (x '), TROCHAIC(' x),ANAPESTIC (x x '), DACTYLIC (' x x), and SPONDAIC (' ').

FORESHADOWING—An event which occurs later in a piece prefigured by an earlier image or event is said to be foreshadowed. It can be a kind of irony. See Chapter 2 (page 49).

FORM—A general word that may refer to any or all of the organizational aspects of the poem—meter, rhyme, imagery, metaphor—or to the type (genre) of poem.

FREE VERSE—Poetry without rhyme or regular meter.

GENRE—A literary form such as an epic, pastoral, or lyric.

HAIKU—A Japanese poetry form: haikus are poems of seventeen syllables, usually in three lines. See Basho (page 11).

HEMISTICH—A fraction, usually one-half, of a regular line of verse.

HEROIC COUPLET—A couplet in iambic pentameter which forms a complete thought that does not run over into the next lines. Pope's "The Rape of the Lock" (page 94) is written entirely in heroic couplets.

HEXAMETER—A line consisting of six metric feet.

HYMN—A song of praise.

HYPERBOLE—A poetic exaggeration, such as Burns's vow in "A Red, Red Rose" (page 25) to love his lover "'Till all the seas gang dry." Often ironic, as in Marvell's line from "To His Coy Mistress" about his "vegetable love" (page 27). See Chapter 2 (page 49).

IAMB (IAMBIC)—A metric foot with an unstressed syllable followed by a stressed syllable. (x ').

IDENTIFICATION (METAPHORIC)—A type of X/Y metaphoric juxtaposition as defined by this text. See JUXTAPOSITION. See Chapter 1 (page 4).

IMAGE—Description. See Chapter 2 (page 50).

INCREMENTAL REPETITION—A REFRAIN where a significant change is introduced upon each repetition.

INTENTIONAL FALLACY—The belief that one can discuss, analyze, or judge a work in terms of what the writer intended it to mean is an error of intentional fallacy. This is because it is virtually impossible to know what a writer's intention really was. In fact, if the poet's intention was to express a sense of truth through metaphor, the intention may defy paraphrasing—it is an intention that can only be understood *as* the insight embodied in the poem itself.

INTERNAL RHYME—The rhyming words are found within a line of verse and at its end. For example, the line, "speaking clearly and most severely," in Auden's "Law Like Love," (page 130) employs internal rhyme.

INVOCATION—An address by the poet to some god, gods, or muse for approval of his work or assistance in its composition. For example, Pope humorously invokes as a muse his heroine, Belinda, and friend Caryll in the opening lines of "The Rape of the Lock" (page 94): "I sing—This Verse to *Caryll*, Muse! is due;/ This, ev'n Belinda may vouchsafe to view:/ Slight is the Subject, but not so the Praise,/ If She inspire, and He approve my Lays."

IRONY—A tension between what a statement means on the surface (X) and its real or recognized meaning (Y). See Chapter 2 (page 48).

JACOBEAN AGE—The period of the reign of James I (1603-1625), which followed that of Queen Elizabeth. Shakespeare was still active during this period, though Donne, Marvell, Cowley, Jonson are generally associated with it.

JUXTAPOSITION (METAPHORIC)—Linking two or more unlike terms together in a metaphoric context can be done by comparison, association, identification or contrast. See Chapter 1 (page 4).

KENNING—An old English formula metaphor, such as "whale's road" meaning the "sea." Hopkins uses a similar device in "Spring and Fall" (page 140).

LAMPOON—A portrait ridiculing someone in biting language.

LITERAL—Adhering to the usual or primary meaning of a word or expression. In a literal statement there are no connotations, no overtones. Literally, for example, an owl is a species of bird. Figuratively, it may suggest any number of other things: death, wisdom, night, etc. See AMBIGUITY, CONNOTATION, DENOTATION, and FIGURATIVE LANGUAGE.

LITERARY CONVENTION—An idea, situation, or image that has been used repeatedly in literature. See page 92.

LITERARY-NATURAL IMAGE—Natural images that have been associated with religion, myth or historical events: the Styx, Mt. Olympus. See Chapter 2 (page 50).

LITERARY-TECHNOLOGICAL IMAGE—Images involving technological objects that have been used often in literature: a lyre, a sword, a bow. See Chapter 2 (page 50).

LOCAL METAPHORS—The individual metaphors in a poem as distinguished from the CENTRAL METAPHOR governing it.

LYRIC—See Chapter 6 (page 204).

MASCULINE ENDING—A line of verse ending with a stressed syllable.

MEASURE—Often used as a synonym for meter or to indicate any system of counting the sound in a line of verse.

METAPHOR—See introduction to Chapter 1.

METAPHYSICAL POETS—A group of seventeenth-century poets (including Donne, Marvell, Herbert, and Cowley) said to have written in a "metaphysical style" because of their use of outlandish, extended metaphors; abstruse, logical-sounding arguments; and dramatic diction. See also STYLE.

METER (METRIC)—The pattern of stressed and unstressed syllables in a line of poetry.

METONYMY—A metaphoric relationship in which the name of one thing (X) is used for another thing (Y) to which it is closely related. Pope's description in "The Rape of the Lock" of the feuding factions at court as "Wigs" and "sword-knots," in the line "Where Wigs with Wigs, with Sword-knots Sword-knots strive," is an example.

MOCK EPIC—A poem in which trivial events and characters are mocked by being presented as if they were of epic proportions. See Pope's "The Rape of the Lock" (page 94).

MONOMETER—A line of verse consisting of one metric foot.

MUSES—In Greek mythology, the nine goddesses who presided over the arts.

MYTH—A metaphoric story to explain natural phenomena, such as the myth that when the goddess Proserpine returns from the world of the dead to visit her mother, Ceres, spring arrives.

NARRATIVE POEM—A poem that has a plot, that tells a story. See "The Lady of Shalott" (page 207).

NEAR RHYME—See SLANT RHYME.

NATURAL IMAGE—Involves objects in the world that have connotative depth: the sea, stars, flowers. See Chapter 2 (page 50).

NATURAL, NONLITERARY IMAGE—An image that involves things generally thought of as prosaic or ugly, unpleasant or lacking in intrinsic depth: fecal matter, fungus. See Chapter 2 (page 50).

NEOCLASSIC PERIOD—The period of literary activity between the late seventeenth and late eighteenth centuries. Writers of this period generally held classical literature (the literature of the Greeks and Romans) in high esteem. They valued art, polish, and wit in literature and believed that the end of art was to communicate to people in a pleasing, informative fashion: "What oft was thought, but ne'er so well expressed," as Pope put it. Neoclassic poets tended to write in restrictive forms and followed rigid conventions like the heroic couplet. See also AUGUSTAN AGE.

OBJECTIVE CORRELATIVE—A term introduced by the twentieth-century poet T. S. Eliot. He wrote: "The only way of expressing emotion in the form of art is by finding an 'objective correlative'; in other words, a set of objects, a situation, a chain of events which shall be the formula of that particular emotion." In part, it means making the more or less abstract emotion concrete, as Keats does, for example, in "Ode on Melancholy" (page 20).

OBJECTIVE—In so-called objective poems, the poet presents ideas, images, and metaphors without seeming to become personally involved, that is, without our sensing the poet's voice. See SUBJECTIVE. The distinction between these two terms as applied in criticism is often vague, particularly since, in using them, critics run the risk of the INTENTIONAL FALLACY. For example, what seems to be a poet's confession may be more an imagined confession than a real one; that is, what seems to be subjective may really be an objective vehicle for conveying poetic insight.

OCCASIONAL POEMS—Poems written for specific events or on the occasion of deaths, dedications, birthdays, coronations.

OCTAVE—See PETRARCHAN SONNET.

ODE—A poem in praise of a person, idea, or thing. The classical ode had a rigid form with three parts: a strophe, antistrophe, and epode. Early English poets, however, developed the form such that each ode was allowed to find its own pattern of line lengths, number of lines per stanza, and rhyme scheme.

OFF-RHYME—See SLANT RHYME.

ONOMATOPOEIA—An onomatopoetic word is one formed in imitation of the sound made by, or associated with, what it refers to, for example, "buzz," "crackle," "hiss," and "boom."

OTTAVA RIMA—Verse in iambic pentameter, rhyming *a b a b a b c c.*

OXYMORON—Related to paradox, a combination of contradictory terms, for example, "pleasing pain" and "living death."

PARADOX—A statement that seems self contradictory as Donne's statement in one of his sonnets, "death thou shalt die." See Chapter 2 (page 49).

PARODY—A form of burlesque which makes fun of a particular work or style by imitating it grotesquely. See the Shepherd poems (pages 90-92).

PASTORAL—See ECLOGUE.

PENTAMETER—A line of verse consisting of five metric feet.

PERSONA—The speaker in a poem; the mask the poet adopts so that the reader will not assume it is the poet speaking personally.

PERSONIFICATION—Ascribing human characteristics (X) to nonhuman entities (Y). See "Ode on Melancholy" (page 22).

PETRARCHAN SONNET—A sonnet composed of an OCTAVE (eight lines) and a SESTET (six lines) and rhyming *a b b a a b b a c d e c d e.*

POETIC LICENSE—The poet's freedom to depart from ordinary speech patterns (diction), from the logic of everyday reality, or even from conventional poetic forms in order to achieve an effect. In other words, it is difficult to criticize a poet who is illogical or ungrammatical or who does not stick to tradition—as long as (s)he is "effective." Keats's image of pleasure "turning to poison where the bee-mouth sips" (page 20) is an instance of poetic license since, while the image violates reality, it is true to our intuitive perceptions.

PORTMANTEAU WORD—A made-up word in which two or more meanings are compressed into one term. Lewis Carroll's word "uffish," used to describe the Bellman in "The Hunting of the Snark," is a portmanteau word, suggesting perhaps "if-ish," "selfish," and maybe even "uppish" (uppity).

PRIVATE SYMBOL—An image assigned special meanings or connotations by the author. See Chapter 2 (pages 52-53).

PROSODY—The study of sound pattern, rhyme, meter, verse forms and other formal aspects of poetry.

PUN—A play on words of the same or similar sound but different meaning. See Chapter 1 (page 23) and Chapter 2 (page 49).

PYRRHIC—A metric foot with two unaccented syllables (x x) .

QUANTITATIVE VERSE (METER)—Verse measurement based on the length of time it takes to pronounce syllables in a line. A measure used in Greek poetry.

QUATRAIN—A four-line stanza, perhaps the most common stanza in English poetry.

REFRAIN—See BALLAD.

RENAISSANCE—Historically, the period following the Middle Ages. The term is often meant to suggest the rebirth of activity in the arts. The English Renaissance occurred in the sixteenth century and included Wyatt, Surrey, and Sidney among its poets.

RESTORATION PERIOD—The period at the end of the English commonwealth (1660) when an English king was returned to the throne. Dryden and the Earl of Rochester were poets of this period. The Augustan age followed, during which time Pope and Swift flourished.

RHETORICAL FIGURES—The arrangement of words departing from ordinary usage for special effects of sound or sense. See ALLITERATION, ALLUSION, APOSTRO-PHE, CHIASMUS, INVOCATION, ONOMATOPOEIA, RHETORICAL QUES-TION, RHYME, AND ZEUGMA.

RHETORICAL QUESTION—A question asked not for the purpose of receiving a reply, but as a means of emphasis to make a point—for example, "And last year's snows, where are they?" from "Ballad of the Ladies of Old" (page 43).

RHYME—Words with a similar sound, such as "white" and "night."

RHYME SCHEME—The pattern of END RHYMES.

RIME-ROYAL—A stanza of iambic pentameter, rhyming *a b a b b c c*.

RISING METER—IAMBIC and the ANAPESTIC feet are rising meters.

ROMANTIC PERIOD—In English poetry, the Romantic period is thought of as having begun in 1798, the year of the publication of Wordsworth and Coleridge's *Lyrical Ballads*. The Romantics (including Wordsworth, Coleridge, Keats, Byron, and Shelley as major figures) generally favored innovation and individualism in style, as opposed to the traditionalism and classicism of the Augustan age. Emphasis was placed on feeling instead of wit and on natural landscape as opposed to city culture. The period is considered to have ended with the beginning of the Victorian era in the 1830s.

SARCASM—Heavy, obvious irony. See Chapter 2 (page 48).

SATIRE—A work in which the subject is made to look ridiculous; the attitude of a satire is one of contempt or scorn for the object of the satire. Pope's "The Rape of the Lock" is a satire on English high society, among other things.

SCANNING (SCANSION)—The method of analyzing stressed and unstressed syllables to discern metric patterns.

SESTET—See PETRARCHAN SONNET.

SHAKESPEAREAN SONNET—A sonnet composed of three QUATRAINS, and a COU-PLET and rhyming *a b a b c d c d e f e f g g*.

SIMILE—The technical word for a metaphoric comparison employing a term such as "like" or "as" between the X and the Y. "My luve is like a red, red rose" is a type of metaphor technically called a simile.

SLANT RHYME—Also called OFF-RHYME or NEAR RHYME. "White" and "night" are an exact rhyme. "White" and "wait" are a slant rhyme.

SONNET—A famous fourteen-line verse form. See PETRARCHAN SONNET and SHAKESPEAREAN SONNET.

SPENSERIAN STANZA—A stanza containing lines of iambic pentameter, with a rhyme scheme of *a b a b b c b c c.*

SPONDEE (SPONDAIC)—A metric foot with two stressed syllables (' ').

SPRUNG RHYTHM—A mixed meter with a stressed syllable alone or in combination with two or three unstressed syllables. Sprung rhythm was made popular by Gerard Manley Hopkins (page 140).

STANZA—The poetic paragraph. A division of a poem consisting of a group of lines.

STOCK RESPONSE—A cliché reaction to a work; any reaction based on the reader's habits or opinions rather than a genuine reading and consideration of the piece.

STRESS—Accented syllable in a line of poetry.

STROPHE—See ODE.

STYLE—The word "style" refers to the characteristic way an author expresses herself. A poet's style may consist in part of the poet's tendency to use certain types of images or metaphors (technological, literary, natural) or certain combinations of these types. It may consist in part of her tendency to take a certain tone (e.g., ironic, serious, confessional, polemical) in her works or to use formal or colloquial diction. Style may have to do with the poet's tendency to express things simply and matter-of-factly or to stud his works with ornate images and allusions. The term "style" can also refer to the characteristic methods of expression of an era or period of poetry. For example, the tendency of some seventeenth-century poets to use technological CONCEITS (extreme metaphors) is one element of what has been called the METAPHYSICAL STYLE.

SUBJECTIVE—A subjective poem is one in which the poet seems to be telling of his or her private thoughts, feelings, and experiences. See OBJECTIVE.

SYLLABIC VERSE—Verse counted by the number of syllables in a line.

SYMBOL—An image with an assigned meaning or connotation. See Chapter 2 (pages 51-54) and Chapter 7.

SYNECDOCHE—A type of metaphor in which a part of something (X) represents the whole of that thing (Y)—for example, "All hands were lost when the ship sank." Hands = seamen.

SYNESTHESIA—Expressing one sensory experience in terms of another—sight as sound, taste as sight, etc. Keats, in his works, makes extensive use of synesthesia: "Then glut thy sorrow on a morning rose,/ Or on the rainbow of the salt sand-wave" (from "Ode on Melancholy"). "Glut," a word associated with taste, is applied to objects of sight.

TANKA—A Japanese poetry form; tankas are poems of thirty-one syllables, usually in five lines (pages 10-11).

TECHNOLOGICAL IMAGE—Images involving objects fashioned by man. See Chapter 2 (pages 50-51).

TENOR AND VEHICLE—Technical, critical words referring to the two terms of a metaphor. The tenor is the main subject of the metaphor (it may be either the X or the Y term); the vehicle is the term used to express it. In "My Luve is like a red, red, rose," "Luve" is the tenor, and "rose" is the vehicle (page 25).

TENSION—This word is used critically in various ways. In its most general application, it signifies the balance of similarities and differences between elements of the poem—the unlike factor. It is the force that connects the opposing (or unlike) abstract and concrete elements of the piece.

TERCET—A three-line stanza, usually having the same rhyme for all three lines.

TERZA RIMA—Tercet stanzas link together by the rhyme scheme *a b a b c b c d c d e d*, etc. Shelley's "Ode to the West Wind" is in terza rimas as is Dante's *Divine Comedy.*

TETRAMETER—A line of verse consisting of four metric feet.

THEME—A term generally used when discussing the abstract concept or idea we think a poem is about. Donne's "A Valediction: Forbidding Mourning" (page 82) could be said to have been written on the theme of parting. The theme of Keats's "Ode on a Grecian Urn" (page 158) might be stated as: "Man dies, but art is eternal." Obviously, there are many ways to state the theme of a work, and disagreement is possible on what the theme really is. Theme is what a poem is "about."

TONE—The atmosphere of a piece or the author's attitude toward his or her subject matter as manifested through the poet's use of metaphors, images, puns, paradoxes, metrical patterns, etc. See introduction to Chapter 2.

TRAVESTY—A type of burlesque or parody that supposedly mocks a heroic or lofty work by treating it in degrading terms.

TRIMETER—A line of verse consisting of three metric feet.

TROCHEE (TROCHAIC)—A metric foot with a stressed syllable followed by an unstressed syllable (' x).

TROPE—The class of metaphoric language including CONCEIT, HYPERBOLE, METAPHOR, METONYMY, OXYMORON, PARADOX, PERSONIFICATION, PUN, SIMILE, and SYNECDOCHE. A trope takes language beyond its literal meaning into the area of connotation and association.

UNDERSTATEMENT—A type of irony. See Chapter 2 (page 49).

UNLIKE FACTOR—The effect of the *differences* between the X and Y terms in a metaphor. See Chapter 1 (page 5) and Chapter 2 (page 51).

VERS DE SOCIÉTÉ—Light verse, generally occasional.

VERSE—A regular metric line. Often used as a synonym for "poetry."

VICTORIAN PERIOD—The period from the 1830s to 1901, the reign of Queen Victoria. It followed the ROMANTIC PERIOD. The Victorian era included the poets Arnold, Browning, and Tennyson.

VIRGULE—A line (/) used to indicate the division between one line of poetry and another when written out in a prose paragraph.

VOICE—Can be used in two ways: (1) to indicate the speaker or narrator of a poem and (2) as a synonym for TONE.

ZEUGMA—The technical word for a single term which relates to two other terms in different ways: "Or stain her honor, or her new brocade" (Pope's "The Rape of the Lock," page 94). Somewhat like a pun, a zeugma operates metaphorically. In Pope's line, the abstract significant word "honor" (X) is contrasted to the trivial concrete "brocade" (Y) on the basis of a similarity between them (both can be stained).

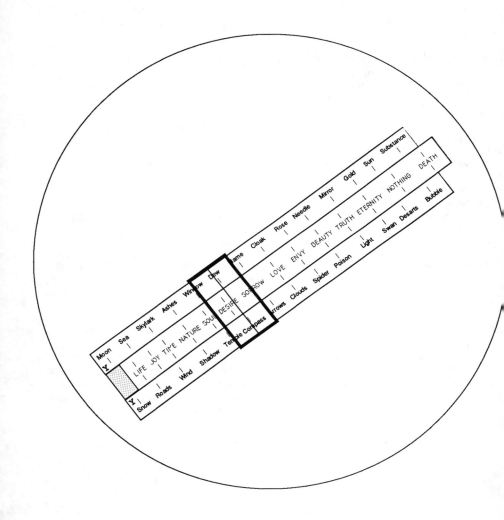

Indexes

Index of Poets

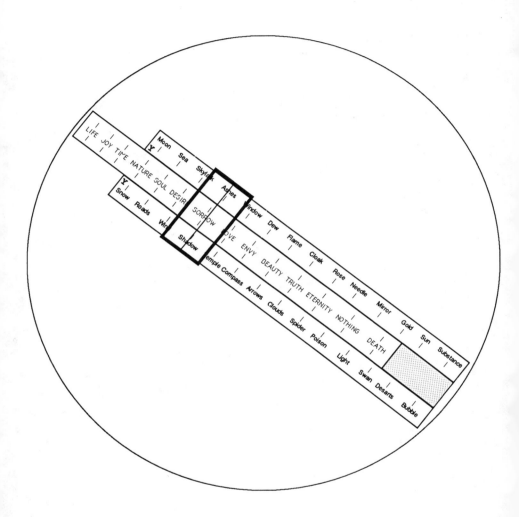

Index of Poem Titles

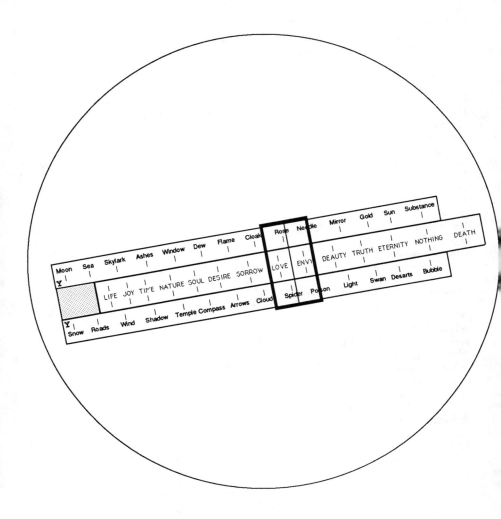

Index of First Lines

It was a long time ago, 248
It was only important, 178

Just as this ruler measures off the floor, 87

Kite like a soul, 10

Law, say the gardeners, is the sun, 130
Looking up from the gorges the sky winds like a thread, 206
Love that doth reign and live within my thought, 250

Márgarét, are you grieving, 140
My galley charged with forgetfulness, 122
My mistress' eyes are nothing like the sun, 31

Never seek to tell thy love, 204
No, no, go not to Lethe, neither twist, 20
Nothing! thou elder brother ev'n to shade, 75

Oh my luve is like a red, red rose, 25
O Light! (which mak'st the light, which mak'st the day, 128
On either side of the river lie, 207
One's grand flights, one's Sunday baths, 226
One's life, a single, 11
O Rose, thou art sick!, 70
O What can ail thee, knight-at-arms, 182
O who shall, from this dungeon, raise, 218

Perfect pearl, a pleasure for princes, 45
Pile the bodies high at Austerlitz and Waterloo, 198

Rime, the rack of finest wits, 73

Season of mists and mellow fruitfulness, 201
See how the orient dew, 125
She sits embroidering them, 163
Silence is not an empty room, 63
Some man unworthy to be possessor, 186
So we'll go no more a-roving, 82
Spring night, 11

Tell, where, what country is Flora, 43
That's my last Duchess painted on the wall, 195
That time of year thou mayst in me behold, 81
That which her slender waist confin'd, 156
The Auctioneer of Parting, 121
The clerk Bukashkin is our neighbor, 38
The Indian weed withered quite, 40
The long love, that in my thought doth harbor, 250
The lush, green landscape is breached by a silver river, 194
The night, a street, a pharmacy, a lamp, 199

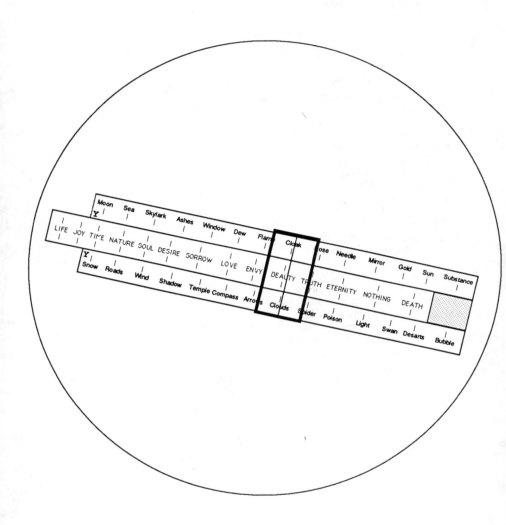

Chronological Index of Poets

William Blake (1757-1827)
Auguries of Innocence, 33
From Milton, 61
The Sick Rose, 70
The Tiger, 181
Never Seek to Tell Thy Love, 204

Robert Burns (1759-1796)
A Red, Red Rose, 25

William Wordsworth (1770-1850)
Composed Upon Westminster Bridge, 253

George Gordon, Lord Byron (1788-1824)
So We'll Go No More A-Roving, 82

Percy Bysshe Shelley (1792-1822)
Ozymandias, 56

John Keats (1795-1821)
Ode on Melancholy, 20
Ode on a Grecian Urn, 158
To Autumn, 201

Alexander Pushkin (1799-1837)
The Flower, 153

Alfred, Lord Tennyson (1809-1892)
The Kraken, 174
The Lady of Shalott, 207

Robert Browning (1812-1889)
My Last Duchess, 195

Walt Whitman (1819-1892)
When I Heard the Learn'd Astronomer, 55
A Noiseless Patient Spider, 143

Charles Baudelaire (1821-1867)
Correspondence, 70

Matthew Arnold (1822-1888)
Dover Beach, 192
Philomela, 161

Emily Dickinson (1830-1886)
The Auctioneer of Parting, 121
There's a Certain Slant of Light, 157

William Wills (1900-1919)
  In Praise of Marriage, 87

Gerald Francis (1901-1920)
  Poetry and Melancholy, 24

Langston Hughes (1902-1967)
  As I Grew Older, 248

Stanley Kunitz (b. 1905)
  The Science of the Night, 215

W.H. Auden (1907-1973)
  Law Like Love, 130

Stephen Spender (b. 1909)
  Subject: Object: Sentence, 72

Muriel Rukeyser (1913-1980)
  The Power of Suicide, 243

John Berryman (1914-1972)
  Dream Song 176, 228

Gwendolyn Brooks (b. 1915)
  My Dreams, My Works, 66

William Cassegrain (1916-1985)
  Lucid Prodigy in Snow, 180

Robert Lowell (1917-1977)
  The Death of the Sheriff, 230

Richard Wilbur (b. 1921)
  The Writer, 137

Richard Hugo (1923-1982)
  Blonde Road, 174

Denise Levertov (b. 1923)
  Merritt Parkway, 224

Allen Ginsberg (b. 1926)
  Death on All Fronts, 189

James Merrill (b. 1926)
  Laboratory Poem, 58

W.S. Merwin (b. 1927)
  Toro, 149
  For the Anniversary of My Death, 224